VOLATILITY ILLUMINATED

MARK WHISTLER

Mark Whistler is a trader, author and analyst.

Whistler has appeared on CNBC and is a <u>regular contributor to FXStreet</u>.com, discussing currency trading and global markets. From time to time, Whistler assists with content as a contributing Senior Market Strategist to<u>TradingMarkets.com</u>.

His books include:

- <u>2034 The Corporation Post 2012</u> (CreateSpace, 2009)
- <u>The Swing Trader's Bible</u> (John Wiley & Sons, Inc.)
- <u>Trade With Passion and Purpose</u> (Wiley, 2007)
- <u>Trading Pairs</u> (Wiley, 2004)
- Profit from China (Investment U/Wiley, 2006)
- Profit from Uranium (Investment U/Wiley, 2006)

Mark Whistler is also the founder of <u>WallStreetRockStar.com</u>, <u>fxVolatilty.com</u> and <u>InstitutionalIndexResearch.com.</u> Whistler is also a regular columnist for <u>Investopedia.com</u>. In his spare time, Mr. Whistler operates <u>Eats For The Streets</u>, a growing organization - dedicated to helping homeless across America and the <u>MarkWhistlerGallery.com</u> , an unbiased Internet art gallery open to all artists (globally) seeking to display their works.

Library of Congress Cataloging-in-Publication Data:

ISBN 1441490795 EAN-13 X 9781441490797

Printed in the United States of America, New York, New York

First Edition June 2009/First Printing June 2009

LIMIT OF LIABILITY / DISCLAIMER OF WARRANTY (EXTENDED)

In addition, the indicators, strategies, columns, articles and all other features of Company's products (collectively, the "Information") are provided for informational and educational purposes only and should not be construed as investment advice.

Examples presented on Company's website are for educational purposes only. Such setups are not solicitations of any order to buy or sell. Accordingly, you should not rely solely on the Information in making any investment. Rather, you should use the Information only as a starting point for doing additional independent research in order to allow you to form your own opinion regarding investments. You should always check with your licensed financial advisor and tax advisor to determine the suitability of any investment.

HYPOTHETICAL OR SIMULATED PERFORMANCE RESULTS HAVE CERTAIN INHERENT LIMITATIONS. UNLIKE AN ACTUAL PERFORMANCE RECORD, SIMULATED RESULTS DO NOT REPRESENT ACTUAL TRADING AND MAY NOT BE IMPACTED BY BROKERAGE AND OTHER SLIPPAGE FEES. ALSO, SINCE THE TRADES HAVE NOT ACTUALLY BEEN EXECUTED, THE RESULTS MAY HAVE UNDER- OR OVERCOMPENSATED FOR THE IMPACT, IF ANY, OF CERTAIN MARKET FACTORS, SUCH AS LACK OF LIQUIDITY. SIMULATED TRADING PROGRAMS IN GENERAL ARE ALSO SUBJECT TO THE FACT THAT THEY ARE DESIGNED WITH THE BENEFIT OF HINDSIGHT. NO REPRESENTATION IS BEING MADE THAT ANY ACCOUNT WILL OR IS LIKELY TO ACHIEVE PROFITS OR LOSSES SIMILAR TO THOSE SHOWN.

ADDITIONAL NOTICE TO FOREX/CURRENCY TRADERS

Trading foreign exchange on margin carries a high level of risk and may not be suitable for all investors. The high degree of leverage can work against you as well as for you. Before deciding to trade foreign exchange, you should carefully consider your investment objectives, level of experience and risk appetite. The possibility exists that you could sustain a loss of some or all of your initial investment and therefore you should not invest money that you cannot afford to lose. You should be aware of all the risks associated with foreign exchange trading and seek advice from an independent financial advisor if you have any doubts. ..

THE INFORMATION AND STRATEGIES IN THIS
BOOK DO NOT MAKE ANY PROMISE, OR
GUARANTEE. MARKET CONDITIONS
CONTINUALLY CHANGE AND THUS,
INFORMATION PROVIDED IN VOLATILITY
UNLIMITED COULD CHANGE AS WELL.

YOU SHOULD SEEK PROFESSIONAL ADVICE
PROACTIVELY, DURING AND AFTER
ATTEMPTING TO IMPLEMENT ANY
STRATEGY/INFORMATION NEW TO YOU AND
YOUR TRADING KNOWLEDGE, OR STYLE.

NEARLY 95% OF ALL RETAIL TRADERS LOSE.

PLEASE DO NOT ATTEMPT TO TRADE FOREX IF
YOU FEEL THE AFOREMENTIONED EVEN
REMOTELY APPROACHES YOUR RISK
TOLERANCE. THE BEST ADVICE TO MOST
INDIVIDUAL'S CONSIDERING TRADING FOREX
– IS UNLESS YOU HAVE PROFESSIONAL HELP –
DON'T.

ACKNOWLEDGEMENTS

Sandy and Ed – Thank you! I love you!

Karen, Mike and brilliant Ryan! I love you!

Thank you FxStreet…Maud and Vicki… Your patience is amazing! Thank you Marcel ter Beek for your feedback and patience! Thank you Michael Soni for your time and guidance (and the initial 'poison tree' metaphor.) I really appreciate all that you've done! Thank you Alvin Yu, Adam Huo and all of ECTrader.Net in Guangzhou, China. To Francois, thanks for still believing in me… We're almost there!

To Mark and Tanya Harrison… Mark I am very excited for your new book on Mortgages to hit shelves soon! Mark, you're an incredible writer! Thank you Ed Carson for your friendship, past guidance and continued support.

Thank you to TradingMarkets.com and to Investopedia.com - Chris! Thank you Carl Killough, your trading is brilliant buddy – perhaps one of the best I know!

Thank you to everyone who I have not mentioned who stuck by me during the composition of Volatility Illuminated… The project pushed every ounce of everything I have to the brink… I cannot thank you enough for not giving up!

Last, but not least, thank you Joe O'Connor for editing the 1st version of the probability article!

TABLE OF CONTENTS

PART ONE

PARADIGM AT SEA

CHAPTER ONE

WHY SUPERMAN WEARS HIS UNDERPANTS ON THE OUTSIDE

"BELIEVE NOTHING, NO MATTER WHERE YOU READ IT, OR WHO SAID IT, NO MATTER IF I HAVE SAID IT, UNLESS IT AGREES WITH YOUR OWN REASON AND YOUR OWN COMMON SENSE."

~ HINDU PRINCE GAUTAMA SIDDHARTA

J ust possibly, a significant portion of the information we've been traditionally taught to think of as 'accurate' in trading, investing and life, might be flawed...especially what we perceive as the best possible order for our underpants.

I hate to say it, but it's true. After ten years of research, trading, analysis, writing six books and over 1,500 articles about various aspects of markets, I am convinced the mass public - and most of the experts - are snowed.

The present epidemic of misinformed masses is precisely why over the following pages, I will present multiple cases showing how the majority's perception of information and markets is drastically flawed.

In addition, while many believe 21st century technology has created a more productive, 'progressive' and intelligent society, in reality (at least, as seen from the trading floor) the greater public seems to actually be regressing in ability to accurately perceive major market moving events significantly beforehand.

Underlying causes are both complicated and numerous; however, our contemporary light speed of information, increasingly 'factory setting' dependant mindset and growing naive trust of 'fast-mass media' all stand out as bold culprits behind humanity's swelling herd behavior.

On the outset, retail traders often complain of increased volatility in today's market, seemingly from nowhere.

The retail trader is correct about one thing; volatility is becoming fiercer in markets, especially Forex.

While we personally have zero ability to halt erratic market swings (a larger archetype than we are, of course), we can attempt to see today's erratic Volatility Illuminated through diligent, open-minded and perseverant investigation. To do so though, we will need to find new flashlights capable of cutting through the thick fog, which has now settled upon markets.

Unfortunately, in today's trading environment – even with all of our high-tech everything - most retail traders, media pundits and even professionals simply cannot see three feet beyond their nose, let alone light a reliable path into the distance.

Fact is, analysts, retail traders, media and even many high-finance professionals feel empowered with their 50,000 watt technical analysis and 'reliable information' fog lights.

We're really talking about the blind and oblivious mass acceptance of mucky, grimy, tampered, booby trapped, credulous and opinionated information, simply because such *is* 'the accepted standard'.

The problem is- the big shiny lights do nothing more than actually create a 'blinding screen' on the face of the brume.

All too often, media, analysts, and masses don't even have a clue the tool they're depending on for guidance- is really the problem.

Even if you are aware of the situation, don't bother attempting to mention the problem; you'll just hear something like:

"It's commonly known this thing can light up a cliff 1,000 miles away. Besides, I'm 'certified' to use it; didn't you see my credentials in the capital letters after my last name? And I wasn't trained to use the big light- just anywhere; my school was ivy."

You might reply, "Don't you mean 1,000 miles- on a clear night?"

"This bulb is the best money can buy...and I've got credentials," the financial professional replies.

Just to be nice you offer, "I know the bulb is expensive, but I have an extra one here in my pocket- it's designed for fog... You're welcome to borrow it."

The troop leader turns away with an abase chuckle- while rolling his eyes in the vision of his witless 'mega-fog-light' followers.

You can't be angry though; you just feel bad for the whole group.

Sadly, the general public is attracted to the same media/analyst *big light* too, all believing there's no way mainstream media and Wall Street professionals could be so obtuse, as to <u>not</u> truly know what they're doing…and off into the night they march.

Making matters worse, brokers and financial news portals have generously provided all customers with the exact same *personal wide beam fog light contraptions* for use during their little expedition into the darkness.

Nevertheless, the identical wide beam spots only make the crowd more dim-sighted by adding another layer of glare to the front side of the fog. Really, the mega-light fanatics are creating a sort of floating (though radiant) sheeting only a few feet into their speculated direction.

Because *the masses do,* in fact, all have their own little lights they think are worthwhile, while the 50,000-watt media monkey's prod from behind, they all start dashing into the fog…

Clueless of the cliff just a few feet away…

Over the following pages, I will attempt to provide a very, very special flashlight…. Not only does it perform well, but it works in rain, snow, fog and of course, on a clear night.

Moreover, I think once you switch it on, you're going just stand there speechless and shocked, as you begin to see the terrain (beyond the fog), for the first time, in a long time.

You will also likely look over at the larger media/analyst/retail troop marching credulously into the night…and say nothing.

You would normally laugh at the current situation, but you can't – it's devastating.

You're standing there with your light – you can see – and because you can, you know the herd…the retail traders and investors, all with their identical broker issued spots and the media with their analyst fueled 50,000-watt mega-mouth beams…are all swaggering into the foggy night, totally clueless they're just a few feet from a massive ravine.

Even if you try to help, almost none will believe your little light works better than the larger lightshow of the collectively credulous circus.

Let me ask you a question…

Is it possible – even remotely possible– that perhaps our perception and digestion of, and action upon much of the information we have been taught to believe as accurate and reliable…may have been flawed from the start?

Let me tell you about a guy I know; he's perhaps not the brightest of the bunch… He is a trader though, and he has never done anything else his entire career. When I asked him why he trades for a living, his reply was:

"To make $40 billion dollars beating markets."

In reality, 'not so bright guy' is me.

I'm still a long, long, way from my goal of $40 billion, but with the information in this book (and years of experience and disciplined money management) I believe I will someday make my $40 billion goal real. Why do I yearn for $40 billion dollars? Because I've always had another dream:

Buy a black jet; paint a 'skull and crossbones' on the tailfin and fly around the world giving $39 billion away to help people - all people.

Perhaps I'm crazy…

Regardless of sanity, in pursuit of turning the previously mentioned dreams into reality, I have chosen trading as my genie of action.

Over the years, one major heartache I've found - trading for a living - is when one rubs markets three times, the only thing that comes out of the 'wishful thinking market lamp' is a margin call… Not a dude in tights joyfully granting three wishes. In my time, I've seen more grown men cry on trading floors than I care to remember. I've also seen **one** make hundreds of millions of dollars. I am not the 'one' yet, but I intend to be.

With all of this in mind, the information you are about to read in the following pages was derived from countless hours grinding it out with the market, in an effort to create my own magic lamp. What I'm talking about is the culling of thousands of hours of research, real-time trading (I do not back test, or trade demo to prove a strategy), breakouts, blowouts, headaches, elation and in the end, insights that I would have never found without having taken the rocky, unstable, non-traditional route that I have.

After just short of 4,500 days of eating, sleeping and breathing markets; after endless research, writing, analysis and of course trading – at the ripe old age of 35 – I posses something more than a head full of gray hair…

I have a hidden treasure.

– A very special light, really.

As hidden treasure goes, often very few know it exists, when it does exist, which is why it was so hard to find...

Because I had to find it myself...

If there were others I crossed along the way - who already knew - they didn't let on.

And I understand why one would want to protect knowledge of the treasure's existence, and location.

Not many people seek to give their money away, just to give it away.

For those who do know of the treasure's existence though, sometimes they even intentionally burn their maps to keep others from coming into possession of information containing the whereabouts.

Without a map, the chances of finding the treasure are virtually zero, especially when one doesn't know to even look for it in the first place. What's more, for those who are seeking the treasure, sometimes even when they're standing directly over it, they still won't be able to see it.

That's how it was when I began looking...

Every once in a while over the years though, I would unexpectedly catch glimpse of an amazing shimmer within markets; something so bold, luminescent and brilliant, I would stop everything to investigate it.

But it was always gone in a brief second.

By the time I located what I thought was the source, no evidence of the glow remained.

The light was so brilliantly overwhelming though, I simply couldn't get it out of my mind's eye. I began looking for the magnificent illumination each day - and night - sometimes not sleeping for two, and even three- days at a time.

Many of those around me wondered if I might be going slightly nuts...

A few times, I think I might have wondered too.

I even spent the entire month of November in 2008 at the World Trade Center in Guangzhou, China working with several programmers and traders on the trading floor of

ECTrader- to develop and code the information I'd uncovered to that point...

This fall, I'll travel half way around the world to work the Chinese traders and programmers again... Not only are they some of the nicest guys in the entire world, but I've never met better programmers...ever.

Even after China, I was still missing few critical pieces though... But over this past winter and spring...

I finally compiled enough information to clearly see Volatility Illuminated in a way the masses have yet to.

I can tell you this... Towards the end, it was almost as if daylight were growing from the horizon- after a long dark night... Before I completely realized it- there was light everywhere.

In my arduous search over the years, there were moments so difficult; I almost gave up many, many times. Honestly, the search to see Volatility Illuminated was so grueling; I sometimes wonder how I made it through, without quitting.

You don't have to go through what I did though... And I hope you don't. And won't.

It is my hope - that with the information in this book - you will be able to clearly see Volatility Illuminated, without having to endure all that I did.

While compiling this book, I've asked myself - at least a dozen times - why I'm giving up any of the information I've found? My search was arduous and at times – literally – painful...

Strangely, every moment along the way, both good and bad, was the precise event required to dislodge (sometimes in the most unexpected of places too!) a little piece of information that I desperately needed to take another step forward with Volatility Illuminated...

Even an understanding of why Superman wears his underpants on the outside...

Again though, I have asked myself repeatedly why I'm giving up what I worked so hard to find?

1. I am presenting the information here because I believe I can say with a confident voice, most have never seen Volatility Illuminated before, at least, as I will present here. In addition, I believe retail traders sorely need the information right now.

2. I'm a trader. I trade for a living. Writing this book is a trade too. You get information- I get money. If I blow up doing something stupid five years from now, thankfully I will have hedged my position with a few bucks from these words.

I think it's a good trade... And by laying size out at the offer, obviously, with all of my years of sacrifice, research, and hard work, I'm long Volatility Illuminated. Now, I'm offering out of some of my position into strength - precisely at the 38.2 Fib Retracement. If the demand the tape has shown in the last few days of May is real, I may later regret not lifting my offer higher - now - but for the time being, I think it's fair.

Yup, everything is a trade.

I can't say I'm putting absolutely everything I've discovered in these pages…but it is definitely enough…

Likely, more than enough to finally give the little guy…

The retail trader…

– Something of value to help level the playing field in today's media-mania, monster truck institutional orderflow markets.

On another note, I am almost certain those in the financial media do not know about the treasure you're to going learn here… Otherwise, they would have already brought it to the market's attention. I've heard a few pundits lightly brush on one aspect of the treasure or another – almost as if they'd sensed it was there, but I do not believe any have ever found it (or even heard of it) completely.

Moreover, I believe there are a few great investors and market minds 'in the know' about the concepts to follow…though likely keeping quiet.

What's more, in my research, I've come across various pieces of the treasure - here and there - but I have never found much compiled all in one place…in an easily understandable format. What little of the treasure I have heard mentioned in conversations and radio, caught glimpse of on television, spied in magazines or newspapers, or found on the Internet – was not (I do not believe) geared for, or meant to grab the attention of retail traders.

Before we go too far, I need to give you a few warnings about the treasure in this book…

- It won't make you instantly rich this hour, but it could over time.

- You can't sell it on eBay today, but you can try.

- You cannot take the treasure all for yourself, though many people would.

- You cannot horde it in your upstairs closet at home; it won't fit in a shoebox.

- The treasure (by itself) likely won't even buy you a hotdog on the corner, but someone might offer to give you all the hotdogs in the world just to know what it is.

I would like to mention something else… You will not be able to see the treasure at all, if you only want a 'gimmick' to make money quickly. The treasure is not a 'gimmick' - it is real - but to see it, you must have the desire to truly understand markets and trading.

While writing this book, I often handed the manuscript to a small handful of 'test readers' for feedback. One of the test readers made a comment similar to:

"You may want to remove, or change the bullets about it won't make you rich and you can't sell it on eBay, because some people might think *well what good is it then?* or *I don't want to waste my time then* and then you might lose some readers."

I really appreciated the comment, because my friend was truly attempting to step into the shoes of the masses… I thought about removing the seemingly self-defeating bullets, but then concluded I would not.

Why?

Because my friend's perception of many potential reader's likely fickleness was spot on. However, the reason the treasure remains buried day-after-day, month-after-month and year-after-year to media, retail traders, analysts, and the public is precisely in the comment itself.

The treasure has remained hidden because one will not be able see it if they are only seeking an easy, automated, 'no effort', instant gratification solution to markets.

The treasure is mostly invisible to the retail eye because upon first glance, it appears worthless, though really, it holds immense potential riches and value.

The treasure is not simple; yet it's also not so complicated that almost anyone can't understand, or use it.

The only people who will not be able to see or use the treasure are those who never wanted to see it in the first place. The desire to see Volatility Illuminated - means you must have already - somehow - wanted to know (and see) markets better. Those who have never truly desired to understand markets and trading (and were not willing to put in some good old-fashioned hard work) just wouldn't know to even look for Volatility Illuminated in the first place.

- Media only cares about being in the middle of a 'hot story' and most pundits and analysts never really trade their own money...

- The bulk of retail traders hardly ever really 'think' about information they receive and act upon, and rarely truly attempt to learn fundamentals of markets...

- Many investors seek something, or someone to do the work for them...

- Often, if retail traders, professionals, and/or media can't see value in something instantly, they throw it away...

Thus, the treasure is most often invisible to the common eye.

I bet many readers have personally walked by it a dozen times and never even sensed something amazing might be nearby.

I know I did. On a rare occasion, I still do.

The treasure is so obvious though- once you see it, you might ask how you missed it all this time?

It is possible; however, that even after reading this book, some still will not be able to see it, even if I directly point it out, as best I possibly can.

How could it even be feasible for an 'obvious' trading treasure to exist, as I am mentioning here (something of great potential value), right infront of all of our eyes, and yet invisible to the masses?

My conclusion is the treasure remains invisible to the masses, because to see it - and to use it – means one must first not only have the desire to see it, but also acknowledge that the common perception of the information we receive (as even 'mostly valid') could be flawed...

- Wrong about the information we accept daily.

- Wrong believing what we've been taught is accurate.

- Possibly wrong about some of the things we think and feel at this exact moment.

- Maybe even wrong about our own memories right now.

How many are now thinking, "...*that sounds fascinating, please show me.*"

And how many are really thinking, "*Are you crazy? Whatever, this is hocus-pocus. My memories have nothing to do with markets.*"

Like the masses were historically wrong about the world being flat, the sun revolving around the earth and wrong about slavery - as being even remotely acceptable or moral, before the final Emancipation Proclamation and 13th Amendment came to life in 1865.[1]

(By the way, the 1860 United States consensus showed 393,975 individuals owned 3,950,528 slaves. The 1860 document also shows that there were just over 31 million people in the population. Only 8% of the population owned slaves.[2] What the aforesaid means is -as always- a small percentage of wealthy corrupt – sway the opinions of the masses and hold the majority of power in society, economics and politics.)

Much like the masses thought the world economy was absolutely doomed after the crash in October 1973, especially as major indices skidded south into the end of 1974. But in January of 1975, markets rocketed higher.[3]

Probably why Warren Buffet, the brilliant and amazing investor often says, "Buy when others are fearful and sell when others are greedy."[4]

Much why many will happily repeat Buffet's words, but then never act on the advice personally.

To step apart from the masses, one needs to take action.

Almost everyone tells children to follow their dreams, but so few truly do as adults.

Even after I show you the treasure, it will take time and effort to unlock the power within. Volatility Illuminated will not work instantly for those who want nothing more than a lotto-ticket, or 'plug-and-play indicator' -so they can mindlessly know when to buy and sell, without really adding any effort.

However, if you truly desire to see Volatility Illuminated and you're willing to put considerable effort into understanding the 'philosophy' behind such, the greater your chances of using the treasure to pull millions out of markets.

To see Volatility Illuminated though (and then utilize the information effectively) a paradigm shift will likely be required in your mind. No matter how hard I try, I can't help you see it if you totally believe what you've been taught about markets and trading (in terms of fundamentals, technical analysis and information), is absolutely *right and proper*.

Just know this, if you're willing to open you mind, please don't fear Volatility Illuminated may be too complicated to comprehend. I am proof of the pudding that you don't have to be a rocket scientist to get it. I am also virtually certain you don't need to be a seasoned Wall Street pro, or even college educated, for that matter...

All you need is the ability and willingness to challenge the traditional paradigms of what you have been taught about investing, markets and trading in today's high-tech, *light-speed information* world.

Again, in Volatility Illuminated, I hope to completely change the way you look at trading and markets and I seek to give you the tools you need to trade perceptively and profitably.

I have put hundreds of hours into the theories, concepts and strategies you are about to read. Moreover, I've spent nearly as much time tactically planning and organizing how to convey the information to you in this book. I did not write this book *just to write a book*. This book was written to deliver concepts to the masses that have been missed, overlooked, held back, or simply not discovered - to date.

With this in mind, every word, every sentence, paragraph and chapter has a specific reason for its placement within the larger work.

In Part One, we will cover some basic groundwork behind Volatility Illuminated, flushing out why some of what we accept as truth *is not*, while also seeing how instances of fundamental and technical analysis can be helpful to our trading, but really require *more*.

In Chapter Two, we will discuss why technical indicators are built for failure, are indeed currently failing, and how you can overcome the destructive reality at hand by taking time to step back from markets with clear eyes. We will also touch on why and how technology is really creating a larger *blind mass*, rather than helping.

Next, in Chapter Three we will cover why the much of what we think we know *could be an illusion*. I'm talking about our own memories even. I hope to challenge our unquestioning acceptance of our understanding and perceptions, not only of our own minds, but the reasoning and sensibility behind much of the information we take in daily.

In the remainder of Part One, we will walk through two technical strategies (Fibonacci Pitchforks and Quad-CCI Momentum) that I've found work reasonably well. However, I won't just present the positive aspects of Fibonacci Pitchforks and Quad CCI, but also seek to show how at times, almost all pure technical analysis breaks down. It is here that we will open the door to volatility, probability and the movement of distributions (statistics).

By the end of Part One, you should have moments of excitement, coupled with questions about whether anything 'really works' in this book, markets and/or in attempting to see and predict volatility.

Then, in Part Two, we will dive into descriptive statistics (in terms of distributions), while tackling volatility and probability right away.

In Part Two, I seek to not only present Volatility Illuminated in an easy-to-understand format (for those who do not have hordes of experience), but I also hope to show why tenured traders may want to rethink some of what they've been taught to believe as truths of information, markets, trading and volatility, as well.

I will also present some theoretical ideas combining physics and markets...

Don't worry though, no calculus or math will be required.

As you will see though, through Einstein's Theory of Special Relativity, I will prove that the entire paradigm of information colliding with markets has changed, partially through the acceleration of information over the past 100 years.

As we move through the first chapters of Part Two, you will also begin to learn why and how mass, acceleration, force and energy all 'critically' apply to trading today.

Again, you won't need to understand the math, but readers absolutely must take the time to understand the philosophy and theoretical modeling behind the concepts within Volatility Illuminated. I have done my best to explain the entire paradigm in plain, everyday language.

In addition, we will also combine physics (specifically mass, acceleration, force, and energy) with volatility, probability, subset distributions, and institutional benchmarking to form **Whistler Volume Adjusted Volatility** (WVAV) and **Whistler Active Volatility Energy • Price Mass** (WAVE • PM.)

The information you are about to read **is not** a regurgitation of old ideas, like most books on trading.

The ideas presented in Volatility Illuminated are fresh, groundbreaking, innovative, and are really my life's work.

Moving on, in Part Two, our discussions will move from physics to volatility/probability and distributions...opening the door to institutional benchmarking and VWAP.

The information on VWAP is intended to be delivered in a humorous format, though really, could be game changing for most readers.

After many, many hours thinking how to present the information to you, I finally came up with the story of Captain BIOVAP and Doctor Watermelon Stuffer, as the relay. (Trust me, if I explained it from a professional technical market perspective, not only would 70% of readers not get it, but the other 30% would be asleep by the time I was finished...)

However, do not take the information lightly.

Really, 'the theory of stuffing watermelons into mufflers' is why most retail traders lose.

Fact is, they never understood the game from the start. **When you understand Doctor Watermelon Stuffer, you understand institutional trading**.

With the aforementioned in mind, we will then break into WVAV and WAVE • PM.

My intent with WVAV is to show how and why we can integrate mass/energy concepts into VWAP, thus locating levels of volatility and probability, possibly providing insights many institutional traders have even missed.

The concepts you are about to read about are designed to help all traders; meaning both institutional and retail.

I will also show how and why WVAV and WAVE • PM allows one to see when markets are about to trend, when trending has ended, and even when to expect consolidation.

Through WVAV and WAVE • PM, readers will learn probability trading, perceiving volatility and orderflow (ahead of the game) and perhaps most important: how to use the information within - real - day-to-day trading.

By the end of Volatility Illuminated, you will posses information about indicator and information failure, volatility and probability, institutional orderflow, mass, energy and force in markets and distributions – all pulled together in a simple, understandable format and methodology...

You will understand what Whistler Volume Adjusted Volatility (WVAV) and Whistler Active Volatility Energy • Price Mass (WAVE • PM) are, while also seeing why the totality of the entire paradigm; the strategy, methodology, theory, philosophy, and signals are like nothing else markets have ever encountered...

You are about to set eyes on the critical underpinnings of market movements and trading – which virtually all media, retail investors and professionals never, ever see.

What you are about to read is powerful, useful, actually works in real time and can help you succeed in trading - once and for all.

But you MUST be willing to consider that everything you've been taught to date…is skewed.

Now that you know what to expect in the pages to come, I'm very excited to explain:

...why Superman wears his underpants on the outside...

...and also, why it matters so much - to you - right now...

...as you're about to discover...

You may want to consider wearing your underpants on the outside as well...

THE MAJORITY IS ALWAYS WRONG – ESPECIALLY RETAIL TRADERS

The 19th Century playwright Henrik Ibsen penned:

"The majority is always wrong."

Again, the 'majority' thought the sun circled the earth before Galileo.

The 'majority' thought the world was flat before the days of Columbus, even though other great thinkers had shown evidence of a sphere planet long before.

Around 330 BCE Aristotle surmised the earth was round and in 240 BCE, Eratosthenes created a reasonable estimate of the earth's circumference...

And yet, the masses still believed the earth was flat- for almost 2,000 years more.

It would be rude to say something like, *'people are cattle'*, which would never surface in the pages of Volatility Illuminated. After all, a statement like *'people are cattle'* would infer the masses simply move when prompted to do so, by almost nothing more than the directional stampeding of the larger group.

Actual people couldn't possibly be that mindless could they?

Would you ever mindlessly accept news or even [gasp!] believe in a mainstream media opinion, simply because the bulk of society had accepted the information as valid?

It's hard to believe for one moment, human beings might be that silly. **People would never credulously accept inaccurate social, political, or economic trends, merely because such had become 'progressive', or the 'accepted standard', would they?**

However, with each passing day and every laborious hour of research, I begin to **believe** they would. At the end of the day, the majority is **almost always**…wrong.

Perhaps, it's not completely the larger group's fault though. The more I look at the totality of information delivered to investors and traders; I see where and how they have been set up for failure (within trading and markets, economics and politics) from the start.

I'm not just talking about Forex either; I'm talking about all markets.

Some people refer to the phenomenon of the general investing public seemingly always on the losing end of the stick, as proof trading is nothing more than a 'zero sum game'.

Perhaps the common perception that markets truly are a 'zero sum game' is precisely correct, for those who've never been exposed to any information, other than the noxious rattling of media and so called 'professionals' who have an agenda.

Consider this for a moment:

If one eats apples from a tree with poisonous roots, chances are the apple is poisonous too, right?

After all, a poison tree probably only produces poison apples…

For the average investor –in the short run- the apples sure look pretty though and they're just so tasty, investors keep going back for more – even if they'd fallen sick from eating the apples once before.

The tree -like all trees- follows the seasons though. The tree blooms in spring, grows luscious apples during the summer, sheds its fruit in fall, and then grows dormant when the coldness of winter arrives. Spring always comes back though, even if the winter was longer than most on record.

When spring does finally arrive, media is always there to tell the world about the new fruit budding.

Investors are reluctant at first, remembering the sour fruit that had made them so sick the previous season…

Many are even still recovering from the poison they couldn't digest, or barf out...

But the media is there – touting the trees and the season, often reporting **this season** could be the **best** and **longest** and **safest** yet.

However, smart money already staked claims on many trees and their potential production in late winter, or early spring, often before the 'season' of today was even in the minds of most.

As summer unfolds and the apples begin to take form, media comments on how they look tastier than ever. While the apples are developing, they're not poisonous though, as shown by media eating gorging on the fruit as quickly as it can, while touting to the world how delicious and safe they are this time around.

At this point, the lure of the flavorsome fruit is becoming irresistible for most... Towards the end of the summer, media is at the harvest in full force touting '*the grandest bloom yet*', while also mentioning that this season's apples are not only the safest ever, but could still grow even larger.

Media even starts to present the possibility winter may never come again. Finally, giving into the media bolstered temptation – investors can't resist any longer. They buy apples...hordes of apples.

But the apples have a secret...

The apples from the poisoned trees are safe to eat only so long as the temperature remains warm...

But when the first cold sets in, the cores release a deadly toxin into the meat of the fruit.

Those who were the last to buy don't have a clue what just happened under the surface of their purchase, as they bite in…

Sometimes, even institutions buy tainted fruit too, thinking they know better than the public where the poisoned fruit is, and is not. But they're wrong too.

So I ask, why do the people keep buying apples from the exact same tree that produced poisonous fruit the previous season?

And then, I have to ask an even more important question…

In the paragraphs you have just read, did you… even for a moment…consider that perhaps it was not the tree, or the apples, or even the roots, which were truly poisonous…

Perhaps the tree wasn't really poisonous at all…

*But the soil **the tree is growing from**…is.*

THE PRINCIPLE OF
BUOYANCY IN MARKETS

I believe that back testing is a joke. Everyone has perfect 20/20 hindsight. Thus, in developing the trading strategies here (from a retail perspective); I made sure to test each and every one with real money. I'm not going to barf out a win/loss percentage, Sharpe Ratio, or any of the other canned junk people use to bolster whatever it is they are selling...

Because all that matters is today. Right here - right now. Past results are no indication, or guarantee, of future performance.

This book is not about a 'system', this book is about truly learning markets and becoming skilled at seeing Volatility Illuminated, once and for all. Moreover, in my humble opinion, learning to trade comes down to the quote:

The law of flotation was not discovered by contemplating the sinking of things, but by contemplating the floating of things which floated naturally, and then intelligently asking why they did so."

- Thomas Troward

Interesting quote right? Right. Except that at times, it's the opposite of trading. I hate to say it, but without a clear understanding of why what's happening is happening, trading is the opposite of buoyancy.

The reality of the situation is:

Traders and investors have a limited amount of time and money; however, markets have an unlimited amount of time and volatility.

If you simply toss your money into markets, thinking you've picked a safe entry and given your position a liberal stop, just so you won't be unnecessarily taken out and then step away… Chances are, markets will -eventually- hit your stop, or produce a margin call, much sooner than your sanity and/or wealth can 'wait out' the pain of a massive pullback.

I remember a long time ago, just after I started trading; I hit a three-month rough patch where I couldn't seem to make a decent trade to save my life. One day, angry, upset and whinny, I decided to just flip a coin during the entire US session and take my trades in whatever direction the coin prompted.

My theory was this: I should have a 50/50 shot, up or down, in picking the direction of my trades. However, I also figured my odds would be even better because I have something 50/50 probability does not account for: money management skills.

I figured even if I didn't like the trade, I could just place a strategic stop (cutting losses quick and letting winners run) and I'd surely come out ahead in the end.

Nope. I was just about even on the day...but it was a painful *even*.

See, if you don't have a real reason to be in the trade from the start, you won't have a solid reason to know when to get out. (And vice versa really.)

Anyway, randomly tossing cash into markets is more like 'the theory of sinking things', over that of buoyancy.

Here's what I want to tell you about the concepts coming in Volatility Illuminated...

Over the years, I have taken some big losses to uncover the information you are reading... I'm not even going to talk about the wins, because in the latter half of the book, you will see where, how and why the principles work. I don't need to tout what most people only do – past wins.

But I will touch on the losses – because they are what matters most to see Volatility Illuminated...

I've already 'contemplated the theory of floatation' for you...and as we roll out the principles of Volatility Illuminated over the following pages, you will see likely what works, without me having to run my mouth about my winners. If I were to only discuss my wins, the occurrence would be like giving you a set of keys to a supercharged 357 Mustang and an open highway, but then *forgetting to mention* the car has no brakes.

Throughout the years, as I was developing all that you're reading, every single time I lost, I would ask myself a massive pile of questions- in an attempt to uncover *why* the trade did not work.

Every single time I went through my little self-interrogation (with honesty) I constantly found one question as the main culprit behind almost all losses:

Was my information wrong?

There's really only two answers to the above:

1. Yes, my information was faulted, and/or...

2. My information was correct, but my understanding and application of the information was not.

Amazingly, it was the question, *"Was my information wrong?"* that not only caused many headaches, but was the catalyst for success.

It was the sinking of things that brought the volatility theories of flotation (which you're reading right now!) to light.

Again, it was in constantly asking the one question (that produced two more questions) that unearthed the hidden and mysterious volatility within markets that often plagues most traders for all of their days.

Funny thing those old self-introspection and honesty questions; here's what they produce:

Growth.

In the end, I not only found answers to why and how retail traders lose, but I also discovered the answer to, why Superman wears his underpants on the outside too.

The answer is this:

Superman wears his underpants on the outside because really, he knows he can beat up anyone who makes fun of him for wearing Underoos™ on the outside of his pants.

Just kidding…

Really, Superman wears his underpants on the outside because he is the inverse of mass humanity. Superman is everything we are not. Superman is the inverse of greed, ego, fear, dishonesty… All the things that keep retail traders from winning big.

Unfortunately, as regular people we are not, *"Faster than a speeding bullet, more powerful than a locomotive, or able to leap tall buildings in a single bound."*

But Superman is…

Hold on a second though… We might actually be able to do the marvelous things Superman does… What I mean is…how do you know - for sure - you can't? Have you ever tried?

With your underpants on the outside of your slacks?

Regardless if you've ever run down the street next to a passing locomotive –with your underwear atop your jeans- please know this…

In essence, we are penetrable organs and bones on the inside, while the world is seemingly impenetrable (to us) on the outside.

Superman is the opposite, impenetrable on the inside, and penetrable to the world from the outside.

Superman - as a walking bag of biology - is stronger than the world surrounding his physical form.

Logically, we can diagram Superman in relation to the outside world as:

Body $\rightarrow$ Pants $\rightarrow$ Underpants $\rightarrow$ World

On the other hand, we can diagram regular people (non-superheroes) in relation to the exterior world as:

Body $\rightarrow$ Underpants $\rightarrow$ Pants $\rightarrow$ World

or

World $\rightarrow$ Pants $\rightarrow$ Underpants $\rightarrow$ Body

Do you see what I'm saying?

Let me break it down, just in case...

What we are: Breakable.

What Superman is not: Breakable.

What we are: Slow, brash, opinionated, and mortal.

What Superman is not: Slow, brash, opinionated, and mortal.

What we are: Stuck on the belief our underpants should go on the inside of our jeans.

What Superman is not: Stuck on the belief his underpants should go on the inside of his trousers.

It makes sense that as metaphor of Superman's extreme difference to regular humanity- is his preferred order of underpants, relative to what most people would ever consider in their own lives. Precisely what most would scoff at others for considering, or doing...

Here's where I'm going with all this underpants business...

To truly understand why much of the information we believe to be valid within trading and markets is flawed, we have to be willing to invert what we have previously accepted as valid.

What I'm saying is that metaphorically, if we want to understand volatility and markets, we **must** be willing to consider the possibility that what we have learned and believe as 'truth' and/or 'the right way', may not be so correct after all.

Again, let me clarify.

I'm not saying the information you have received is just plain wrong…

What I am proposing is perhaps a different paradigm exists within trading, markets, and the validity of information we accept from mainstream media, and to transcend and evolve in our ability to comprehend, predict, and profit within Forex, equities, options, futures, whatever…we must be willing to accept an inversion of what we have come to know as truth.

Perhaps, what we believe to be true - right now - may not be.

To see where and how some of the information we receive and accept within markets may be faulted, we must be open minded enough to accept new paradigms.

If we can remain open to new ideas, we might be amazed at what we are about to find in the following pages.

Bottom Line: If you want to be a superhero, you're going to have to be willing to wear your underpants on the outside, knowing you are doing precisely the opposite of what the masses believe is valid and/or acceptable. Again, 'the majority is always wrong', which is why they wear their underpants on the inside.

The masses believe that '*underpants on the inside*' is the only way to go about day-to-day business. The 'underpants on the inside' crowd even laughs at anyone who wears their drawers on the outside.

Those who wear their underpants on the outside - have superpowers. Mr. BVD's atop khakis and Ms. Brassiere over blouse can fly.

The undergarment-rerouted-to-the-exterior minority, are really the inversion of credulous, blind and herd-following masses- who simply accept common dogma as *truth* because it is *the accepted standard,* even though it's wrong.

Super-traders know much of the information presented to the masses…is flawed…especially when it comes to markets. Most retail traders and investors are the inverse of super, which is why so many lose in markets…and then even keep coming back for more, again and again, without ever questioning what's really happening under the surface.

With the aforementioned in mind, we will now move into Chapter Two, where we will discuss how many technical indicators are failing in the current market, while uncovering why so many traders are likely suffering, when attempting to trade simply from common technicals.

Chapter Two will open our initial discussion on volatility, though we will only scratch the surface for the time being. Then, in Chapters Three and Four, we will cover two technical combinations (Fibonacci Pitchforks and Quad CCI), discussing how the indicators help traders, while also touching on why current market volatility could be causing false signals as well. Over the following pages, I ask you to break from what you currently believe as valid and true, concerning information, indicators, and markets...

I'm pleading...

If even for a moment, while reading this book, please wear your underpants on the outside, like Superman.

At least, metaphorically, anyway...

CHAPTER TWO

WHY INDICATORS ARE FAILING IN THE CURRENT MARKET

The initial version of this chapter was printed in Forex Journal in the spring of 2009, but has been revised significantly since.

When it comes to trading Forex, it's no secret retail traders struggle desperately and most often, lose. The aforementioned statement is dismal, I know.

However, it doesn't have to be that way...

With a little understanding of "*why*" retail traders seemingly (endlessly) toil, shifting the paradigm may actually be easier than many think. In short, when we truly take a moment to step back from technical trading and examine how information and indicators impact the decisions of the masses, a clear picture of why traditional chart-based signals are 'built for failure' from the start, should arise.

By understanding the true paradigm of technicals, and then making a few slight adjustments, traders could potentially find themselves suddenly empowered to navigate markets with confidence and clarity.

RETAIL VERSUS INSTITUTION

SEPARATE TAKES - SAME INFORMATION

Foremost, it is important to note that institutions move markets, not retail traders. However, with many institutional and retail traders acting at similar time, it would almost appear as if they were trading from the same signals. Upon first glance, it would appear as if traditional indicators do indeed provide reliable signals for market movements.

In reality though, traditional indicators (like MACD, Stochastics and CCI) are providing "false signals", especially on shorter-term time frames. Institutional order flow has nothing to do with 'technical signals' and is truly derived from perceived risk aversion and future fundamentals.

Despite the true reality at hand, some retail traders continue to believe traditional technical analysis accurately looks into the fundamental mindset. What you MUST understand though, is common retail technicals have nothing (at all!) to do with institutional trading and do not accurately look into the minds of institutional traders.

At the core of the issue, common technicals never accurately see into the minds of institutions, simply because the technicals are derived from an empirical event that has already occurred (lagging indicator) within price action, while fundamentals attempt to mitigate fundamental risk of today, while attempting to step in ahead of possible fundamental events of tomorrow.

Retail traders often lose, because even if they are able to perceptively step into the minds of institutions, trading successfully commands the trader is not only able to see the true fundamental paradigm, but also know <u>when and where</u> to implement a position to capitalize on such. In non-technical language, one may be able to accurately distinguish that a particular currency will lose value over the next year because of deterioration in fundamentals; however, successfully acting on the information is much, much more difficult, when considering the inherent volatility within Forex markets today. Looking at our first image, readers will note the significant rally in the EUR/USD into December 2008. The euro's momentary recovery can be attributed to a dead cat bounce from torrid selling in the previous months, coupled with the momentary loss of belief the US Dollar would continue to avert risk throughout the global economic crisis.

Conspicuously, even if traders were able to accurately predict the U.S. Dollar was about to boldly recover from late fall rally in the euro, blindly taking a position could have been devastating, if implemented based on fundamental outlook alone. The single daily candle highlighted in late December shows almost 400 PIPs of volatility, which should serve as empirical evidence of the excessive volatility at hand within Forex markets.

The larger issue is simply while institutions and retail traders may have unearthed similar fundamental information (though often institutions have greater clarity) retail traders who act on technicals or fundamentals alone, will constantly fall victim to the inherent volatility within Forex today.

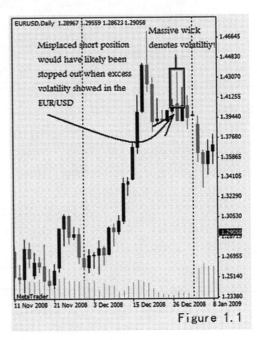

Figure 1.1

What's more, the indicators retail traders act upon are often significantly different than that of institutional traders, something many are not even aware of.

For example, when looking at descriptions of services banks and institutional companies provide for larger FX participants, one will note the first two technical strategies/indicators are almost always Volume Weighted

Average Price (VWAP) and Time Weighted Average Price (TWAP).

However, the charting packages most retail traders use almost never contain VWAP and TWAP, as indicators. In fact, even MetaTrader (arguably the retail standard), does not contain VWAP and TWAP preloaded. Traders can find the code in the back of this book, on the Internet, and on my Websites fxVolatility.com and WallStreetRockStar.com; however, the aforementioned are not delivered already installed within the software's various custom and traditional indicators. The point here is the main *indicators* institutional traders are not only looking at, but also acting upon, are rarely visible within the retail trader's world. Most often the retail trader must actually intentionally seek out the indicators; but how can one find what one does not even know exists?

There's even more to the story, and as readers are about to witness, the paradigm behind retail technical analysis may have been flawed from the start. Even worse, the common technical indicators most retail traders covet could even show greater amounts of false signals in the future.

LOCK, STOCK AND DOGMA

To understand why technical indicators are becoming more and more troublesome in volatile markets, one must take a step back from the entire situation and examine the "nuts and bolts" of the larger situation at hand.

Constance Brown just about says it all in her book titled Technical Analysis for the Trading Professional (McGraw Hill, 1999), where she asks:

"Why does it appear to us that conventional technical indicators are failing us as we approach the 21st Century? What has changed?"

- Constance Brown

Technical Analysis for the Trading Professional

As a brief side note, while Brown's book is almost a decade old, the information is still extremely innovative, as she often examines the "truth" behind how and why indicators produce signals. Even more important, Brown also attempts to uncover how and why traders act on the information received.

In the case of failing technical indicators, Brown hypothesizes technical indicators are failing because too many people are acting on the same information - at the same time. She points out virtually every charting program comes with the same pre-loaded indicators, with the same pre-set variables. What's more, she also unmasks the unfortunate reality that **many traders never even bother to question, or change the preset variables within the pre-loaded indicators.** In essence, traders simply accept the "factory settings" within their indicators as dogma.

At first glance, it would seem common sense that many people acting on the same information – at the same time - would create a sort of 'self-fulfilling prophecy' within technical signals. However, the reality of the situation proves differently. Really, some people acting on the same information at the same time may create a slight amount of 'self fulfilling prophecy'; however, when too many people move in the same direction, at the same time, the real outcome is volatility. Think of it like this: If a troop of ten men run are running on the street together and suddenly need to stop before a busy street, all ten will likely be able to do so. However, if 1,000 men are running on a street and a few in front attempt to stop before a busy street, the mass of bodies in motion behind the will likely bump into one another, with the greater whole pushing the few in the front into the intersection. Someone call a paramedic.

Why would trading be any different? When a hundred thousand traders take the same position, at the same time, based on the same information, and suddenly the market moves just slightly opposite the herd's expectation, what will the obvious outcome be?

You probably guessed it; the large mass-herd of traders moving in unison creates a *pop* of volatility as the collective whole attempts to switch directions.

Making matters worse, once the herd is pushed slightly into the intersection; electronic stop orders begin tripping across the world, like grids of lights rolling into darkness, as a mass blackout ensues. The "mass effect" of too many people acting on the same information, coupled with the domino effect of electronic stop orders being tripped globally, creates excessive volatility within intraday trading.

While retail traders do not carry enough weight to propagate an all out "trend" in the world of Forex, they do create short-term volatility. I like to call it **Herd Induced Intraday Volatility, or the "HIIV Effect."**

Retail traders move like a swarm of bees and so when I see a clear signal from a common technical indicator on a 5, 15, or 30-minute chart, I look for the HIIV effect of volatility to begin stinging.

By the way, with stop order rule changes coming (for U.S. retail Forex platforms) in July of 2009, the 'rolling blackout volatility' effect could wane, while overall reversal volatility could increase as traders hold losing positions as long as possible (it's just human psychology) until major critical technical points are hit.

While the removal of stop orders in U.S. trading platforms may help bolster longer periods of trending, **<u>major</u>** points reversal points could surface with fierce volatility…

HIIV EFFECT IN ACTION

For traders having trouble believing the technical 'herd effect' I previously described actually exists, please take note of the following example.

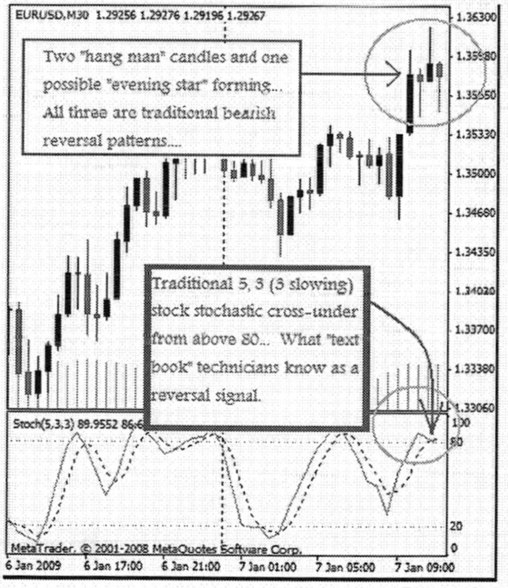

Figure 2.2

(By the way, one needs to do nothing more than scan 5, 15 and 30-minute charts to discover plenty of examples of the HIIV effect.)

Looking at Figure 2.2, traders will notice the 30-minute chart is clearly showing signs of a potential reversal pending, at least in terms of traditional technical indicators, like candlesticks and stochastics.

One cannot miss - even for a second - that the 30-minute chart is displaying three bearish candles (two red hangmen and one evening star). In addition, using the pre-loaded stochastic indicator (5, 3, 3) traders see a clear cross of the K-period (blue) under the D-period (red).

The aforementioned stochastics cross-under is occurring at the 80-line, the exact point many technicians believe produces a reversal.

Seems like a clear short-entry point right?

Hmm...

Look at Figure 2.3, which shows the EUR/USD rallied significantly **after** the appearance of the two hangmen, one evening star and a stochastics +80 cross-under.

There are two events occurring in this scenario:

First, institutional order-flow (read: fundamental mindset) likely believed the carry trade differential and risk facing oversold levels of the EUR/USD were prompting short covering and short-term relative range trend continuation, if even only for a moment.

Second, when the false signals appeared, many retail traders likely took short positions, expecting a larger reversal to ensue.

However, when the reversal did not show, those same traders were forced to cover positions...en masse, thus helping fuel the torrid bull candle eight bars after our short signals (Figure 2.3). Often, when false signals surface, we see a slight amount of "wiggle" shortly after, while traders and institutions attempt to decipher the reality of the situation. As the dust begins to settle though and traders realize the technical indicator was false, a sharp move occurs as panic sets in. Again, the panic HIIV effect can be seen in Figure 2.3, eight bars after the final false hangman short signal.

The EUR/USD quickly (and sharply) rallied from the 1.3580 (roughly) area to the 1.3680 region in one 30-minute bar.

For the EUR/USD the aforementioned pop is '*faster than usual*', thus we can infer many traders were caught going the wrong way.

Figure 2.3

What's more, Figure 2.3 also shows stochastics trending downward during the bulk of the ensuing upward momentum, even after the false signals appeared.

Does all of this mean technical indicators can no longer be trusted whatsoever?

Not necessarily; however, there are a few critical points to consider. Foremost, common sense tells us that most retail traders attempt to take intraday positions, without taking much notice of long-term fundamentals. What this means is many traders likely take positions against the larger-trend, simply because their misunderstanding (or lack of will to do the proper research) hinders the mass contingency of "at home traders" from seeing the situation clearly. Moreover, retail traders often watch shorter-term timeframes, more often than they take note of the 4-hour, daily, weekly, and (even less often) monthly charts. Without a clue of the larger technical and/or inherent fundamental pictures, they are really just 'trading blind.'

FINDING SANITY WITHIN THE CHAOS

What all of the previously mentioned translates to is an inferential conclusion where technical indicators (at least those commonly used by the mass army of retail traders) will provide false signals more often on shorter-term timeframes, over longer-term counterparts. Simply put, retail traders who are taking positions on shorter-term intraday timeframes (based on stock indicators), are actually making the situation worse, and only adding to intraday volatility – even more. It's important to note retail traders are not the sole blame for volatility, as many institutions can also make silly decisions as well. What's more, in today's trading environment, the historically transparent environment of fundamentals (GDP growth, inflation, interest rates and underlying economic reports) have many professional analysts scratching their heads with the added variables of present and future national debt, credit related (out of the blue) bombshells, inflation, deflation and risk aversion.

Thus, in the current Forex paradigm, the HIIV effect coupled with fundamental uncertainty are creating the "perfect storm" for erratic intraday movements and HIIV-derived volatility, contrary to traditional market-movement common sense.

When coming to terms with the fact that technical indicators are - indeed - failing in today's markets, many readers may perhaps be wondering if there is any way to truly put the odds back on their side?

The answer is yes. The solution is three-fold. **First,** Retail traders can help remove uncertainty by spending more time attempting to learn and understand the larger fundamental paradigm, while also trying to perceive where future fundamentals will land. By doing so, retail traders are attempting to not only decipher why present volatility exists fundamentally, but also map future possibilities for seemingly unanticipated moves beyond today's price range.

Second, retail traders must also begin taking greater notice of institutional indicators such as VWAP (and other benchmarks), understanding that institutional order flow trumps all. Taking greater notice of VWAP (and other benchmarks) could provide at-home traders with superior insights into the institutional mindset and thus, potential future price action.

Third, retail traders must take the time to understand the philosophical and theoretical underpinnings of volatility/probability, while also seeing how the dynamics of markets demand the application of the principals of physics, helping put the odds of success back in their favor. All three aforementioned points could be of great benefit in helping defeat false technical signals, seemingly random price action, and the lack of volume/order transparency retail traders are faced with daily.

With everything we've covered in Chapter Two in mind, please make sure to remember common technical indicators (especially on shorter-term timeframes) are providing greater amounts of false signals, with each passing day.

It is arguable trading purely from technicals once allowed retail traders to clearly see the fundamental paradigm unfolding via price action; however, within today's Forex volatility, the bar for success has been moved much, much higher.

All participants must now pay attention to fundamentals, institutional-grade technicals, volatility/probability, and market-physics to truly trade profitably in the constantly changing markets of the 21st century…all of which we will cover in the upcoming chapters.

CHAPTER THREE

BEHIND THE CURTAIN

" Imagination can not only make people believe they have done simple things that they have not done but can also lead people to believe that they have experienced more complex events."[5]

– Elizabeth F. Loftus

In Chapter Two, we discovered how and why technicals are prompting false signals in today's markets. Really, I would be very shocked to learn <u>most</u> readers were already aware of the failure(s) happening, and had taken the time to identify specific instances of such, while also really considering the 'philosophy behind' false signals in today's markets.

When I discussing failing indicators at speaking engagements, or occasionally in educational Webinars, I generally always ask how many people were aware of the situation. Surprisingly, many will indicate they already had 'some notion' there was a problem; however, virtually none have taken the time to investigate the matter more deeply themselves.

Really, we've become so 'default dependant' that we often do not question what's happening behind the curtain, even something inside of us is telling us we should. I'm not just talking about indicators, I'm talking about the information we receive through media daily too… I'm even talking about our own memories.

Throughout Chapter Three, you're going to see some concrete evidence of why and how our own memories fail us from time to time. In addition, we will also see how and how some of the information received daily from media is not really telling us the full truth. The two together are a deadly combination for investors and traders. To transcend the modern paradigm of 'faulty information' potentially coming from inside our own minds (propagated by external information and media), we must be willing to look behind the curtain- **always**, even if we are part of the curtain, in and of, ourselves.

THE PHILOSOPHY OF LOOKING BEHIND THE CURTAIN, EVEN IF IT'S NOT SOCIALLY APPROPRIATE

Information and memory failure are not only subjects that keep me up at night, but were part of the motivation behind releasing the information in this book, in the first place. Over the past few years, it feels as if I am finding more and more evidence showing that even if one *intuitively* feels the information they are receiving is faulted, hardly anyone actually takes the time to investigate *how and why* the propaganda is flawed.

I think it must be like having a tick embedded in one's back… One might know the little bugger is present after having spotted it in the mirror after stepping out of the shower. However, because the little thing is so hard to get to and because it's not overly bothersome at that moment, he or she ignores it, hoping it will just go away. I would think the host would ask another for help to remove the tick, which they cannot reach with their own hands.

However, for many, actually asking another for help just seems awkward, perhaps because for whatever reason, they're embarrassed that the tick is there in the first place. Drawing attention to the annoyance just seems too uncomfortable to approach. Here's the thing though, 'the tick' could be carrying bacteria and every minute it is ignored, the greater the probability the carrier could be infected with a malady like: Lyme Disease.

Let me tell you what I know about Lyme disease…

Just a few weeks after I first moved to East Hampton (at the tip of Long Island) in 2008, I developed a funky little 'bulls-eye' rash on my shin. At the time, I didn't think too much about it, as I figured it was likely just a funky bruise from biking, or something. A few months later, I remember going to bed one evening feeling a little strange, like I was just a 'more tired' than usual.

I didn't get out of bed for five days...

I had no idea what was happening. Fact is, I had no idea I'd been bitten in the first place... Prior to moving to East Hampton, I'd never lived any place where Lyme disease was a threat, and thus, had no idea to even be on the lookout for anything peculiar, much less actually able to recognize possible symptoms. (Stay with me for a moment and you will understand why this little story is so important to trading and our perception of information.)

I finally pulled myself out of bed (feeling completely wrecked) determined to find a doctor in my new hometown; however, I still didn't know what the problem was... I remember thinking I must have caught a wicked strain of flu or something... While searching for doctors online – and just by dumb luck really – I stumbled on a Webpage detailing the symptoms of Lyme disease. After only a few minutes of reading, I was convinced Lyme disease was the problem, and thus, I suddenly felt slightly better (at least) having some insight into the catalyst behind my illness. Luckily, a great friend was there to help find a doctor who could help and the next day I was treated with antibiotics.

I caught the Lyme infection early and after only seven days of antibiotics, I was fine. However, for those who aren't able to properly diagnose the condition, or ignore the symptoms completely… The effects of Lyme disease (over the long haul) can be devastating.

Often, doctors unfamiliar with the illness misdiagnose Lyme disease as Chronic Fatigue Syndrome. Their patents are mistreated and eventually…end up feeling the full force of the bacteria overtaking their bodies.

The point behind all of this is very, very important. If you can't read the symptoms, you can't diagnose the illness. The bull's-eye rash on my shin was a dead giveaway that Lyme disease was present for anyone who'd seen one before, or if they had been educated on such matters. In my case, however, I had never lived anywhere the disease (or ticks) were present and had never been educated on symptoms or preventative measures.

Fact is, because I didn't even have a clue of the possible danger lurking, even when a symptom blatantly showed up on my own body.

Here's what's so important about this little story… The increased volatility of today's markets is a symptom of unclear and misleading information, nervousness of the investing public and troublesome economic and business conditions. In addition, increased volatility within today's markets is also a symptom of a larger problem whereby individuals, traders and even institutions are not able to clearly and accurately find confidence in markets. Bad information is the bacteria in the bloodstream. Also, remember in the close of Chapter Two, when I mentioned VWAP (an indicator of institutional movement) as not readily available in most retail platforms... Just another example of how the retail trader is not only missing vital information, but perhaps not even aware the missing information exists at all.

I have to ask another question now, though it might seem a little odd...

On a personal level, is it possible your perception of markets is flawed, or even worse...

Your own memory might be failing you right now, and you don't even know it?

Don't laugh... I'm serious, *'just what if?'*

Do you believe most of what media delivers – news, polls and opinions – is/are true and valid? What about financial news? Moreover, do you believe your memories of past financial news and events are rock solid?

Chapter Three is geared to soften hardened and cynical hearts, while cracking open the most riotous brains to the possible paradigm- *that we might all be snowed.*

As competent adults, friends, husbands, wives, analysts, traders, executives and market participants- overall, we like to think of our minds as rational, with little error. What I'm talking about is personal confidence in our recollection and perception of past, present and future reality. But what if…

What if some of the things we think we know as real - were never real in the first place? How many of us could actually admit to ourselves (or others) that even though we believe we are mentally adept, we were, and perhaps still are, wrong about our own memories even.

I'm not just talking about trading psychology here, I'm also talking about human psychology…

Perhaps what I'm about to show is part of the reason hardly anyone really knew the financial crisis was coming. I know plenty of guys who currently tout *'they called it all along'* and *'they knew something was wrong way beforehand'*, but do not have any extra zero's in their bank and/or trading accounts to actually prove it.

Yet, they all seem to have perfect 20/20 hindsight. Out of the thousands of professional and retail traders I know – only **one** trader that I know of – placed a bet in markets before the crisis started…

My friend Carl purchased index put options ahead of October of 2008, specifically because he foresaw a greater problem stirring in markets, than most perceived.

I'll never forget the day in October 2008 when Carl called with news of his windfall. He is the **only** trader I know of who actually **took action** on the information his intuition was picking up on. **All** of the other traders, they're just kidding themselves. They didn't see it coming ahead of time, or they would have made money, but that won't stop them from telling you differently.

Now, I would like to give you an example of how the information we receive from markets – and from ourselves – could be flawed. To do so, I must back up in time and tell you about a market event – as it unfolded in my life…

THE STORY OF BLACK
MONDAY - 1987

Do you remember the crash? I hate to admit this, but I was only in high school… I do remember the crash though, because my father traded futures actively. One afternoon when he picked me up from school, he seemed lost in thought. The day was Monday, October 19, 1987 – the day the Dow Jones Industrial Average (DJIA) barfed 508 points, or 22.6%.

During the majority of my high school years, every Monday my old man would pick me up after the final bell and we'd go have a burger and talk, you know- *man to man*.

He'd then drop me back of at school for tennis, wrestling, or whatever other practice I needed to make it to…

I have to say though, those Mondays *sucked.* I'm kidding really, as my old man is gone now and I'd give a ton to have just one of those Monday's back…

Back then, however, I didn't feel quite the same. Every Monday, as the end of classes would near; I'd consider finding a bus to throw myself under, just after the final bell let out. See, the entire Monday ritual with my father was about more than just having a burger and chatting; I was also required to hand over a piece of paper containing all of my grades (I wasn't the best student); freshly signed by each of my teachers. Every week, good old Mark got more than a burger; Mark received a well-done earful about his hideous grades, always in the middle of a restaurant.

October 19th, 1987 was very different from all the other Monday's though… On Black Monday, My old man– the speculator, the stock operator, the futures trader and the aerobatics pilot…never asked to see my grades. As we sat down to eat in the old 1950's Deco diner, he was studying one thing and one thing only: The Wall Street Journal. But the paper wasn't fresh from a store, it looked well worked over, as he'd been writing on it all day. There were notes everywhere: calculations, ratios, lists, letters and as I recall, even a few items circled with curse words scribbled to the side.

The burger joint was deserted - just enough - that I remember hearing the ceiling fans rocking back and forth over the soft clamor of a mid-afternoon shift change in the background.

Dave ordered a cup of coffee (black) from behind his paper; I ordered a Stewart's root beer. Do you remember? The kind that comes in a bottle, with orange swirly writing on the neck, stamped with '1924'.

My brew arrived with a straw and my old man's Joe-gorging in cream and sugar. I remember him looking over the paper at me (I was waiting for the grade card demand), down at his mug filled with cream and sugar, to the side, and then to our gum-smacking server, who was already on her way back to the kitchen. I'm not sure if he smiled or sneered, but he drank the blunder anyway.

Silence was all I had with my burger that day, as I watched Dave's same dish toil in abandon at the edge of the table. Silence –dead silence– like the kind where you're cautious not to swallow too loud.

As I was eating, I unconsciously reached for my Stewart's. As I was siphoning the last bit of soda, I accidentally made a huge *schlurgle* sound, the kind that only comes from a straw. Normally, a schlurgle would not have been a big deal; today though, the *schlurgle* was like dropping a piano in morgue…

Words cannot describe the displeased look the grade-czar shot across the table- just after I'd broken his concentration with my noisy mouthful of root beer. I think I made my first official trade at that moment; I'm pretty sure I was long and strong all of the 'run for your life' calls in the entire world.

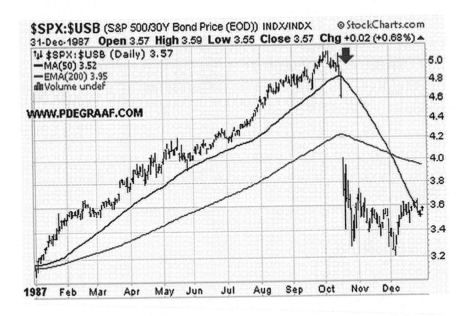

Just at the moment I thought Mr. Financial Paper *gawker-atter* (and International king of staring contests) was about toss me and my empty bottle of Stewart's all the way to Africa, he suddenly diverted his peepers over my shoulder. Thankfully, the waitress had decided to check on his uneaten hammy. Saved by the forgotten burger; talk about a bull market! Before she could say anything though, he'd already shook her off like a pitcher does a curve ball.

Then, unexpectedly- he called back after her…

"Get the hoodlum market-maker another stout, please would you."

"Whoa! Did Dave just order another Stewart's?" I recall my next thought as, *"this is a setup for sure… No doubt about it, I'm leaving in a body bag."*

"C'mere, I want to show you some things…" That's all he said while the waitress was acquiring another bottle of suds… Even after he ordered the second soda, I have to admit, I waited a few moments before moving over to the chair next to him. My old man was a great guy, but the second soda order was definitely out of place for our Monday talks… Taking my new seat, I looked up just in time to catch the waitress winking at my old man.

His face remained stone cold.

Then he began, *"Today, you learn about life, money, fear, greed and most of all…opportunity."* Over the next few hours (and like six more Stewart's!), he explained everything he possibly could about Black Monday.

We talked about principals of psychology, markets, stocks, trading, order flow, how market makers stopped picking up phones, futures, derivatives, economics, common sense, mass herd mentality, media Chicken Little, global money shifts, and most of all…the thing he pounded into my head over and over…

"*Mark,*" he looked directly into my eyes in a way that let me know I was about to hear something very, very important, "*today, Black Monday… It <u>will</u> come again in your lifetime…once, maybe twice…*"

He paused for a moment and then nodded in quiet kind of way with a content smile, before turning back, "*you'd better be looking for it, because it's going to happen – eventually - and most people will be caught off guard.*"

Then he smiled again, "*You should be able to make money on the way down, but if you miss it – while most people are running scared from newspaper headlines, you should be looking for some of the greatest opportunities- to be presented in decades.*"

In my entire life, I can't remember a more memorable afternoon than Black Monday with my pop.

That afternoon, I think we both suddenly figured out that while I wasn't the most punctual student, markets touched my soul in a way my classes never had. I don't know why, but <u>I just got it</u>. That dark day of market devastation with my father, I became a stock operator forever. I was born a speculator from the crash of 1987.

I can't remember everything my old man said that Monday, but I do vividly recall him also speaking in terms of gravity, airplane engines, speed, aerodynamics, weather, instruments… All in context of markets, but in terms I'd already come to know from him– flying. The trader turned aerobatics pilot, my old man, my father, Dave, made sure to present the information in concepts I'd already learned, to help it all sink in.

Occasionally, I wonder if 58 years beforehand, another young guy possibly made the same mistake of loudly schlurping the last swig of root beer too…while in the company of his father, recoiling from the aftermath of Black Tuesday, 1929.

Today, when I drink a root beer, I think of the crash of 1987 and how in an ironic way, the historical global market plunge was really the conception of my life's path. My old man died in his plane a few years after on July 4, Independence Day… That might seem like a little more information than is required here, but it taught me something else…

If you're going to love something, love it all the way- and **never** give up.

I sometimes wonder if my life would have taken another turn, if the crash of 1987 had never occurred. Maybe I'd just be shining shoes for a living now.

It doesn't really matter though- whether we're traders or shoe shiners, because eventually a crash is going to catch us all…unless we can see it coming beforehand.

But to perceive the future… We have to be certain of the past…

THE CONFESSION OF
MASS MEMORY FAILURE

There's a point to the entire story you just read...

Presenting a little insight into where I'm headed with all of the aforementioned mumbo jumbo; we must all question not only the information we receive daily, but our own memories as well. In short- while so many of us believe that our recollection of historical events within our own lives is infallible, the empirical evidence on the table could be saying something incredibly different.

Shortly after the turn of the present century, an article appeared in the UK Guardian where writer Claire Cozens penned, "*A group of US scientists has discovered that advertising can alter people's childhood memories, making them remember events that never happened.*"[6]

The above excerpt is specifically referring to the 2002 study by Kathryn A. Braun of Harvard Business School, Rhiannon Ellis of University of Pittsburgh and Elizabeth F. Loftus of University of Washington titled:

Make My Memory: How Advertising Campaigns Can Change Our Memories of the Past.[7]

In the study, the authors assert:

*"But times are changing, and some marketers are beginning to realize that memories are constructive. Some have even benefited from the fact that their consumers' memories have been manufactured. **Take, for example, Stewart's root beer. They report many adults seem to remember growing up drinking Stewart's frosty root beer in bottles. This is impossible, because the company only began full-scale distribution 10 years ago, and prior to that only fountain drinks were available.** It could be that glass bottles adorned with sayings like 'original' 'old-fashioned' and 'since 1924' provide consumers the illusion of a past that they might have shared as a child. In fact, the vice president of Stewart's marketing swears he remembers drinking their soda after Little League games in an area where distribution was unlikely, but admits, 'Memories are always better when they're embellished' (Prince, 2000)."*

Fact is, I never drank Stewart's root beer in my childhood and neither did any reader here, unless you specifically went to one of the Stewart's soda fountains, or you're under the age of 19, as of 2009. [8]

However, while all of the story about my father and Black Monday is absolutely true (to the best of my memory), the fact that I really do seem to remember drinking Stewart's root beer on the afternoon of the 1987 crash, shows that we are all fallible to memory inconsistencies. Here's the thing- I would have likely gone through my entire life thinking **I was** drinking Stewart's root beer in my childhood, had I not come across Loftus' article in my research. Really, I had no reason to even question my own memory, especially about such trivial things such as the type of soda I drank in my childhood. However, now that Pandora's box is open, a little detail like a memory of root beer brings up many, many larger questions.

I'm not talking about questions about the solidity of my memory, as I'm pretty sure most of it is in pretty good shape; what I am discussing here is that my 'little slip' of a minor detail- when coupled with millions of forgotten 'minor details' by the mass investing public…might really be a much larger problem. As I write this, I am truly wondering how many readers **believe** they personally could never have any *'itty'* inconsistencies in their memories?

My direct question is this: I have admitted my memory is flawed, can you?

The thing is, until I stumbled on the research from Loftus, I would have never even thought to question the memory I was holding in my own mind, as flawed… Much like when I first noticed the little bulls-eye bruise on my shin, I no idea to even consider the possibility of Lyme Disease…

Fact is, the greatest threats to our health, our success, our livelihood and our longevity…often stem from events, happenings, understanding(s) and occurrences **<u>inside</u>** of our own minds and bodies, which we are not aware of.

True, the tick was an external catalyst poisoning my body, however, the inability to recognize the symptoms was a failure in my knowledge, mind and constitution in that I had not even taken five seconds to consider the inherent dangers I should be cautious of in my new surroundings... I can blame the tick forever, or I can take responsibility for not having proactively sought out the tick, before the tick found me.

After I read the article by Loftus (*and almost all of her downloadable work on the University of Washington Website, which I highly recommend*), I took the afternoon off and simply went for a long walk. Though my mind (for whatever reason) <u>still</u> sees a Stewart's root beer bottle in my hand almost twenty-two years ago, the evidence at hand has presented a different truth, which I absolutely must accept, **<u>even if by doing so, I am admitting to myself that my own memory is sometimes flawed</u>**.

I can say with confidence that my memory of drinking root beer on the afternoon in 1987 is valid; however, I must admit that the detail of the brand is not. Interestingly, as Loftus shows in her work, much of modern memory failure may actually be propagated by advertising... What's more, her studies also show that memory failure is not only real, but devastating to many who have been accused (and convicted) of a major crime, even though they were truly innocent. (More on this in a moment...)

My next question to you is this: How can market participants trust their memories of the trading and economic events from yesterday, if modern research is proving our memories are highly capable of failing?

Would you believe memory failure is so plausible that *real adults* could even misplace reminiscences of Mickey Mouse and Bugs Bunny? What about those who '*swear on the Bible*' in Federal court?

The 'Facts of Root Beer' are Undeniable

From Stewart's Official Website, Stewart's states:

"Root Beer was only available at Stewart's root beer stands and later, at Stewart's Drive-Ins.

In 1990, Cable Car Beverage Corporation acquired the bottling rights for Stewart's and began selling Stewart's Root Beer in 12 oz. amber glass bottles."

Claire Cozens of the UK Guardian also wrote: "*Adults shown a mock advert in which Disney World visitors shake hands with a Bugs Bunny character became convinced they had done the same as a child.*

But shaking hands with the famous cartoon character could never have happened because the giant rabbit is a Warner Bros creation and does not feature in any Disney theme parks."

What I'm really trying to hammer home here is our memories can deceive us... **all of us.**

Just when we thought we had '*steel traps*' for minds, another paradigm surfaces encouraging **all of us** to question what we remember (and believe) in our own minds.

A DATE WITH BLIND DEVOTION

You may have heard the cliché; *Wall Street has a short memory*... Well your damn right it does and so do investors who keep coming back time-and-time-again to eat poison apples from the same damn tree that put them in the hospital only a short while ago.

Fact is, when markets begin to move (mortgage markets, dot com stocks, commodities stocks- the likely upcoming REIT penny stock surge, whatever...) the masses seemingly perceive the potential to make a few bucks, and as momentum begets momentum, suddenly become infected with (what I like to call) *exuberance-induced-amnesia*... Joey-Q-Public lines up one more time to take on the same reckless and misinformed investments all over again.

Remember the Internet stock market dump at the turn of the present century? The only difference between the dotcom.bomb and the recent mortgage crisis was instead of owning paper, the same exuberant '*want rich, will buy blind-quick*' mass investing public rotated what was left of their wealth from ravaged tech stocks into houses.

The **same** investors went back for the **same** poisoned fruit (in a different wrapper), thinking it *couldn't possibly* be venomous again.

But it was…

And it will be…

And they will go back for more- again and again and again…

Why?

Because their memories and deeper understanding of the situation are not only synthetic and flawed, but manufactured from media, as well.

I **seriously challenge** you to ask your colleagues, family and friends what the dotcom.bomb was all about?

I'd bet you will receive answers with sounds of *'artificially inflated'* and/or *'overvalued Internet stocks'*, perhaps *'Enron'*, and most likely: *'daytraders'*.

On Wikipedia.com, there's a page titled Dot-com Bubble, which cites the main reasons for the whole debacle as, "*A combination of rapidly increasing stock prices, individual speculation in stocks, and widely available venture capital created an exuberant environment in which many of these businesses dismissed standard business models, focusing on increasing market share at the expense of the bottom line.*"[9]

Please read the above explanation one more time, I'm going to point out something huge in just a moment.

Moving on, please take a moment to read the first line of the paragraph following the passage you just read: "*The venture capitalists saw record-setting rises in stock valuations of dot-com companies, and therefore moved faster and with less caution than usual, choosing to mitigate the risk by starting many contenders and letting the market decide which would succeed."*

Here's what we have to understand. In the first statement, the only mention of *Joey*-Q-Public's personal responsibility is 'individual speculation in stocks'. Then, in the second statement -*the big explanation*- the blame is **clearly** headed in one direction: Venture capitalists.

Just like Stewart's root beer product placement influences memory and just like pictures of Bugs Bunny at Disney Land influence memory- mainstream media always finds an escape goat for tragic events in markets, which is/are the only things investors really remember, after the fact. In essence, just like I can't remember clearly whether it was Stewart's I was drinking on October 19, 1987, investors can't, don't, or don't want to remember they were **individually** the ones who bought their dotbomb.com stocks in an exuberant greed-fueled-feeding-frenzy. The bottom line is, because media recollection of the event now directs blame at overzealous Internet entrepreneurs, greedy venture capitalists and daytraders, most people have replaced their personal responsibility and reality of the situation with the manufactured memories delivered by Internet, television, print and radio. The 'product placement' here is that of 'shift the blame', where investors forget he and/or she were (and are) responsible for their own losses, by buying into the hype in the first place.

Why does this happen? Why is manufactured memory the accepted standard?

Foremost, information is everything.

Take a moment to look at the larger outline of the Wikipedia article…

Little 8.2 'Media' is ***nothing*** more than three reference links at the END of the article…

The links are:

- e-Dreams
- SatireWire
- Startup.com

I don't want you to think I'm shifting blame here, because I'm absolutely not. Individuals are solely responsible for their own investment decisions.

Period. However, based on the previously mentioned article, we can also assume two critical points – one intuitively and one empirically:

1. Empirical – As Loftus' studies show, human memories are not only capable of error- but are pregnable. (FYI, for those who are not yet believers, I will present even more evidence in just a moment.)

2. Intuitive - On the whole, people are lazy, greedy, move in herds, credulously believe media, are addicted to exuberance, and frankly, never question **anything** unless the same media actually tells them to question such.

I encourage you to look beyond my above Wikipedia cite regarding for a greater dotcom.bomb explanation. Please Google the term. You will not likely find a substantially wide variety of truthful explanations.

What's more, the register of explanatory articles is seemingly devoid of pieces covering how media predominantly promoted, hyped, exaggerated, publicized fueled, and inflated the whole Internet stock mess.

If historical coverage of the event seemingly absolves media from any responsibility –as playing a major part in the catalyst of the Internet bubble- does that mean mainstream financial (and non) media wasn't a huge part of the problem? Will the masses forget the circuslike 'pitchman' role financial media played throughout the whole event?

Perhaps they already have.

Speaking of memories, do you remember in Chapter One, when I mentioned the 50,000 watt mega-media-mouth bulb? Well here's the thing- Financial media is always the first in line to promote any bubble whatsoever, because the bubble itself is exuberance, and exuberance means ratings, and ratings mean advertising dollars. Exuberance equals revenue for media.

What's more, when appearing on television, pundits are often **told** to *ramp up* the tone of the discussion...

And because pundits want *and need* exposure they do. Here's an example *-a VERY real example-* of how I know, from the inside... Just so you know though, I am not going to mention the network's name, as I don't want to have to use all of the proceeds from this book fighting a lawsuit. Nevertheless, here's what most people don't see...

Pundits are contacted by producers to appear on news and talk shows based on expert status, producers exchanging information with one another, inside station 'go to' lists and/or if the pundit happens to be in the middle of news, or has produced news (like an article for a major financial Website) of notable mention.

Sometimes, the Producers will call the evening before to notify the Pundits that they are invited to appear, though most often; the calls come in last minute just hours before the slot. (By the way, usually there is no compensation for appearing on CNBC, FOX Business, or various other networks, as an outside contributor, the trade is exposure for time.) The producer briefs you on the subject you will be speaking on- sometimes providing a little reading material, or questions; however, more often than not- the pundit is only aware of the subject and intended scope of discussion. *And that's okay, after all, pundits are supposed to be experts.*

But here's what many might be surprised at... On more than one occasion, I have actually been told to '*really speak out*' and even '*argue fiercely*'. What the average Joe doesn't know (sitting front-side of the television), is this:

- **Producers know what they want and they know who they can get it from.**

- **Pundits who do not play ball- do not come back.**

- **If you are told to argue, you argue.**

- **If you are told to be loud, you are loud.**

I encourage you to watch the financial news with a fresh set of eyes. Are the commentators and pundits seemingly excited and/or speaking above one's normal 'inside voice?' (Key network personalities generally do not have to play the same game of fetch, just FYI)

Are there multiple participants in the studio, who seemingly 'debate' or almost 'argue' opinions, even though it seems like there's not much to argue about?

Do you think the elevated levels in their voices are purely because they are passionate about markets?

Alternatively, is it possible the producer perhaps guided the 'energy level' of the segment, or show beforehand? You better believe it.

Is yelling 'fire' in a crowded movie theatre effective?

✓ You better believe it.

✓ **People move fast when they're fearful...or in the case of exuberance: hungry.**

There are two problems with yelling fire though:

1. Unless you want to go to jail, you have to find someone to blame your outburst on...

2. If you do get away with yelling 'fire' in a crowded theater (which you most likely will, because it's dark and the patrons are paying attention to something else really), if and when you do it again, you're going to have to yell even louder, because you've already pulled the stunt once. The savvy *stampede starter* might switch up his tactic to something like:

 'Look out! He's got a gun!'

Same thing - different wrapper.

(By the way, I'm not very good at manufacturing emotion – and thus, the networks don't call very often anymore.)

In my research on the dotcom.bomb explanations easily available on the Internet, there was **one** excellent article that came up on the #1 Google search page that deserves significant mention…

The article was published on April 24, 2000 in New York Magazine; arguably not a mainstream source of financial news. (Taking note of the article's date, the words were penned in the heat of the moment and have a significantly different tone than Wikipedia's *reflection*.)

The subheading of Michael Wolff's article Dot-Com Bomb reads:

"We've all been waiting for the next Great Web Wipeout. But the Orwellian technology geeks never imagined the fuse would be lit by an old-media magazine article."[10]

The first thought that comes to mind is, "Here's a guy who really *get's* **it**," meaning our love affair with media-fueled exuberance.

Wolff asserts:

"Mania is always a pure play. It's reality confusion. It's blind devotion. It's a media thing.
To me, the key constants of this manic phase have been the vast, astounding, messianic, mesmerizing certainty on the part of technology-industry people on the West Coast (together with their cursed, Orwellian language) side by side with the profound insecurity on the part of the media that has reported the Internet story. While stupid about technology, stupid about finance, stupid about the nature of the hype itself, these people (we people) have been absolutely willing to believe."

Wolff's writing is just brilliant…

I believe he should be given a gold medal for the words:

"It's reality confusion. **_It's blind devotion._** *"*

At the heart of the issue, blind devotion means total and complete <u>unquestioning</u> trust, completely forgetting the events of the past.

Forgetting the confusion created on the way up (*and then on the way down as well*), by the same 50,000-watt-mega-fog-mouths' only a few hours, days, months, or years ago.

What the 'mega-fog-mouths' will not do -**<u>ever</u>**- is publicly admit they were part of the problem.

Wolff caps the statement with the words, *"stupid about the nature of the hype itself, these people (we people) have been absolutely willing to believe."*

Dear readers, what will you remember about the financial crisis three months, six months, and even five years from now? With so much information coming at you from all angles (national debt, credit swaps, predatory lending, GDP loss, global tribulations, asset nationalization, reckless spending, woefully high unemployment and foreclosure rates), what will you really remember- especially when considering all of the information you haven't even received yet... I can tell you one thing for certain; as markets truly start to recover, who do you think the first 'pitchmen' to talk it up will be? Yup- media. You will then be bombarded with a completely new suitcase of information...and memories. In six months, nine months, or a year, will you really remember the events in detail – other than retrospective mega-fog-mouth headlines?

If you do forget a year from now, fret not, I can guarantee you media will provide you with a fresh serving of 'retrospective specials', just to jog your memory. Perhaps help re-create your memory. *Oops, did I just say that?* I'm sorry, like media, I can't remember what I just said, even though I just said it.

Let's focus on something else though...let's focus on you becoming a millionaire.

Let's focus on how much money you can make trading...

How much money you can make **right now.**

I mean right now.

I know three stocks, all under $5, that will triple in the next thirty days. Here they are:

1. Nasdaq: IJCTSW – I Just Changed The Subject With…

2. NYSE: ESYWF – Exuberance, So You Would Forget

3. OTCBB: MPS – My Previous Statement.

Fear and exuberance are tactics commonly used to divert one's memory from five seconds ago, to what could happen a few moments from now… Good financial writers **know it** – effective media **knows it**…

I hope you do too.

Please take a moment to consider the following excerpts from two separate articles by Elizabeth Loftus –

In the 2003 article **Our Changeable Memories: Legal and Practical Implications** (Nature Reviews: Neuroscience), Loftus states, "*The history of the United States justice system, like those of other countries, is littered with wrongful convictions made on the basis of **mistaken memories.**[11] Huff recently estimated that about **7,500 people arrested for serious crimes were wrongly convicted in the United States in 1999.** He further noted that the rate is thought to be much lower in Great Britain, Canada, Australia, New Zealand and many other nations, especially those that have established procedures for reviewing cases involving the potential of wrongful conviction.* "[12]

And also…

"*The U.S. Department of Justice released a 1996 report after analyzing 28 cases of DNA exonerations and concluding that **80 percent of these innocent people had been convicted because of faulty eyewitness memory.**"*[13]

The reason I've placed the above two quotes from Loftus in this book- is because I want traders to understand that if people **who are swearing on oath...in a court of law** are potentially falling victim to memory failure...

It **IS** plausible our recollection of similar technical signals, or market conditions that may have surfaced two weeks ago...could be wrong. In addition, it is possible the hyped (regurgitated and fresh) news we take in daily is altering our memory of the past, and thus, our perceptions of the present...and future.

Given the **massive** ramifications of accusing someone of a crime while on the stand (meaning an innocent person could go to jail for a long, long time), we can infer the witness was either **almost one hundred percent sure** their memory was correct, had some other type of mental, or psychological defect to allow such to occur. Alternatively, perhaps –somehow- their memory was artificially altered... Aliens did it.

Just kidding. In reality, as Loftus research shows, the power of suggestion (in recollection) can change what we remember about –and how we recall- past events.

On another note, media is often the 'psychological defect' witness I just mentioned, in that media has no problem accusing anyone, and everyone, else to divert attention from their own participation in the crime spree, metaphorically speaking.

Investors who continually go for the same poisonous apples -repeatedly- either **do not know** their memories have been impregnated, or sadly, cannot and/or will not find the personal courage and strength stop the vicious cycle of <u>**blind devotion**</u> to media. In essence, the acceptance of blind devotion is admittance to not only historically believing in, but also having (consciously) allowed our memories to have been manufactured by synthetic sources.

One would think nonchalantly believing in a hyped hot stock tip, or media touting of an economic number *intraday* is one thing, however, recalling a false memory in a court of law would likely see a much more serious 'other' requiring significantly greater consideration and importance.

However, because <u>**it is proven human memories can fail in a court of law**</u>, where there are potentially dire consequences, what does the evidence of such fallibility mean about the plethora of *less important* information we're constantly receiving every day?

By the way, somewhere buried in this chapter is a good explanation for why I lose my keys every three days…. Kidding…well…somewhat anyway.

Beyond the paradigm of our memories as fallible, there could be another '*add-on*' to the entire situation- making matters even worse…

What if the information we receive daily isn't even **precisely** correct in the first place?

Given that we have just clarified there is indeed considerable possibility that our memories can fall victim to 'manufactured recap' (based on media tributes, or revisits), what are the chances of correctly analyzing history to make accurate decisions (today) if the information was flawed from the start? Even more worrisome, what if almost no one had any clue that information was flawed from day one?

There's just no way the masses – investors and media – could be that blind, is there?

If the information we have accepted as truth– suddenly presents another picture, how many would honestly accept the reality of the new situation and how many would actually attempt to justify the previously accepted untruth?

Part of the current volatility paradigm within markets is that of the public's mass anxiety in reaction to events, propelled by media… Like all the quiet warnings of a pending credit disaster --prior to the fall of 2008, most investors and traders ignored the possibility…until it became front-page news.

However, by then it was too late and those 'in the know' had already profited and/or exited positions, precisely at the moment common investors were coming to terms with the realization the apples they had eaten (again) were poisoned.

Before we delve into the next section further examining 'how memory is contaminated' I would like encourage all readers to take some time to explore Loftus' work. Readers can find multiple articles and resources on memory failure, along with links to Loftus' three books on her University of Washington Webpage.

For additional information, please visit:

http://faculty.washington.edu/eloftus/

I firmly believe Loftus' research is nothing less than *game-changing* and I sincerely hope she receives a Nobel Prize for her efforts - seriously.

MEDIA MADE MALADAPTIVE MEMORY

Please take a moment to read the following statement by Loftus closely: "*More specifically, when people experience some actual event — say a crime or an accident — they often later acquire new information about the event. This new information can contaminate the memory.*"[14]

Let me ask you a few questions...

- Have you ever lost when trading?

- Have you ever watched as your portfolio freaked out in a global financial crisis?

- Have you ever seen the Dow Jones Industrial Average plummet from over 14,000 to under 8,000 in a matter of months?

- Have you ever witnessed excessive volatility within Forex that either manifested, or accelerated a loss?

If you are an active trader, you likely answered yes to all of the above questions. I would like to present the possibility that after-the-fact *'manufactured memory'* often plays a significant role in many traders' ability to adapt to, evolve with, and overcome volatility, when markets change paradigms. In essence, the average trader's (and mass public's) inability to rapidly adjust to continually shifting market conditions is derived from two sources:

1. Maladaptive fear and blind devotion.

2. Lack of knowledge and experience.

For the duration of Chapter 3, we're only going to focus on #1 above, *maladaptive fear and blind devotion.*

(The totality of Volatility Illuminated is geared to help overcome #2.)

For those who are not familiar, *'maladaptive fear'* is a type of unnecessary, manmade **bad fear**, which is often harmful in our lives. On the other hand, 'good fear' is known as *adaptive fear.* Again, 'bad fear' is termed *maladaptive fear.*

As a working definition, "***Adaptive fear*** *is a nuanced emotion that diminishes during times of relative safety, while* ***maladaptive fear*** *lurks beneath the surface all the time, quick to make its presence known whenever there is discomfort, the unknown, or change.*"[15]

Maladaptive fear is really the product of a traumatizing circumstance, where after a devastating event has taken place in our lives, when faced with a similar situation (or possibility of), our brains and bodies manufacture the symptoms of biological fear, even though nothing is truly *'to be feared'* at all.

In the book, Injuries in Athletics: Causes and Consequences author Semyon Slobounov states, "*fear is one of the major components of psychological trauma that may or may not develop as a result of traumatic injury.*"

The importance of the previous statement rests within the words, "*as a result of.*"

Maladaptive fear or *conditioned fear* is a byproduct of an event that can literally alter our brain chemistry to react to future events. Again, bad fear is separate from adaptive or *healthy* fear, in that when we are feeling adaptive fear, we are (literally) usually faced with physical peril.

Specifically, according to Rosen & Schulkin (1998) "*Fear responses (e.g., freezing, alarm, heart rate and blood pressure changes, and increased vigilance) are functionally adaptive behavioral and perceptual responses elicited during danger to facilitate appropriate defensive responses that can reduce danger or injury (e.g., escape and avoidance).*

However, pathologic anxiety, as a form of an exaggerated fear state, may develop from adaptive fear states as well. If that happens, the hyperexcitability of fear circuits that include several brain structures..."[16]

I cut off the sentence a little there, as the passage delves into brain chemistry terminology (if you'd like to continue reading, please see the endnote); the point is that beyond our normal 'healthy fear' levels, constant upsurges of the adaptive fear state can mutate into maladaptive fear, where we begin to feel anxiety and fear (constantly) even when we really don't have anything to truly fear at all.

Do you think media plays a significant role in pushing the greater public into a state of maladaptive fear?

You should – but you should also know media does the same with **'maladaptive exuberance'** too.

In essence, a maladaptive state is where we perceive current events as correlated, or will possibly have the same outcome as previous – traumatizing – events, even though the current event is completely independent from the previous event.

But maladaptive fear cannot exist without first having a trauma take place…

In the case of media, the trauma does not always have to come in the form of 'instant shock', like 9/11 (*every single person I know –including me- was literally glued to the tube*) or the financial crisis, as a slightly duller example. However, the *trauma* can be a slow, grinding campaign of fear, or exuberance propaganda.

Why do you think the evening news is filled with so much negative crap? Because as a society we not only buy into it big time, but also have become addicted to *needing to know* the negative crap, so we're not blindsided by trauma.

But the trauma **is** the slow creation and conditioning of maladaptive fear by the daily negativity and fear grinding. If you're always worried about something, you're likely trusting of the anyone has an '*in*' to information, **or news** that helps alleviate your anxiety, or make you feel safe, by presenting you with *more* information about negative information.

Case in point: I've randomly pulled two screenshots from major news Websites … (*I've left their names out as I try to avoid a lawsuit for the second time in this book.*)

Again, I did NOT search for the news, I simply hit two major websites as I was writing these words and snapped the screens with no doctoring, or digging to manufacture evidence. The point, as you will notice on the following page, 70 to 90 percent of the information we're being fed by media today- **is fear based wretchedness**. However, the *same* fear peddlers will likely change their campaigns into **exuberance-based wretchedness**, just after enough of the fear junk has been deployed so that the public is well conditioned into a reasonably stable state of constant anxiety...

(By the way, I pulled the two following images only minutes apart – from different continents – to show fear-media isn't just American, it's global.)

In the first example from a major European publication, nine of the 11 headlines are CLEARLY negative...

That's 81% negativity in terms of the information delivered at the moment the screenshot was taken.

(I grabbed the headlines on May 27, 2009 – just FYI)

It's amazing...scary...and devastating to see the maladaptive anxiety conditioning paradigm in action.

Figure 3.4

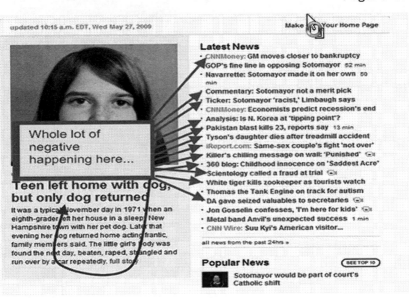

Figure 3.5

The above major U.S. publication is slightly better in the fear department; however, **65% of the headlines are still negative.**

All of this leads us to Media Made Maladaptive Memory (MMMM)

 Media Made Maladaptive Memory is created through the conditioned acceptance of hype, negativity and/or whatever else we are being pitched at every moment by media that is seemingly **imperative** to our immediate protection or well-being, but is really doing nothing more than creating un-necessary anxiety.

*(By the way false **Media Made Maladaptive Memory** is not a professional term- it is my term, which I made up to try to explain the entire paradigm in greater detail. I'm only telling you, because I hope to be a part of the solution, not a cog in the larger problem and I don't want you to think I'm citing a professional psychology term, when I'm not.)*

Here's what I'm saying though: mainstream '*modern*' media is possibly creating maladaptive fear (and anxiety) within the masses, who are constantly begrudged with fright, panic and dread through televisions, the Internet, radio and newspapers.

I ask, is the constant bombardment of negative, or almost synthetically positive (exuberant) headlines a form of intimidation in and of itself? I thought public intimidation was illegal, though perhaps I'm wrong.

I seem to remember reading something about civil rights somewhere… Perhaps it was Title 18 of the U.S. Code Section 241, Conspiracy Against Rights, that said something like, "*This statute makes it unlawful for two or more persons to conspire to injure, oppress, threaten, or intimidate any person of any state, territory or district in the free exercise or enjoyment of any right or privilege secured to him/her by the Constitution or the laws of the United States, (or because of his/her having exercised the same)."*[17]

Honestly though, I can't remember exactly what it said...

Merriam-Webster dictionary defines intimidation: *"intimidate, cow, bulldoze, bully, browbeat mean to frighten into submission."*[18]

Here's what I'm not doing: Insinuating whatsoever that media is breaking any laws, after all, this is America and media has the right to free speech, just like everyone else. When we see 65 percent and 80 percent of headlines touting negativity though, we might want to at least (personally) take notice that there's a type of 'influence' taking place.

If the news just reported news, like non-trivial whatever, would you be interested? The flaw in the human condition is that we are drawn to sensationalism- whether it is fear, or exuberance. The critical point of understanding here as well, is that intimidation isn't always in the form of negative headlines. Remember my previous discussion on the dotcom.bomb?

Well, if you were trading prior to the turn of the century, you likely remember terms like "new economy."

Mainstream media was **all over** 'new economy' mania touting rising indexes and rocketing stocks, while Internet companies poured in the advertising dollars... In January of 2000, sixteen dotcom companies forked over (on average) $2.2 million each for 30-seconds of fame during Superbowl XXXIV.[19]

Momentum begets momentum and nothing attracts a crowd, like a crowd.

The problem is not only are our memories 'influenced' by whatever negative, or positive hype is taking place in the moment, however, the controlling emotion of the present is actually the catalyst helping to keep the 'extreme anxiety' helix in motion... See, while in the thick of exuberance, media is your best friend- all the inside scoops, stories and tips... The pitchmen are all too happy to sell the greatest show on earth, and dear friend...the trend will never end...

I don't care if it's Internet stocks or real estate; all trends do eventually end.

Case in point, the last three letters of trend are:

e n d

When the bubble bursts, your old media pal (who was peddling tickets to the show the whole way up), will immediately puke out the words: *I told you so.*

And as quick as lickety-split, hawker-media will turn tides, being the first to change face and tell the crowd, 'it was that dirty old rich fatso Ringmaster.' The same media-mouth that was selling the tickets to the circus-leader's show (only moments ago) will suddenly become 'a vigilante of the people', asserting that it's imperative to *take down* the portly *'Richie Rich'* who did you wrong.

Someone, somewhere, always swindled the public; never the public or media themselves. During the Internet era, it was highflying entrepreneurs and venture capitalists; individuals had nothing to do with the stocks they personally bought while riding high atop fluffy greed clouds. In the current crisis, individuals were duped by predatory lenders, with the larger criminals being credit-swap traders and investment banks… All those people who bought too much house, just because 'they could', had nothing to do with it.

Fact is, in the first moments of any bubble bursting, media will immediately find the biggest scapegoats it possibly can (as quickly as possible) immediately, diverting the public's memory from the ham-bread hype Mr. Internet and television were handed out, all the way up. Then, as the bubble draws out, media drowns the masses in negativity… After all, idol minds are the devil's workshop and an idol mind- might begin to remember that media had almost as much to do with the 'irrational exuberance' of the bubble, as those they are currently hanging.

The conditioned maladaptive fear shtick works perfectly and just as the crash rounds out of the bottom (and as quickly as Jekyll turns to Hyde); those swell old media mouths and pundits are back on the bull bandwagon again, circus exuberance in hand…

Old 'mega-mouth' might even mention he's learned his lesson and *this time*, he can help you spot the poison apples.

The evidence shows -repeatedly- the deflection of blame for crashes and bubbles, coupled with the **constant cyclical maladaptive fear and exuberance conditioning** ensures no witnesses will remember the *truth* from the scene of the crime…

What's more, the 'confusion' of blind devotion is an ongoing game that must be continued daily- even when there is no apparent 'fear' and/or 'exuberance'.

And as you're about to see, even the 'accepted standard' of statistical information regularly delivered to masses is part of the larger 'confusion' puzzle keeping the investing masses from ever seeing the truth clearly.

THE ACCEPTED STANDARD OF NOTHINGNESS

It's blind devotion really- to take in information and never question how the information is compiled… Reflecting back on the same Loftus' quote from the opening of this chapter:

"Imagination can not only make people believe they have done simple things that they have not done but can also lead people to believe that they have experienced more complex events." [20]

When the EUR/USD plummets 300-PIPs intraday (after the release of a consumer sentiment survey), retail traders who were caught going the wrong way can easily fall precisely into the aforementioned trapping.

See, the 'event' was the loss. Was the cause- the consumer sentiment report? Not really, the true cause was the breakdown in the way information is collected and delivered. The subsequent event to the sentiment report, which preceded the market move, was sell side traders firing out orders because the market was moving away from their benchmark. (I know this sounds a little foreign right now, but by the end of Chapter Eleven, it will likely all come clear. The larger explanation of the motivations behind institutional buying and selling demands a thorough explanation, which we will get to in Part Two of Volatility Illuminated.)

IMPORTANT NOTE:

*Over the following pages, you are about to read how one commonly coveted 'economic indicator' is slightly flawed... Let me rephrase that... The report is not flawed in itself- actually, it is calculated exactly as the 'industry standard' says it should be. However, the **'industry standard'** in itself, is slightly misleading and probably needs to be reconsidered. Again, I am not saying the report, or the organization, is misleading the public, nor am I attempting to pick a fight with the organization. I am merely speaking to the accepted standard of gathering, analyzing and deploying information to the public. It may be possible that 'polling data' within media (including politics) might need a little reshaping to help deliver a more accurate picture to the public.*

Let's take a moment to talk about the scope and accuracy of the fundamental data we receive in markets.

According to the Philadelphia Fed, the University of Michigan Consumer Sentiment Survey is:[21]

Consumer confidence surveys measure individual households' level of confidence in the economy's performance.

The monthly Survey of Consumers is a nationally representative survey based on approximately 500 telephone interviews with adult men and women living in households in the co-terminous United States (48 states plus the District of Columbia). For each monthly sample, an independent cross-section sample of households is drawn. The respondents chosen in this drawing are then re-interviewed six months later.

A rotating panel design results, and the total sample for any one survey is normally made up of 60 percent new respondents and 40 percent being interviewed for the second time.

The Index of Consumer Sentiment (ICS) is derived from the following five questions:*

1. We are interested in how people are getting along financially these days. Would you say that you (and your family living there) are better off or worse off financially than you were a year ago?

2. Now looking ahead--do you think that a year from now you (and your family living there) will be better off financially or worse off, or just about the same as now?

3. Now turning to business conditions in the country as a whole--do you think that during the next 12 months we'll have good times financially, or bad times, or what?

4. Looking ahead, which would you say is more likely--that in the country as a whole we'll have continuous good times during the next five years or so, or that we will have periods of widespread unemployment or depression, or what?

5. About the big things people buy for their homes--such as furniture, a refrigerator, stove, television, and things like that. Generally speaking, do you think now is a good or bad time for people to buy major household items?

Okay, so now, let's go back to the basics; reviewing lecture notes from "Introduction to Statistics," by Steve Stanislav of North Carolina State University, it appears there are really three types of sampling that apply to this type of data collection:[22]

1. Simple Random Sample (SRS) of size 'n' consists of n individuals from the population chosen in such a way that every set of n individuals has an equal chance of being selected and each sample has an equal chance of being selected.

Note: A SRS does not allow for favoritism by samples nor self-selection by respondents

2. Stratified Random Sample - to select a stratified random sample, you must first divide the population into groups of similar individuals called strata/stratum. Then choose a separate SRS in each stratum and combine to form the full sample.

3. Multistage Sample - same concept as a stratified random sample but you divide each strata even further. So random samples eliminates bias, but when a population

consists of humans (as it does on earth), accurate information requires more than 'a good sampling design.'

Hold your thoughts on the sampling space for just a moment, let's take a look at the "surety" behind the numbers we are receiving from the media in the first place...

There are two factors go into figuring out how "confident" one can be that an entire population feels one way, or another: The confidence interval and the confidence level.

Starting with the confidence **interval**, which according to Creative Research Systems is, "the plus-or-minus figure usually reported in newspaper or television opinion poll results." For example, if you use a confidence interval of 4 and 47% percent of your sample picks a particular answer, you can be "*sure*" that if you had asked the question of the entire relevant population...between 43% (47-4) and 51% (47+4) would have picked that answer."[23]

The second factor is the confidence **level**, which according to Creative Research Systems "*tells you how sure you can be. It is expressed as a percentage and represents how often the true percentage of the population who would pick an answer that lies within the confidence interval. The 95% confidence level means you can be 95% certain; the 99% confidence level means you can be 99% certain. Most researchers use the 95% confidence level.*"

So let's say that you live somewhere like, well let's just say: the United States. In the North American country, there happens to be 305,705,463 people, as of the spring of 2009. If you wanted to report –with accuracy- how confident a statistical study could/would be that 95% of the population felt a particular way, you would first find the "confidence interval," which we just covered. However, let's drill into the number a little, just to see if there's anything we might find interesting… If we input the expected confidence level of 95%, with a population size of 500… attempting to calculate how *about half* of the people felt on one matter, or another, our confidence interval would be 4.38. What this means is that if you survey 500 people in America on a subject, you can be 95% sure that between 45.6% and 54.4% of the people would agree.

Funny thing though, if you wanted to be 95% sure that between 78% and 82% of the people in America agreed with your answer, you would need a sample size of 1,537 (the confidence interval would be 2, FYI.)

TO SEE VOLATILITY ILLUMINATED YOU MUST BE WILLING TO

SEE INFORMATION CLEARLY

Okay so here's the deal… The commonly accepted methodology behind the way major polling data is collected is drastically faulted- though it's not the University of Michigan's fault. It's about 'media protocol' delivering partial truth to the masses. Part of the issue is that of the good old *"media business as usual"*, which propagates misinformation to the public.

Really, what I'm getting at, is that given the population's size, we can be 95% sure that about 50% of the people in America agree with the survey's results.

I don't want to bash the University of Michigan here, because it's a general rule of thumb that when sampling a population for statistical results presented to media; one needs to use the 50% benchmark to assume a worst case scenario.

Then again, the media doesn't really tell you this little detail when most surveys are released, do they? Honestly, I couldn't even find the information on Reuter's site. What I'm really saying is that what we have is a two part problem. To pad for error, researchers are forced to use "worst case" confidence levels, which in turn means smaller sample sizes. Making matters even more unnerving, when the results are published, consumers are not informed of the data or confidence levels used behind the information they are receiving.

Take the last sentence in the first paragraph on the December 2008 report, which read, "*Although most consumers view the recent price declines as due to the recessionary downturn in spending, even longer term inflation expectations have decreased. While most consumers expect a rebound in prices when the economy recovers, they now anticipate a somewhat lower overall inflation rate to prevail in the future.*"

Here's the point, according to *The Study of Economics: Principles, Concepts & Applications*, published by McGraw-Hill:[24]

"The most common cause of inflation is too much money chasing too few goods. If everybody had 5 times as much money, but the amount of goods and services produced remained the same, prices would naturally rise by a factor of five. So the answer to avoiding inflation is simply to avoid printing too much money. Easier said than done...

Government leaders like to spend a lot of money on military equipment, roads, subsidies, building projects, etc., because this keeps them popular with their constituents. But getting money to pay for these things is often difficult. Raising taxes is as unpopular as government spending is popular."

So my gripe with the information provided three paragraphs above from the December University of Michigan Consumer Sentiment Report is this: How can "most consumers" believe "a somewhat lower overall inflation rate to prevail in the future," when it's economics 101 common sense that when the Government prints more money (think stimulus and bailout), inflation becomes a deadly threat looming?

Who are these "most Americans" anyway?

Either "most American's aren't aware of the real situation at hand – meaning the survey is a contrarian indicator – or we're not getting the real story.

Listen to this…first, sure, yea right…it makes sense that many American's wouldn't feel like 'too much money was chasing too few goods', after all, almost none of the cash the Government is handing out is showing up on the average American's doorstep. For the little guy –the retail trader- the only real stimulus he's getting is a headache with the slow economic grind down, while watching executives blow hordes of bailout cash on leer jets.

Case in point, by June of 2009, weekly Federal Reserve Data indicated core loans and leases from banks were down almost 8% over the previous three months, and 1.6% over the year ago period.[25] The facts clearly show consumers have not been the benefactors of Government spending, even though (in all) US Government recovery spending was nearing almost $3.8 trillion (Federal Reserve, Treasury, Federal Deposit Insurance Corporation, Federal Housing Administration, Congress and Joint Fed, FDIC and Treasury) into the early summer of 2009. Well you're darn right many consumers aren't aware to be on the lookout for inflation, after all, they hadn't/haven't –personally- seen a nickel of the Government's monetary upchuck since the start of the crisis.[26]

There's something else happening here too; remember those confidence level things? We're talking about basing opinions on whether a 'slight majority' of the public feels conditions are getting better, or worse. But what is 'slight majority' data anyway? Want to know? I'll tell ya…'slight majority' data is just the type that's required to determine the outcome of an election…like if you get 51% of the votes, you win. However, economics **do not** work that way- if 54% of consumers vote the economy is improving, a larger economic '*growth cycle*' doesn't just '*win.*'

And yet; similar methodology is used in polling for economic sentiment, as Presidential elections. Uh… Okay…

At the end of the day, it is important to take all "survey related" reports with a grain of salt. In addition, when we dig into the information delivered by media, in many, many cases we find the information is often '*murky*'… I'm not saying the media is fibbing, what I'm implying is the information delivered does not truly and accurately lay out the entire picture from an unbiased, or impartial standpoint.

What's more, mainstream media tends to have a heyday with "consumer sentiment" reports, which is really a translation of a translation, making big inferences about the total population, which in part, is just another shoveling of nothingness into the individual's lap. What we're talking about is light-speed information changing the total critical mass of market moving disasters pending... Oh, wait, what I've just mentioned doesn't come until Part Two of Volatility Illuminated. ☺

At the end of the day, what I'm really proposing here is that much of the information often 'reported' to the public (regarding fundamentals) isn't really fully explained and thus, it's no wonder the average investor always seems to get the shaft every few years...

Unfortunately, we simply cannot depend on mass media to deliver clear, helpful, reliable information for our investing pursuits...we MUST (as individuals) take the time to truly dissect ALL of the information that could have **any** impact on the positions we are taking within whatever market we are trading... Sounds like a ton of work right?

Right, which is why 95% of all retail traders lose.

What I'm saying is *'man up'* and dig into the details.

Overall, the larger point behind everything you have just read is... Not only is much of the information we are receiving potentially faulted in delivery, but because we are receiving potentially misguiding information from the start, our memories could be hindered in the future, when attempting remember the past.

What we have is a massive problem with the clarity and delivery of information overall, where the individual must take the time to not only understand the information coming forward, but also reflecting upon how major media is reacting to, and then delivering, as well.

Media has a **major** interest in every headline delivered... What I'm talking about is: *the more you staying glued to the tube, the more the tube keeps advertising revenue glued to the network's wallet.*

Thus, we have to not only keep a close guard on our emotions, as we take in everyday information, but we must also understand that the constant bombardment of positive or negative headlines *is* affecting our memories. What's more, when the information of today- is repackaged and redelivered in the future, as a historical recap of what was happening today; if we did not take the time to accurately understand the events unfolding now, we will not remember correctly in the future- and thus, could fall victim to having our memories partially recreated in tomorrow-land...

Referencing the famous line by Gordon Gekko, Michael Douglas' character in the movie Wall Street, it's probably a good idea to second guess almost all of the information surfacing from media, as with slightly closer examination of the facts, we could find 'mega-fog-mouth' actually just slapped some lipstick on a pig...

Now that we've covered why and how we must question almost all information we receive daily, we will now talk about two technical strategies that generally work well within in trading.

However, we will also attempt to understand why the technical strategies can also fail at times, thus leading us into a greater understanding of why volatility and probability and understanding institutional order flow are necessary to (at the very least) double check the technical indicators most view as reliable...daily.

As one final side note, I don't want readers to think I'm insinuating we have 'question everything', like as in we should walk around in a paranoid state of distrust... Please do not mistake my point... What I'm really saying is...common sense sure goes a long ways... That's all really... just plain old-fashioned common sense.

CHAPTER FOUR
FIBONACCI & PITCHFORKS

Forex markets are tricky, there's no doubt about it. Wide spreads, seemingly unexpected volatility and odd hours can all take a huge dent out of traders' wallets. However, with a few simple strategies, both long and short-term traders can potentially make a big difference in their bottom lines. Here we're going to cover two simple trading strategies: Fibonacci Retracements and trend analysis through pitchforks. What's more, we will also overlay the two strategies, creating what we will call the *Forex Fibonacci Pitchfork Strategy*. By utilizing Pitchforks and Fibonacci Retracements in our trading, we may find ourselves suddenly empowered with what is really… an almost laughably simple (but effective!) trading tool.

Getting straight to the meat, Fibonacci Retracements are **probability points** where a currency or stock are 'expected' to bounce back near, after a large move, before continuing in the original direction.

Think of Retracements in terms of Newton's Third Law of Motion: *"For every action there is an equal and opposite reaction."*

Within this understanding, trading carries some of the same principals. However, I would like to add that after a large move, the opposite reaction can quite often lose energy quickly, and thus, is why the 'reactive move' after a larger previous ascent, or decent, can be less than the large move itself. This is not to say that once a large upside pop, or landslide selloff takes place, the currency will not completely retrace the original move, however, without a fundamental event prompting a larger reversal, energy is often lost in the bounce.

Employing Fibonacci Retracements, we can find some guidance as to where the reactive-moves could lose steam and continue in the original direction.

Ironically, Leonardo Fibonacci lived in the 13th century, while Newton worked in the 17th century. Perhaps Fibonacci unknowingly uncovered the truths behind the laws of motion...centuries before Newton's name became a name brand of motion postulation...

FIBONACCI IN NATURE

If you're not familiar with Fibonacci ratios /numbers, the concepts of such are directly consequential from nature, and are found in virtually all organic sciences today. Briefly, a Fibonacci string results from adding previous numbers together, to find the next. For example 1+1=2, 2+1=3, 3+2=5, 5+3=8 and so on... The Fibonacci string would look like: 0,1,1,2,3,5,8,13,21,34,55,89,144,233...

In nature, the spiral of seeds in a sunflower are exactly ordered in Fibonacci sequence, as with many occurrences in organic life.

Fibonacci ratios are thus, derived from organic numerical sequences. For example, if you take any eighth number in the sequence and divide it by the number following it in the sequence (dividing the eight by the ninth); the answer will ALWAYS be 61.8. In the above string, if we divide the eighth number (21) by the ninth (34), we get 61.76, or 61.8 rounded up.

It just is.

Market quants hold that Fibonacci is not only true in organic matter, but also carry substance within day-to-day trading as well. Thus, Fibonacci ratios often lay out of a map for Retracement levels, after a significant move.

However, because bounces must put in lower lows, or higher highs for a larger trend to remain intact, we intuitively also understand Fibonacci ratios only hold true, so long as a trend is indeed- in effect.

Thus, perhaps Newton's Law of Motion that says, "For every action there is an equal and opposite reaction" fails to take into account the loss of energy in *reaction*, when markets are trending.

There could be another factor involved though, which may be overcome by combining Fibonacci with the founder of quantum physics Max Karl Ernst Ludwig Planck's formula E=hv, where "energy is and absorbed in quantities divisible by discrete 'energy elements'".[27]

For the physicists out there, don't worry, there's plenty of goodies for you in following pages. Now, let's look into how one can -very simply- use Fibonacci Retracements in Forex trading, without any complicated math.

THE FIBONACCI
PROPHECY

All of the magical math in the world will never make
Fibonacci Retracements true 100% of the time. Period. Thus,
a little common sense goes a long way when using any type
of mathematical or technical indicator to trade with. If the
market is showing something different from the indicator,
enough people believe in something different from what the
indicator is presenting, and thus, the indicator is wrong.
Fibonacci Retracements are relevant only so long as enough
people are watching and acting on the same information that
the "collective whole" makes the occurrence a self-fulfilling
prophecy. In other words, even if you've opened a trade
based on Fibonacci Retracement expectations, be prepared to
close the position, should common sense warrant such. In
addition, as I've just mentioned that Fibonacci
Ratios/Retracements require some application of a self
fulfilling prophecy, too many people acting on the same
information at the same time, can actually cause excessive
volatility, as noted in Chapter Two.

Fibonacci Retracements work on both short and long-
term periods, for all types of traders. For this chapter
though, we will only look at Fibonacci Retracements for
short-term trading on 4-hour charts.

First, before we even consider using Fibonacci Retracements, we need to be able to spot when a move has occurred that would warrant using Fibonacci Retracements in the first place. This can be as simple as looking at a chart, and visually identifying when a large move has transpired, and/or capitulated.

What I mean by this is, when looking at a chart, if you're expecting to see empirical proof that a move has stalled, you will never be able to do so. You will see some signs, like CCI turning upward from -100 (and vice versa downward from +100) or Stochastics bottoming out, or a candlestick pattern like a hammer bottom, but you will never know absolutely 100 percent for sure. If there were some way to know all the time, everyone in the world would be rich. One way to have a slight bit of assurance though, is to read volatility compression through short-term volatility bands compressing back underneath long-term volatility. The aforementioned is likely foreign sounding to most- as it should be. I will explain concepts of volatility bands -in detail- in the second half of the book. For now, simply log the statement in your mind, for future reference.

Traders can learn to intuitively 'feel' when a move has capitulated though. However, only countless hours of pouring over charts will give you 'the feel'. Once you are able to infer a move is over though, you can begin to apply Fibonacci Retracements for trend re-entries, or profit targets points, if you are trying to trade the rebound.

I would like to mention that attempting to trade a 'bounce' is risky business and is not really the subject matter of this book. However, we will look at a possible reversal trade with Fibonacci Retracements, just to cover all our bases. Really though, when we use Fibonacci Retracements, we should use the technical tool to time our 'trend re-entry' points in an attempt to take positions with the trend, not against.

Looking into when to apply Fibonacci, the below chart shows a significant downward in the USD/CHF (U.S. Dollar / Swiss Franc). What we see is a 'significant move', which is precisely what we're attempting to find when applying Fibonacci Retracements.

Figure 4.1

Based on Figure 4.1, many traders were likely looking for additional downside to come, as the USD/CHF previously took out support in the 1.0950 area. A major breach of support or resistance is often a key signal that more trending is to come.

Some turned the dollar long, others waited for key Retracement levels to be hit, before taking positions…

The bottom line though- is we must be able to identify some sort of 'significant move', before we can apply Fibonacci Ratios at all.

With the aforementioned in mind, we will now take a look at how we can use Fibonacci Retracements to trade a possible 'bounce' or reversal, once a larger move has taken place.

In Figure 4.2, you will see a large downward move, where the Australian dollar declined significantly against the New Zealand dollar.

Figure 4.2

Several indicators (not shown) were prompting the bulk of the damage was done and the pair would likely experience a 'bounce', otherwise known as a short-term reversal.

Regardless, the Retracements can also serve as profit targets for reversal trades.

Perceptive traders could have taken long positions in the Australian dollar –off the bottom of the range- using the low of the range as a stop.

By means of Fibonacci Retracement levels in such a case, traders would use the key indicator as possible profit targeting points. If one had taken a position in the AUD/NZD off lows, when the pair tagged the 38.2% Fibonacci Retracement level, it would have been a good idea to either take all profit, or place a stop slightly below the 38.3% Retracement. The reason for placing a stop just below the 38.2% Retracement is this:

If the bounce is real and a reversal is truly in effect, chances are the upside momentum will persist, however, as Fibonacci Retracements are significant trend re-entry points, and given that positions into retracements are moving again the larger trend at hand, locking in bounce profits is always a good idea.

Again, Fibonacci Retracements are also key levels where 'with the trend' traders will begin wading back into a pair… What I mean by this is if a Forex pair, or stock, just witnessed a massive downside slide, many traders are likely trying to find low-risk short entry points to capitalize on another move downward, should more selling surface. Thus, the 'bounce' trader will experience significant volatility at key Retracement levels, as many 'with the trend' traders attempt to take opposite positions. Thus, bounce trader are faced with several questions as their trades move into retracement levels.

1. Take profit?

2. Fight the volatility? (If he or she has considerable reason to believe more bounce is to come.)

In figure 4.2 and as bounce traders likely expected, the AUD/NZD did hit the 38.2% Retracement within 12 hours of the low. However, the AUD/NZD sold off again (twice actually), before making a run at the 50% Retracement. (*Again, though we won't cover the subjects until further on in the book, sustained rebounding, or prior trending continuation is where volatility/probability will really help traders.*)

The bottom line in the AUD/NZD example is jittery traders were likely shaken out when excess volatility surfaced around the key Fibonacci Retracements.

It's important to mention that those with steadfast stops - just below the low of the original move- would have not lost their positions. The question is though, can you risk the loss, or for that matter, giving up profit considering you could have exited at the 38.2% level?

Here's one way to solve the problem(s). When trading a reversal set your stop as soon as you make the trade (if you have a non-US account able to enter stops and limits)… Then, set a sell order for one quarter of your position at the 38.2% Fibonacci Retracement, so if the trade fails, you will have a small buffer when your stop is hit on the downside. (You will need to adjust the position size in your stop, if the

38.2% Retracement is hit; accounting for the 25% of your position, you just sold for a profit.)

Figure 4.2 (Shown again)

At the same time you made the initial trade, set a sell order for 50% of the total initial position at the 50% Retracement. In the case of AUD/NZD, when the pair first hit the 50% Retracement, you would have taken even more off the table…and would need to adjust your stop order accordingly, as you will now only have 25% of the original position. Then, with the remaining 25%, you can set another limit order to sell at the 61.8% Retracement, or let it ride.

FYI, from my experience trading Forex, the 61.8% Retracement level seems to hold the most weight... If a pair does not reverse the bounce at the 31.8% and 50% levels, and you see a 4-hour bar close near the 61.8% Retracements, there's a good chance the pair will retrace the whole move.

Regardless, the Retracements serve as profit targets for reversal trades, or re-entries for those who believe larger trending will persist.

You must decide for yourself whether you will trade for larger moves, or quickly scalp profits on smaller, sudden volatility pops. It is my experience that traders who take small profit after small profit and cannot hold for larger wins, eventually get killed when they take a bigger loss. Truly great traders know one of the keys to success is:

...little loss, little loss, little loss, <u>big win</u>...

...not vice versa.

Thus, attempting to trade bounces is generally a losing proposition overall. Really, we should attempt to trade with the trend, using Fibonacci Retracements as a tool to help time our entries.

For traders who think the pair will continue the original move, you can place your short orders near key Fibonacci Retracement points, where you hope to reenter in the direction of the big-move trend.

One way to do so is to place an order for 25% of your total predetermined size at the 38.2% mark, 50% at the 50% mark and 25% at the 61.8% mark... This way, you've allowed yourself 'wiggle room' if the 38.2% and 50%

Retracements do not hold. It's important to note though, that if the 61.8% Retracement is breached –**significantly**, the pair will likely retrace the entire move, an event that happens quite often in Forex trading, especially on short-term charts.

The best rule of thumb in this case is as simple as the old market saying: *When in doubt, get out.*

In addition, as we're about to cover, it is a good idea in today's market to actually place orders above Fibonacci Retracements for short positions and below for long positions. By doing so, we attempt to starve off volatility from the **HIIV Effect** mentioned in Chapter Two. I'll explain this in greater detail in the following pages.

FIBONACCI RETRACEMENT VOLATILITY

As we discussed in Chapter Two, indicators **are indeed** failing retail traders in the current market.

Fibonacci Retracements are no less affected… The problem is there are simply too many traders using the same signals, all acting at the same time. Think about it for a moment… If the entire retail community is watching the 38.2% Retracement as a short entry point in a downward move, what's the likely result? The result is many, many traders will also likely act on that same information at the same time, taking short positions in the same places at –or near- the Retracement I've just mentioned. But what happens if a large institutional order pushes the stock, or currency pair slightly above the Retracement? The result would likely be a massive wave of electronic stop orders tripping globally, as retail traders stop out on excessive volatility.

The problem is that as momentum begets momentum, stops also beget stops, meaning once a wave of stops are hit, the actions could cause just enough upside volatility to trip even more stops- slightly higher.

What all of the aforementioned means is that it no longer pays to take a position 'just before' a key technical, or Retracement level.

Too many people are likely doing exactly what I have just mentioned (shorting before the key Retracement) and as soon as a slight amount of volatility occurs, those same traders will be stopped out, thus causing an additional wave of volatility. Then, just a few moments after the entire retail crowd is wiped out, the currency pair will reverse and travel in the initial direction…leaving *at home* traders scratching their heads attempting to figure out how it is they always seem to get stopped out precisely at highs, or lows… Just before the pair moves in the direction they had originally anticipated.

To combat this issue, traders should take positions a little 'out of the money' from key technical levels. What I mean is if you are going to time a short entry with the Fibonacci 38.2% Retracement, it might be a better idea to wait until upside volatility hits 40 or 42%, thus using the **'HIIV Effect'** (Chapter Two) to your advantage. For the 50% Retracement, we may want to use 55 to 58% and for the 61.8% Retracement, perhaps 66 to 68%. The bottom line is because of the HIIV Effect, we simply need to build in a little 'volatility premium' into our perceived entries and exits.

The following chart shows just what I mean… If you were attempting to take a position short in the EUR/USD using the 50% Retracement as your entry, it would have paid to wait until the pair was slightly above the Retracement, before taking the position. The EUR/USD 'popped' just above the 50% Retracement, before falling through the floor. Those who took positions before (just under) the 50% Retracement were likely stopped out on the *quick pop* above and were likely shaking their heads at 'excessive volatility'.

However, the volatility savvy trader simply used the event to achieve better fill short.

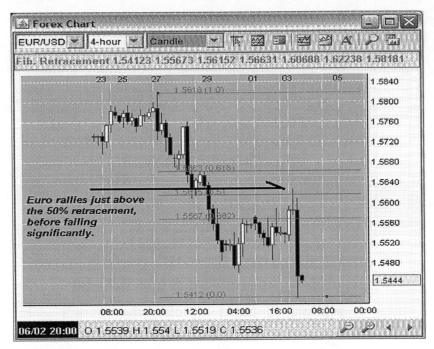

Figure 4.3

AS SIMPLE AS A PITCHFORK

What I'm about to show you is an incredibly simple technical analysis tool; however, it is one that not many traders know about, despite the apparent effectiveness. By implementing pitchforks, traders can quickly identify short and long-term trends, in an effort to find incredible trades, both with and against the trend.

Simply put, using this simple tool, "the trend" could become your best friend, as you will know when to trade with, and/or against the larger trading paradigm at work.

Pitchforks will also help show traders how to analyze the larger trend, by identifying the **'<u>median line</u>'** of the relevant trend in any given range. Many novice traders fail to recognize larger trends within Forex, which can often lead to unanticipated volatility.

With this in mind, we'll start with a explanation of pitchforks, and then use a *'macro to micro'* approach to find our trades.

As you will see, knowing the larger trend, before we look into shorter-term trades can not only help us find more optimum entries, but can also help us keep cool when volatility turns on.

By definition an "Andrew's Pitchfork" is a series of three points in a trend that dissect a sharp ascending move, or downward trough.

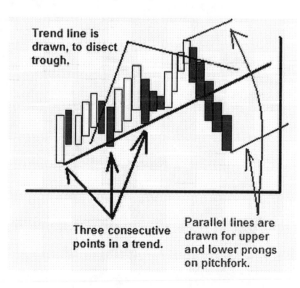

Figure 4.4

The line moving through the middle of the trend forms the middle prong of the pitchfork, and is known as the 'median line.' Then, upper and lower parallel lines are drawn to project ascending/descending support and resistance and targets within the perceived trend.

However, for the purposes of Forex, I have found through trial and error, that the textbook definition does not work well. Thus, with one slight tweak, pitchforks become immensely more reliable for long and short term trading.

The below 4-hour chart of the GBP/JPY chart demonstrates why connecting three points does not always work well...

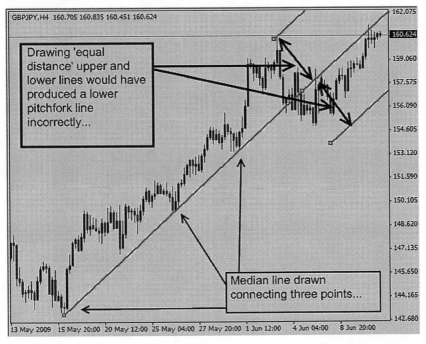

Figure 4.5

As you can see, by simply connecting three 'lows' in the range leading up to the trough, we would have an incorrect pitchfork, as the lower line would not accurately represent the ascending channel.

The reason for the breakdown is simply because we must have equal distance between the median line and the upper and lower pitchforks, the inaccuracy of the median line itself- promotes a breakdown in the lower ascending support line.

We must understand that there is a bit of an **'art'** to drawing pitchforks and at times, we will need to 'cut' the lows of an ascending trend or the highs of a descending trend, to create an accurate median line.

To draw pitchforks correctly, instead of trying to draw a trend line from three consecutive points to dissect the trough, we will simply find **only one point to start our middle trendline with**. The point we will use can be the **lowest point** (or highest, in the reverse case where there is a sharp rally, instead of a trough) **prior to the opening of the trough**. (It's much simpler than it sounds.) Or, we can use the low of the move (which I prefer) and then cut into the some of the lows, or highs of the move, thus forming a more accurate representation of the true trend median.

Figure 4.6 shows what I mean... As you can see in the case of the GBP/JPY, I used the low of the range as my starting point for the median line; however, I did not connect the lows of the range... Instead, I **'cut'** slightly into the lows and dissected the trough at the precise mid-point. By doing so, I have drawn a more accurate pitchfork, as noted in the currency pair running up the lower pitchfork, without a significant gap in-between.

The instance of slightly *cutting* highs and lows is truly the 'art' portion of identifying median lines (and pitchforks) something that you will need to learn by trial and error. However, once you have mastered the ability to correctly identify the –at times- 'mysterious median', you will find much greater success in using this simple, yet effective, tool.

Figure 4. 6

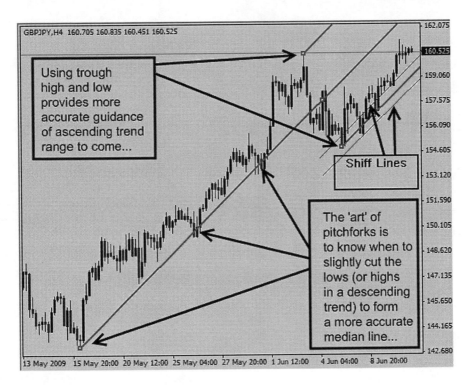

When we are able to correctly identify pitchforks, we will suddenly find ourselves empowered with two possible trading strategies:

1. In ascending trends, buy pullbacks on either the lower, or the middle prong, if a distinctly identifiable trend is in place. By buying pullbacks into the middle, or lower prong in an ascending move, we are really taking on the age-old market advice of *'the trend is your friend.'* In descending trends, sell the rallies up into the middle or upper prongs, and you will be short with the trend.

   We want to put our stops on the opposite side of whichever pitchfork we have taken a position on, while also remembering that at times, there will be a slight bit of volatility breach as well. Like technical indicators are failing and like Fibonacci Retracements are seeing a slight bit of 'excessive volatility' opposite major Retracement levels, as pitchforks become more and more 'mainstream', we will begin to see the same volatility effect taking place. With such in mind, we may want to take our positions just slightly on the underside of a pitchfork in an ascending move, and vice versa on a descending move- just to build a little 'volatility premium' into our trade.

2. If in an ascending trend, the currency pair breaks the lower pitchfork –more than what we would normally assume is not just a 'volatility pop', turn the trade and go short...

Quite often, savvy traders will be piling in as well, and you can ride the wave! If in a descending trend, the pair breaks through the upper pitchfork, a reversal may be occurring and Forex traders can go long.

To isolate entry and exit points for daytraders, draw pitchforks on 4-hour, 1-hour, 15-minute and 5-minute charts to isolate exact points for scalp trades.

The idea behind walking down through the chart timeframes (even if you're a scalper) is simply to have a greater idea of the larger 'terrain' at hand.

There's an old cliché that goes something like, *'It's tough to see the forest when you're in the trees.'*

When we only look at 1, 5 and 15-minute charts we have chosen to remain *in the trees*. However, even if we're doing nothing but scalping, by at least paying attention to the 4-hour chart, we have a better idea what the larger forest looks like (from afar), something that may help us keep our bearings straight when we're in the thick of a trade.

Really, we're talking about a macro-to-micro approach…

MACRO TO MICRO PITCHFORKS

Now that we've covered how pitchforks work and the right way to draw technical tool, let's take a macro to micro approach to finding trades. As you can see in the following monthly chart of the USD/JPY, the dollar appears to have been losing steam since 2001. While the greenback was not experiencing an all out descent, the chart shows the range as more of a 'slowly lowering' occurrence of consolidation. Looking for some sense of support for the larger multi-year range, we see such in the 100.11 area, just above the massive 100 whole number. Moreover, when we look at the larger trend, we see the descending middle pitchfork is very close to long-term horizontal support on the far right side of the chart. Amazing! From this chart we know the long-term trend is down and there could still be more to come... We also know the pair is headed towards 10-year support for the **third time**.

Figure 4.7

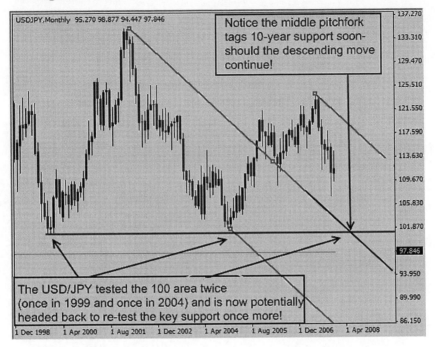

Notice the middle pitchfork tags 10-year support soon- should the descending move continue!

137.270
133.310
129.470
125.510
121.550
117.590
113.630
109.670
105.830
101.870
97.846
93.950
89.990
86.150

The USD/JPY tested the 100 area twice (once in 1999 and once in 2004) and is now potentially headed back to re-test the key support once more!

1 Dec 1998   1 Apr 2000   1 Aug 2001   1 Dec 2002   1 Apr 2004   1 Aug 2005   1 Dec 2006   1 Apr 2008

Next (and please forgive me, as I'm sure Figure 4.8 may seem slightly confusing at first glance) we have the weekly chart. I have actually drawn three pitchforks on this chart, one longer-term ascending trend pitchfork, one medium term descending trend pitchfork and one short-term 'steep' downward trend pitchfork.

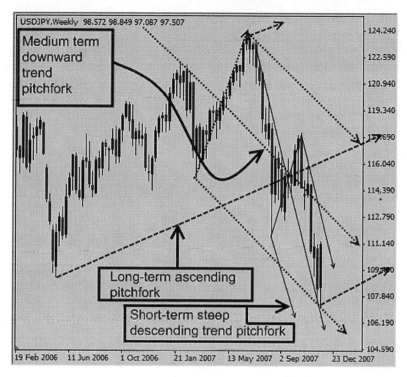

Figure 4.8

Why so many pitchforks you ask?

The point of drawing multiple pitchforks in the first place...is to uncover ALL possibilities, not just the 'one' that appeases what we **want** to see.

By the way, I really believe the reason why many traders never win- is because even when they are given the tools to trade, they make the tools, or technical signals **'fit their preconceived opinion'** of the direction they've already decided (sometimes subconsciously and for no reason really) the currency, or stock *should* move.

Thus, to uncover some sense of truth, we have to examine all options, not just the one, or two that seem to fit the opinion we've already decided fits...

DAILY CHART IN ACTION

As the below chart shows, the USD/JPY tagged the lower pitchfork of the medium-term trend, while also hitting the middle pitchfork of the short-term trend, it's likely a bounce (if even short-term) could ensue. We also know the currency pair possibly put in the bottom pitchfork for a new slow-ascending trend as well...

What we have to remember here is that until the upper pitchfork of the steep descending short-term trend and the middle pitchfork of the medium-term trend- are breached, the trend is still down.

Again, we see confirmation of the downward relevant trend in the daily chart. As you will notice, should the pair continue to bounce; the USD/JPY will encounter resistance in the (roughly) 111.50 to 113.00 area.

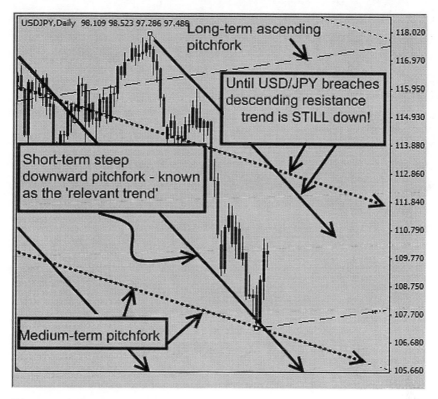

Figure 4.9

See, the whole point of pitchforks is simply to visually identify major trend reversal points and/or trend re-entry points, ahead of the game...

In the present case of the USD/JPY, if the pair is to move above 113.00, we could assume the recent low (which created the lower pitchfork of the longer-term ascending trend) –is real– and a larger reversal is indeed, in effect.

However, until descending resistance of the short and medium term trends are breached, risk prevails for the trader attempting to take a long position. This isn't to say savvy traders can't pick off long moves, however, we have to remember the main trend is still down. This is knowing the 'macro' trend, or reversal points to help in our intraday trading.

As we continue to examine the USD/JPY daily chart, we see the pair recently rode down the topside of the upper prong… Again, it is important to keep in mind that the pair is trading just above the middle pitchfork of the short-term trend on the daily chart, with the medium-term trend still showing downside to come.

4-HOUR CHART

The 4-hour chart begins to shed more light on the current ascending bounce, giving us some idea of what to expect in the near-term. As you can see, I've drawn a 'assumptive pitchfork', thinking ascending support of the recent uptrend could actually be the median line for a possible uptrend to come, should the bounce continue. I've also drawn in two levels of support, one at relative support of the recent trough and one at highs of the 'relative range', while the pair was making new lows. What I'm doing here is attempting to find high probability entry points, should the bounce continue.

What's also important to note, is that I am also marking a final 'give-point' denoted as Support 2 (sometimes known as a critical 'pivot point') where bulls will likely toss in the towel and another re-test of lows is in the cards.

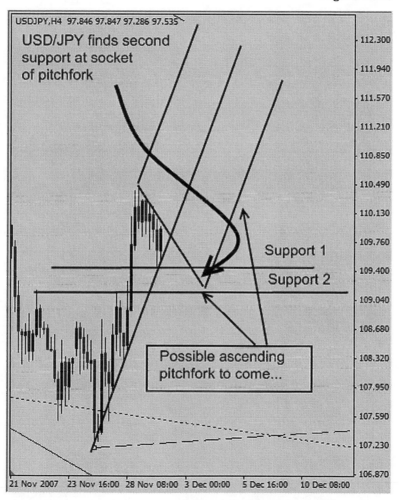

Figure 4.10

Traders may have wanted to wait for a slight bit more 'guidance' to see if the present ascending trend would hold... What you can't see here is how volatility and probability could help determine if more ascending action is to come, or of lateral trading will ensue.

We will cover volatility and probability in Part Two of Volatility Illuminated.

In the next 4-hour chart (Figure 4.11), we can see the USD/JPY held the lower 'socket' of the perceived Andrew's Pitchfork, which it rode all the way into the 111.50 area, before signaling more downside to come...

Figure 4.11

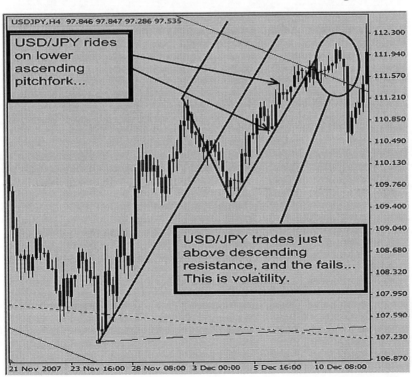

The failure in the 111.50 area was then marked with lateral trading action, which would have prompted us to move the handle of our pitchfork inside the ascending relevant trend to more accurately reflect the true range 'median line.' Then, after the USD/JPY made a significant breach of the lower pitchfork after testing the 114 area, we would have watched support in the 112.50 to 113.00 area of a larger breach of trend…

Figure 4. 12

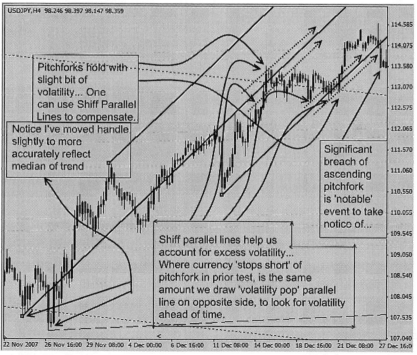

For courageous swing traders, the final stop should have been the highest high of the relevant pitchfork trend. However, for newer traders (who should not be taking on significant risk), zeroing in on a trade, if the pair breaks the prong the trader bought or sold from…on whatever timeframe chart prompted the entry…close the trade.

Chances are there's a reversal looming, or volatility is about to shake out a ton of traders.

Regardless, you don't want to be one of the poor-souls who hangs on, only to be forced to exit at the last moment…taking a whopper of a loss.

Remember: Missed money is always better than lost money!

Overall, the monthly chart showed us the long-term trend was down… and chances are the dollar could take another dive. However, the weekly and daily charts were alluding to a possible short-term pop looming, which confirmed on the 4-hour chart. If some of the information above seems a little jumbled…it is. See, pitchforks are continually changing dynamic tools where we must constantly look for changing ranges and medians… What I have just mentioned is much of the reason volatility and probability help illuminate some of the choppy action that surfaces in trading daily.

We will now apply Fibonacci to pitchforks, to create a more useful tool... However, all 'standard technicals' eventually break down and thus, without the application of volatility/probability; even Fibonacci Pitchforks tend to mislead traders from time to time. Again, please note that we will cover volatility and probability in Part Two of the book.

NOTE

When trading longer-term reversals, it is always best to wait for significant confirmation of a trend change, before jumping the gun. Those who try to trade 'the big picture' without confirmation can fall victim to *presumptuous/impulse-trading* and consequently, can incur large losses.

CHAPTER FIVE

VOLATILITY ADJUSTED FOREX FIBONACCI PITCHFORK STRATEGY

Over the following pages, we will see how Fibonacci Retracements and Pitchforks come together, helping locate high-probability trending re-entries and/or larger reversals. What is truly amazing about overlaying pitchforks on Fibonacci Retracements is the simple fact that by doing so, we are attempting to 'trade with the trend', while also identifying entries that give us clear stop-loss points to maximize risk management within our trading.

The main principal behind the Fibonacci Pitchfork Strategy is to overlay at least two pitchforks on top of Fibonacci Retracements, and then look for larger trend entries near the 50% and 61.8% Retracements.

By doing so we:

1.   Maximize major trend re-entry probability.

2.   Identify if *and when* the larger trend is breaking down and thus, close our losing trade and turn the position in the new direction, attempting to capitalize on the larger potential reversal at hand.

Here's how it works. In the below daily chart of the EUR/USD, you will see a Fibonacci Retracements overlaid on the most recent rally, in an effort to find reentry points for the long-term upward move. We know the relevant trend is up; however, given strength of the U.S. Dollar through the financial crisis, we cannot completely rule out more upside to come… Regardless, given the oversaturation of money supply from October 2008 through the spring of 2009, there could be more strength to come in the EUR/USD while markets attempt to decipher credit quality of U.S. Treasuries and overall 'holding power' of the greenback. With the aforementioned in mind (and please note that I am always considering the larger 'fundamental picture' even though we're looking at technicals) there could be a major point of trend continuation (upside re-entry) looming.

Here's the thing though, we don't have to have an opinion, we can trade the upward, or downward moves profitably using the Fibonacci Pitchfork Strategy with predetermined stops, we just need to be patient about our entries. What I'm saying is that instead of having an opinion and just 'jumping in' we can wait for high-probability entry points. The whole point of patiently waiting for these points to surface, is we are taking positions at major points that even if we are wrong, we can keep stops super tight, to quickly close the position and then turn it in the correct direction…

The below chart (Figure 5.1) is going to look a little confusing at first, but stick with me for a moment, and you will see the strategy is actually quite simple.

The foremost trend we have identified is the present ascending pitchfork, with the handle starting in the 1.2525 area… We know this is the relevant trend, as the recent high strikes the middle pitchfork almost exactly.

What's more, we have drawn a second descending pitchfork (short-term) from the high, dissecting what appears to be a small rally from approximately 1.3805 to 1.4170. We have also drawn a Fibonacci Retracement from 1.2889 to 1.4334. We are now attempting to identify trend re-entry points for the longer-term ascending move, while also looking for low-risk short entry points, should recent selling continue… Also, please note that I have drawn to Schiff Parallel Lines…

While I have modified the definition slightly –to what I find works within Forex- Schiff Parallel Lines are trendlines drawn parallel to middle, upper and lower pitchforks, which are equal distance from the pitchfork as the previous 'blip' recorded. In theory, the stall into a pitchfork or extension slightly beyond, foreshadows a second stall of volatility, or slight pop beyond the pitchfork line in question.

Andrew's pitchforks used to hold ground –on their own-however, as many indicators today, we are now seeing 'pops' of volatility beyond what used to hold, per the traditional definition of the indicator. Simply put, too many people are using the same tool, which is now causing additional volatility. To account for the slight bit of 'extra volatility' in pitchforks, Schiff Parallel Lines seem to do the trick; at least for the time being...

Moving on, also in the below chart, you will notice that I have marked two possible long entry points, one where the short-term trend strikes the 38.2% Fibonacci Retracement, and a second where the short-term pitchfork strikes ascending support of the relative range, while also tagging the 68.1% Retracement...

Again if you remember my earlier discussion of 'excess volatility' in Fibonacci Retracements and in most technical indicators, should the EUR/USD truly drop into the 68.1% Retracement, it could extend slightly below the Retracement, while also slightly violating ascending support on the downside, before starting a new rally...

In today's environment, we have to remember that all technical analysis has a bit of 'art' to it in that excess volatility is creating 'blips' of trading action beyond what used to seem like clear areas of entry and exit. For this reason, volatility and probability, which you will read about in Part Two are major assets in helping to find some clarity, when traditional technical indicators fail.

Figure 5.1

For the time being; however, you can see what I am trying to do in Figure 5.1 is line up trend re-entry signals with the longer-term pitchfork and Fibonacci Retracements. What's more, should the lower pitchfork-line (ascending support) fail, I am also attempting to see where the pair could still begin to rally, as denoted in drawing the simple (dashed) ascending support line of the relative trend.

It's also important to note that if the second Schiff Line (slightly downside and outside of the larger ascending pitchfork) were to fail, momentum short-traders could take positions, looking for a move into ascending support, where they would then want to reconsider their positions, potentially looking for an upside move to surface.

I would like to take a moment to drop in a few words of wisdom... Many new traders never win big, because they don't understand that losses will occur...

However, losses are the one thing (and I mean it...the **only** thing) you can assuredly count on 100% in trading. Losses will happen, however, keeping losses small, and handling situations where our trades are not working is really one of the most constructive steps to becoming a profitable trader. When loses surface, we must remember to keep our emotions in check, while sticking to the original trading plan, knowing our small losses will eventually be offset with large wins.

Moreover, new traders often do not understand that when technical levels are breached –with relative significance- the trade must be closed. Unfortunately, many newer traders can sometimes allow their emotions to override the reality at hand... Here's another trading cliché that I firmly believe in:

The first loss is always...the best loss...

In the above example, the potential damage from holding a long, if major ascending support were to be breached, is simply just too risky. We must remember that every single time we take a position; we have to question *'what if?'* What I mean by 'questioning' is *for every trade we take*, we must have a *'turn it'* plan in place.

The *'turn it'* plan is precisely where we say, "Okay, I mapped out what I thought was the correct technical picture, but clearly the market is saying something different; I will turn the trade the other direction now, without an emotional hold on my previous opinion."

Should ascending support fail, savvy traders would view the small loss as an **opportunity** to turn the trade short, knowing that they were moving *'with the market'* and not attempting to force something that just isn't working.

Experienced traders know that we are never going to be right all of the time, and it is truly *'how we handle positions that are not working'*, which separates those who are profitable, from those who eventually blow up.

With all of the aforementioned in mind, if we now take a moment to drill down into the 4-hour chart, we begin to see a little more 'guidance' into the possibilities at hand. The 4-hour chart shows us that we are currently 'mid-range' within the recent selloff and longer-term support. Moreover, we can also see where a potential long-entry at the 39.2% Fib Retracement sits- at the exterior Schiff Line, drawn just outside of the larger ascending pitchfork. I have not noted the 50% Retracement as a potential long-entry point, as other than lateral support from the relative range, ascending support (noted on the daily chart) is sitting just below at the 61.8% Retracement… The common sense *'sniff test'* tells us that should the pair continue downward in the near term, the 61.8% Retracement (where ascending support sits), would likely be a more realistic target, over the 50% Retracement.

Figure 5.2

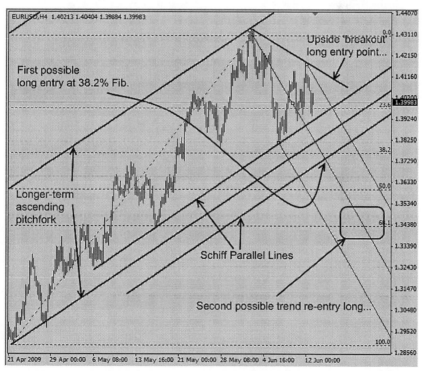

Now, stepping down into the hourly chart, we see just how 'mid-range' the EUR/USD is…

Again, the whole point of drawing pitchforks and Fibonacci Retracements from macro picture down…is to identify high probability entry points, within the larger picture. Some traders might be asking, "What about right now, which direction will the EUR/USD travel?"

The answer is, "I don't know." Well, let me rephrase that… I have a good idea, based on many technical indicators and the present fundamental outlook… However, for the example at hand, we **want** to think:

"I don't know."

Why?

Foremost, even though I personally have a bias towards which direction I believe the pair should travel, we are still mid-range, consolidating after the recent move up. What's more, why would I want to guess here, when I could simply wait for a higher probability entry? Thus, looking at the hourly chart, I have a better idea where the 'higher probability' entries are within the current trading action…and also the longer-term Fibonacci Pitchfork strategy.

As Figure 5.2 shows:

1. I can attempt to take a long position on the lower Schiff Line, just below the lower pitchfork of the ascending trend. At this level, if were are not dropping rapidly, or any EUR/USD bearish news has surfaced, I would likely attempt a long, placing my final stop just below the 38.2% Retracement, which we will call the *support zone*.

2. If the EUR/USD breached the support zone, I would likely then turn the trade short, expecting an extended volatility selloff and a move potentially down into the 61.8% Retracement.

3. If the pair held the 38.2% Retracement (knowing the key Retracement would likely be breached slightly because of the HIIV Effect in today's market), if no news surfaced changing my larger bias from long to short, I may attempt another long trade, looking for the ascending trend to stay intact. I would place my long stop just below my entry, likely in the 44% Retracement area (not pictured), which (with a little common sense) you can calculate by hand.

4. Should the pair fall all the way into the 61.8% Retracement, I might attempt to pick up another long position; however, I would search high and low for some sort of news providing transparency as to why the 38.2% Retracement and ascending support of the lower pitchfork did not hold. Fundamental news is always king and trading without looking for changes in fundamental bias, and/or assuming technicals will <u>always</u> '*tell the truth*' is simply reckless.

5. Backing up to my original long entry (denoted as #1 in this string), if the EUR/USD never actually fell into ascending support and instead breached upper pitchfork descending resistance of the shorter-term relevant range (likely witnessed by a move above 1.4080), I may take a small 'breakout' long position too.

   However, there would likely be news prompting the trade... For a trend to continue (breaking out of consolidation) there is usually some sort of fundamental news to accompany the trading action.

Again, a little common sense goes a long way when overlapping what we see in technicals to the news unfolding within markets.

Figure 5.3

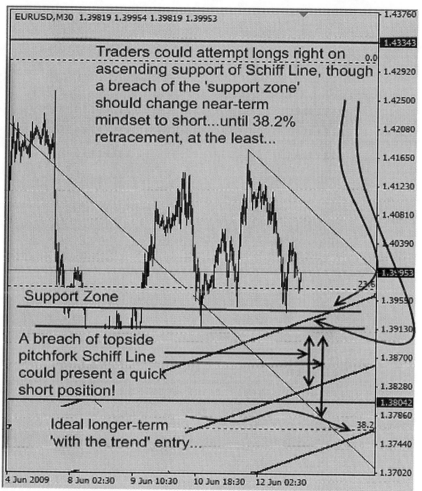

Overall, as you can see, by overlaying pitchforks and Fibonacci Retracements, we have created a strategy that:

1. Helps us identify the 'larger trend' and critical levels within the relevant range.

2. Identified Fibonacci Retracements for the larger move at hand.

3. Located trade entry and stop loss points for 'with the trend' trading, while also enabling us to take quick positions against, should the situation warrant such.

4. Located larger 'reversal points' where we know to look for a shift in fundamental mindset.

5. Created a clear plan for trading with the trend, but also helping to understand when and where we should consider turning the trade, should a reversal occur.

6. Produce a slight sense of peace, knowing that we are trading with high-probability entry and stop loss points…

Again, I would like to mention that even with all of the technical mapping in the world, excess volatility in today's market will cause pitchforks, Fibonacci Retracements and even Quad CCI (which you're about to read in Chapter Six) to breakdown. Thus, in Part Two, we will dive into volatility and probability, providing even more insight into today's market.

Towards the end of the book, we will then overlap Fibonacci Pitchforks and Quad CCI with volatility and probability and as you will see, we will unearth an amazing sense of clarity- most traders never find.

In the mean time, I would like to reiterate a few trading rules that we must always remember...

RULES TO FOLLOW

1. All of the magical math in the world will never make Fibonacci Retracements true 100% of the time. Period.

2. A little common sense goes a long way when using any type of mathematical or technical indicator to trade from.

3. If the market is showing something different than what the indicator is presenting in the current market, the indicator is wrong.

   Signals from indicators do fail.

4. Fibonacci Retracements are only good so long as enough people are watching and acting on the same information (the collective whole) to make the signal true, however, too many people acting on the same information at the same time…causes excess volatility.

5. Again, even if you've opened a trade based on Fibonacci Retracement expectations, be prepared to close the position, should common sense warrant such.

A FEW FINAL NOTES

The trading example in Chapter Five utilized live charts… I did this for two reasons:

1. Anyone can find a trade that works historically; however, real traders know…what looks good historically…hardly ever works in real time… Thus, the example above with the EUR/USD is/was created in real time…

    I do not even know what the outcome will be, as by the time history cements itself, this book will be on the printing press…

2. To show readers that even though Fibonacci Pitchforks lack volatility and probability edge, they do still work…that is, with a little common sense…

CHAPTER SIX

QUAD CCI – THE TRADITIONAL VOLATILITY PARADIGM

Within Forex, there's a term professional traders often throw around when referencing the retail community... Retail traders are frequently cited as doing nothing more than just *'chasing indicators'*. Sadly, so many retail traders fall victim to the mindset of believing trading is easy and/or if they just uncover the *'secret technical code'*, they will never lose again. With this mindset, it's no wonder these same traders unfortunately *constantly* find themselves on the wrong side of the eight ball when volatility kicks in.

However, there is another way to trade...

Throughout Chapter Six, traders will gain more insight into how and why *'chasing indicators'* is such a losing game, while also seeing *how* traders can begin putting indicators back on their side...to overcome destructive volatility that overwhelms most of the retail community daily.

However, it is important to remember that while the Quad CCI strategy you're about to read about is something I personally use, I overlap the strategy with volatility and probability, WVAV and WAVE • Price Mass to gain greater insight into whether the signals produced are real- or are really just *'those old charts fibbing'* - yet again.

While the discussion on multiple CCI time periods is certainly not a *"one stop shop"* to completely navigate the larger universe of trading stocks, futures, commodities and Forex, using the indicator correctly can definitely assist traders when markets are offering little guidance.

Take a look at the below hourly chart of the EUR/USD, which shows the basic *'feel'* of the Commodity Channel Index (CCI), at least, as most traders use the indicator.

For the most part, the indicator is used to look for reversal (or trend re-entry points) when the indicators falls from above +100 back under +100, or up from underneath -100, above -100.

What you will hopefully notice right away is the first 'sell' signal (from the left) and the third buy (also from the left, which I've marked with an asterisk '*'), both provided false signals.

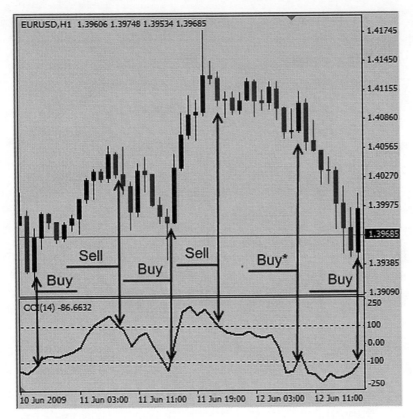

Figure 6.1

To understand why the false signals could be appearing, we need to take a closer look at the indicator overall... According to one major Website, (I'm keeping their name anonymous to not drag them through the dirt, though I have notified them of the error):

"An oscillator used in technical analysis to help determine when an investment vehicle has been overbought and oversold. The Commodity Channel Index, first developed by Donald Lambert, quantifies the relationship between the asset's price, a moving average (MA) of the asset's price, and normal deviations (D) from that average. It is computed with the following formula..."

Here's where we begin to split hairs on a few important matters that I believe you should be aware of...

The Website is correct that CCI was developed by Lambert (in 1980, FYI), moreover, the definition is also correct in that the indicator is meant to help determine overbought and oversold areas... However, CCI was also developed to help find 'cyclical swings' of commodities and other financial instruments. What's more, in the above definition, you will notice the use of the terminology *'normal deviation.'*

Just to make sure I'm not completely losing my mind, I checked about twenty different Websites for definitions of CCI while writing this and what I've found is that **almost all _mislead_ readers** using the same, or similar terminology...**setting you up for failure.**

The problem is likely because most of the information on trading-related Websites is written by people who don't really trade in real life...they don't even know the crap they are regurgitating is <u>wrong.</u>

I like to think of the situation similar to a rocket scientist explaining how to smooth drywall mud almost perfectly...in one shot. Though the task might seem easy overall, unless you've actually done it a few times, there's no way you'd know the tricks of the trade, or the 'inner workings' of how drywall mud sets on the wall and in the bucket, or even how important the 'art' of trowelling is. (I learned the hard way renovating a house many years ago… For the rest of my life, I will have an immense amount of respect for drywallers. And let me tell you, I mean it too!)

Back on subject, in most definitions of CCI, we often hear terms like normal deviation, or standard deviation as part of the equation. However, what we must understand…is that CCI is calculated using mean deviation (or mean absolute deviation MAD), not standard deviation.

Moreover, there is no such thing as 'normal deviation.' (Just to split hairs, Roget's 21st Century Thesaurus, Third Edition lists 'normal deviation' as a synonym for standard deviation; however, standard deviation is not used calculating CCI, mean deviation is.)

Furthermore, what the heck is 'overbought' and 'oversold'? As you're about to see, when CCI is trading above +100 and below -100, whatever financial instrument the indicator is measuring may not be overbought, or oversold at all…

I'm not kidding, the stuff most Websites feed traders is just plain damaging…

To dig into the specifics, CCI is calculated using the 'mean deviation', which is thought of as providing greater accuracy to non-normal (non-Gaussian) data than the more commonly used standard deviation.

In the paper *Revisiting a 90-year-old debate: the advantages of the mean deviation* by Stephen Gorard (presented at the British Educational Research Association Annual Conference, University of Manchester in 2004), the author asserts, "*In those rare situations in which we obtain full response from a random sample with no measurement error and wish to estimate, using the dispersion in our sample, the dispersion in a perfect Gaussian population, then the standard deviation has been shown to be a more stable indicator of its equivalent in the population than the mean deviation has. Note that we can only calculate this via simulation, since in real-life research we would not know the actual population figure, else we would not be trying to estimate it via a sample.*"[28]

I understand why mean deviation is used in CCI (to attempt to compensate for non-synthetic, non-perfect Gaussian price data); however, after spending much of the past year mapping distributions in markets, I would argue the shorter the timeframe measured, the more 'bell shaped' data becomes.

What I'm saying is perhaps the formula for CCI is more accurate with a greater set of data and that perhaps on shorter timeframes, the formula needs to be changed to utilize standard deviation, over mean deviation. Don't worry though, we will change the formula on your charts, without actually changing the formula at all! I'll explain in just a moment...

Below is the formula for CCI, please don't worry about digging too deep into the math... You don't have to crunch the numbers, I would just like for you to understand '**the philosophy**' of what's happening, over the mathematical fun-o-rama calculator super-time. The philosophy is what matters…

CCI is calculated as:

CCI = (TPn - TPSMAn) / (MD * 0.015)

Where

TPn = Typical Price (High + Low + Close)/3

TPMA = SMAn = [(TP1 + TP2 + TP3…+TPn)/n]

Then…

CCI =

[[TP current period – TPMA current period]

Divided by

[((TP1 – TPMA1) + (TP2 – TPMA2) +…TPn + TPMAn))/n]]

All multiplied by 0.015

Okay, so where the heck is all of this going? The whole point of CCI is really to measure the major 'Containment Zone' of a commodity, stock, currency, or whatever… However, like everything else in the market that's totally misleading and confusing, for whatever reason, the whole point of CCI (as explained by 90% of the Websites out there) is as well.

Definitions of CCI state 'cyclical swings', major price movements and reversals, deviation this and that…yada, yada, yada…

Here's what's really happening…

Imagine a teeter-totter that has values from -500 to +500, with zero being the middle. I place a bowling ball on the teeter-totter and get it rolling to the **right side** towards +500 and then tell you that you can't let the ball roll off the end, but the rules are you can only touch the teeter-totter and not the ball itself, what would you do?

Most likely, you would move to our left and push down on the opposite side of the teeter-totter (the -500 side) to get the back rolling back towards the middle.

Now, imagine that I had drawn -100 and +100 on either side of 0 (zero), which right now, because you are pushing down on -500, the ball is rolling back towards.

It would make sense that when the ball is rolling back from the +500 area and crosses over +100 towards the 0 (zero), the ball would likely cross zero right?

Right?

Right…

However, please also imagine that I've drawn the numbers slightly awkward to common sense in that the further from zero we get (conversely, the closer to -500 and +500 the ball is), the more densely I've drawn the numbers grouped together…

As a picture tells a thousand words, I've drawn the teeter-totter for you, as a bit of a visual aid.

Please see Figure 6.1 on the following page and please excuse my art… The main point is via *Chebyshev's Theorem in* statistics, we know that (on average), about 75% all data will rest within two standard deviations of the mean.

(In the case of a normal Gaussian curve, the probability is actually nearly 95% of all data should sit within two standard deviations of the mean, thus, in using mean deviation, Lambert was likely attempting to accommodate for non-perfect bell-shaped data. Moreover, Lambert was likely also using Chebyshev's Theorem to justify the containment range of -100 and +100, implying 70% to 80% of all data, which is why he used 0.015 as the multiplier…)

Just FYI Chebyshev's Theorem states:

"The proportion of any set of data lying with K standard deviation of the mean is always at least $1-1/K^2$, where K is any positive number greater than 1.

For K=2 and K=3, we get the following results:

- At least 3/4 (or 75%) of all values lie within 2 standard deviations of the mean."
- At least 8/9 (or 89%) of all values lie within 3 standard deviations of the mean."[29]

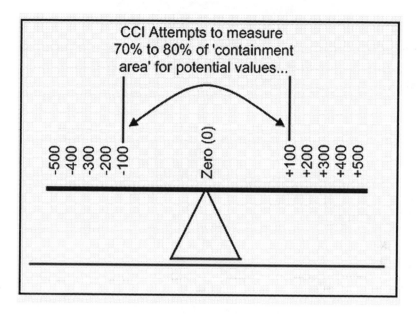

Figure 6.2

Also, please note that in the real CCI, -500 and +500 are NOT the final outlier values the indicator can move to...

Theoretically, CCI could travel infinitely up, or down... However, on a common sense basis, people don't have to buy, but they do have to sell sometime, and thus, prices (and CCI) will never travel infinitely in one direction.

The basic point here is that when CCI crosses back under +100, or back above -100, the theoretical underpinning is prices are moving back into a more 'normal range' after just having witnessed a period of extreme activity. What we're looking at is really just a measurement of 70% to 80% of the expected statistical range for whatever time period we're gauging ...

You might not be jumping up and down in your seat right now, but wait a moment and I think you could be... Though the above sounds both simple and boring, I like to think of anything that could make hordes of money...as the exact opposite...

Amazingly, I would bet (without too much trouble) about **99% of all retail Forex traders don't ever even know what they're looking at** when they use CCI to trade with... No wonder they have such a difficult time making money with the indicator!

Honestly, by simply reading these pages, you're in the 1% elite who actually know what they're looking at when they are trading with CCI...

So what we know is this... CCI is NOT indicating overbought or oversold whenever the indicator moves above +100, or below -100. Instead, CCI attempts to measure illuminate the 'Containment Zone', which is intended to be 70% to 80% of the total range. Again, the 'Containment Zone' is denoted as the area in-between -100 and +100 in the oscillator.

What I'm saying is this... In theory, when CCI is trading above +100, the stock, currency, commodity, or whatever is thought to be trading towards the top of the larger, typical range, and is in essence trading at, or above +1.2 to +1.5 standard deviations (using the term *standard deviations* merely for the sake of example, knowing standard deviations are not used in the actual calculation of the indicator.)

Conversely, when CCI is trading below -100, we generally assume the financial instrument measured is trading below the larger, normal range and is experiencing a period of volatility, denoted most often a sharp or prolonged selloff.

Here's where CCI gets very interesting for those who understand what they're looking at…

On the below chart (and I apologize for the likely confusion- it was difficult to get everything in the image even remotely clearly) you will notice what looks like fire, or hair, or something growing from the left side…

What the mysterious wig-looking thing truly is showing…is an actual representation of the 'distribution' of the price data on the chart. What we've done is literally – visually mapped- the distribution of data, so that you can see the distribution unfolding through trading action…

Here's what readers MUST make clear in their minds:

What we are really looking at when we look at _any_ price data…is data. The data is forming one HUGE distribution over all time, or a series of subset distributions, on smaller timeframes.

Notice there is outlying data towards the upper and lower end of the distributions; however, the bulk of the data rests in the middle; hence the higher mountain-like '_peak thing_' towards the center.

What you are seeing is –in essence- the **Central Limit Theorem** in action. In statistics, the Central Limit Theorem says if we pluck a small subset of data out of a larger skewed range (the totality of market data is skewed, since time is skewwy skewness in itself), the subset should –for the most part- retain a Gaussian bell curve like shape. What you are seeing on the chart is exactly the case in point. For those who are interested, in the final chapter of Volatility Illuminated, I will discuss subset distributions further (which are really amazing and complex animals in markets); reserving the '*mega-in-depth-conversation*' for last. *(In reference to my own 'best for last' hype just deployed – and if you remember Chapter One, I have a 50,000 mega-fog-mouth-lamp too! Just kidding. Anyway, the topic of distributions exposes Poisson distributions as a regular facet of markets as well, thus, given the extent of the discussion required, I will hold off on the exchange until the end of the book.)*

Now, taking a look at Figure 6.3 (below) we are able to easily identify that –indeed- trading action is **-data-** forming distributions. It is vital to 'show' the distributions, so that readers visually perceive why understanding (at the very least) the conceptual framework behind descriptive statistics is so important in day-to-day trading.

The bottom line is to be better traders -on the whole- we absolutely **must** understand that the action unfolding on our charts is really nothing more than: data.

Moreover, as you're also about to see, CCI is really an attempt a measuring 'mean reversion' and or 'divergence' of the data. Divergence is *fancy-talk* for 'trending', 'moving outside of the Containment Zone', or '*geez Zeb, lookie that thang go.*'

I personally think the below chart (Figure 6.3) has many, many implications within trading and volatility; which I hope you will see too.

Figure 6.3

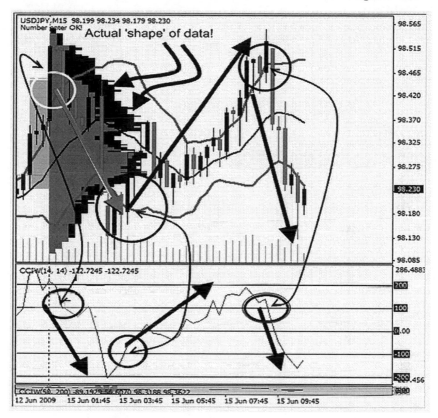

Please take a moment to notice the lower oscillator, where I have attempted to draw lines from the actual CCI 'convergence points' at +100 and -100 (meaning the points at +100 and -100 where CCI breaks from outside the containment area…back within) up to corresponding squiggly lines in the actual chart itself.

Though my connecting lines (from CCI to the squiggly lines on the chart) are not straight, a vertical line drawn on each would connect the points. What you will notice is the CCI convergence points line up almost precisely with the USD/JPY turning back into the middle range (upwards and downwards) of the channel looking thing that is overlapping the actual price action on the chart.

What are the channel lines on the actual chart and how is it that they (almost precisely!) identify the same mean-convergence type of action as CCI?

Believe it or not [insert dramatic pause] I've drawn Bollinger Bands on the USD/JPY chart as well.

However, what so many traders don't understand is that Bollinger Bands are really a visual display of potential distribution wingspan- as denoted through the visual mapping of standard deviations. (I will discuss Bollinger Bands -in detail- in the second half of the book, just FYI.) Sadly though, so many retail traders never even change the input variables (standard deviations) within Bollinger Bands, while also failing to even understand what the indicator is presenting in the first place.

Bollinger Bands come preloaded in every charting package (on the face of the planet) at two standard deviations, which most traders never even *think* to change…

However, in my humble opinion, to truly unlock the 'power' of standard deviations as a measurement of volatility and probability within trading, we must change the pre-loaded default variables. Again, I will discuss standard deviations in great length in Part Two of Volatility Illuminated.

Anyway, I have changed the values in the below bands to **1.25 standard deviations...**

By doing so, I'm measuring just over 70% of the total potential '*containment*' of the distribution at hand.

Does what I've just mentioned sound a little like CCI?

It should, because we're basically looking at the same thing; however, CCI is calculated with mean deviation (or [MAD] for Mean Absolute Deviation), while Bollinger Bands are calculated using standard deviation.

Overall, yes I had to tweak the standard deviations setting in the Bollinger Bands slightly, but really, the two are one in the same. (FYI, just in case you might be wondering, the Bollinger Bands are measuring 14-periods of data, just as CCI in the chart.)

Here's where the story gets even better... Have you ever had trouble identifying trend? Or, have you taken a position that suddenly goes against you and you look back and say, '*ohmygosh that was ridiculous, what was I thinking?!*'

If you've ever been in this place of brilliant trading euphoria, what I'm about to present could help tons.

See, when looking at shorter-term periods, many traders often mistakenly take a position against the longer-term trend, based on CCI reversing down from the +100-oscillator level, or up from below the -100-oscillator level and thus, find themselves in big trouble when the longer-term trend resumes.

And really, I understand why they're making this mistake...after all, if they had learned about CCI through just about any trading related Website on the Internet, they would think above +100 is overbought and below -100 is oversold. Really though, above +100 means *"moving above the first standard deviation"*, while -100 means *"moving below the first standard deviation"*, both of which mean, *"subset distribution on the move – alert – alert!"*

So how do we defeat this potentially misleading and costly pitfall? We identify trend.

Note: Please always remember to walk down through all your chart timeframes (macro to micro) from monthly to weekly to daily to 4-hour to hourly to 30-minute to 15-minute to 10-minute and so forth... Walking down through the charts is the best way to identify trend from the wide-scope monthly all the way into the minutia of the minute.

Again, we're simply attempting to keep the forest in our mind's eye, when we're in the trees.

Specifically to identify trend though, please look at the below 4-hour chart of the EUR/USD... I have added in 1.25 14-period standard deviations with 14-period CCI. What I think you will notice is that when the EUR/USD is traveling near the mean, we're basically 'trendless.'

What's more, in those peculiar times when CCI is actually trading below -100, it is precisely when the EUR/USD was staging the largest and fiercest moves downward...

Conversely, just when the EUR/USD traded to the top of the 'Containment Zone', we failed.

But how many people would have known to associate the move downward below -100 in CCI as 'big selloff to come'?

Figure 6.4

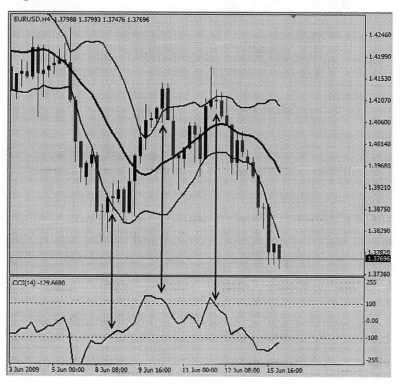

What's more, how many would have known to spot the 'failure coming' at the top of the range as well? I can assure you not many…

Here's why…

Because we're taught to use CCI as a tool for reversals, or trend-reentry (still a type of reversal) we're not taught that the breach of -100 and +100 actually means the stock, currency, commodity, or whatever is really headed towards, or trading outside of the first standard deviation, which is exactly when and where the steepest moves occur. We're taught to *look for CCI to cross back into the middle from above +100, or below -100.*

I would like to argue; however, some of the best trades are waiting for CCI to slip outside of +100 and   -100 and then trading 'with the trend' or with momentum, or 'volatility'. Then, when CCI comes back across +100 and -100 (after we've participated in the trending move), we can close our positions and let the 'containment-area trendless chop-chop traders' slug it out.

On the top of the range, you will also quickly notice that we were already in a descending trend when the EUR/USD was trying to make new highs… But really, the EUR/USD wasn't making new highs, it was just trading to the top of the Containment Zone in an already descending trend, which is also likely, one of the best places to enter 'with the trend' for those who just love those mean reversion 'CCI crossing back towards zero' types of positions.

I don't know about you though, but there's nothing I hate more than getting stuck in choppy lateral trading, so often, I look for the breakout, or breakdown from the Containment Zone, after (and only after) an identifiable trend is in place.

Okay... we should now see that at times, identifying trend (with CCI) can be almost as easy as simply adding 1.25 standard deviations to our charts and keeping an eye on BOTH CCI and the Containment Zone.

Why is it called the *Containment Zone*?

Because I just made it up... Okay, other than that, unless you have some insight into fundamentals, volatility/probability, order flow, or hopefully another technical analysis magic trick, the only thing you get in the Containment Zone is a date with Mean Joe Green...

Where the 'mean' sits...is where the 'bulk' of our data should sit. The 'Containment Zone' is statistically (if we're measuring 1-standard deviation on either side of the mean) where approximately 70% of the data should reside. And in the case of the 1.25 standard deviations, we're really looking at a little over 70%.

What I'm saying is if you're taking a position at, or near the mean, without having a really good reason for doing so, the position could just as easily reverse against you, as work in your favor. If you're on the mean, you're on the hill, on the top of the triangle, at 50/50...tossing your cash into the mystical Forex roulette wheel.

As I just stepped away from my screens for a cup of coffee... I realized that perhaps I'm being a little harsh on old Mean Joe Green... There are actually times when we can take a step into Green's house and walk away unscathed... With the aforementioned in mind, we'll take a few moments to show how we can take positions into the mean, while also using CCI in a more traditional fashion. However, we're not going to use the 'same old' *one-line in an oscillator* trick…

Just to be on the safe-side, we're going to overlay four CCI's to form the '**Quad CCI Strategy.**'

Does this thing sound like a wicked new Bic® Razor, or what?

STANDARD STAN AND THE FOUR HORSEMEN

When I first started writing about CCI a few years ago, there were only two… Somehow, the dynamic duo grew into '*The Four Horsemen*'. I guess if I write a sequel to this book in a few years, there might be two more… *Maybe I'll call it: Six Pack CCI.*

Yes, I know I'm not funny.

Jumping right in, over the following pages we will learn how to use CCI to identify trend…to defeat **false** **CCI** signals, while also attempting to time positions 'with the trend' both *inside and outside the Containment Zone.* All of which can be efficiently accomplished by applying ~~two~~ four CCI time periods to the same chart.

Our goals in doing so are to:

1. Prevent ourselves from taking positions against momentum.

2. Time our trades with short-term 'wrist-rocket' thrust from the larger market momentum.

3. Clearly determine whether the trend is up, down, or sideways.

Foremost please note that I have provided MetaTrader code for 'two CCI' at the end of the book, while having also made the code available on www.WallStreetRockStar.com and fxVolatility.com.

After the code is copied into your MetaEditor / MetaTrader Indicator folder, you should be ready to go. Also, please note that if you do not have MetaTrader, you can simply stack four CCI indicators windows in one of the various free charting applications available on the Internet. For those who use the popular charting Website Stockcharts.com, you will only be able to stack three CCI's one above and below the chart and one in the actual chart window... I've already prepared a chart for you and you can access it at:

http://stockcharts.com/h-sc/ui?s=$INDU&p=D&b=5&g=0&id=p53666348969

Moreover the code I am supplying only contains two CCI's in one widow, this is to prevent excess confusion with too much happening in one oscillator window. To see all four CCI, please stack two windows, as you will see I have done in the examples throughout the remainder of the chapter.

If you are using MetaTrader (it's free, by the way... [and] some brokerage demo accounts [United World Capital, for example] will allow tracking stocks and commodities too), after you have placed the files in your Indicator folder, please close and reopen MetaTrader. Assuming the file is in the right folder, the indicator will show up in your "custom indicator" drop down menu within your charts. Add the Two CCI code twice, using 14 and 100-periods in the top window and 50 and 200-periods in the lower window.

Standard Sam, the Deviation Man will help keep The Four Horsemen in check as the trading day rolls out...

To see Standard Sam, please add a 50-period Bollinger Band(s) to your chart, set at 1.25 Standard Deviations (STD). Also, as you have likely noticed, I am using a chart of IBM (NYSE: IBM) to show that the quad CCI strategy (*really though, all of the strategies in this book*) work with stocks, futures, and commodities too.

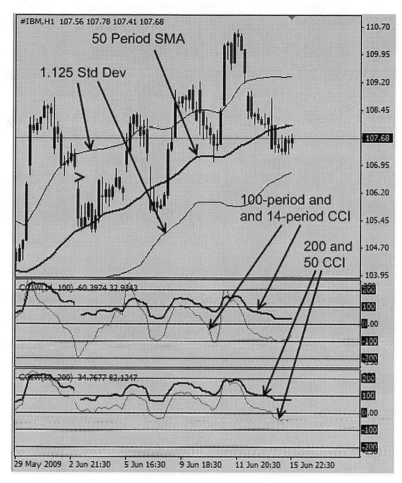

Figure 6.5

As you can see, in the lower two windows, the 100-period and 200-period CCI's are denoted in the thicker black lines, while the 14-period and the 50-period are shown as the thinner in each window.

Then, on the actual price portion of the chart, you can see that I have drawn the 50-period moving average and two 1.125 standard deviations, which as you likely already have guessed, should line up with the 50-period CCI as the casing of the 'Containment Zone'.

Readers should immediately notice that the two thicker CCI lines (the 200-period CCI and the 100-period CCI in separate windows) are both traveling above zero.

Plain Jane, the trend is up. Here's what I would like to mention for newer traders… If you're having trouble deciphering trend direction, drop in quad CCI on an hourly or 4-hour chart …. If the two longer-term CCI's (200 and 100) are above 0, common sense tells us there's more bullish momentum, than bearish and vice versa for below zero. While this may sound simple, don't scoff, I know plenty of 'tenured traders' who jump at every volatility spike, like it's a massive trend change… However, it takes more than a quick 'spike' to move the 200 and 100-CCI's above, or below the zero line, thus the resilience of the indicator within itself, can be a great buffer for 'on edge' nerves, analysis paralysis, and/or muddled vision for whatever reason.

Looking at the below chart…

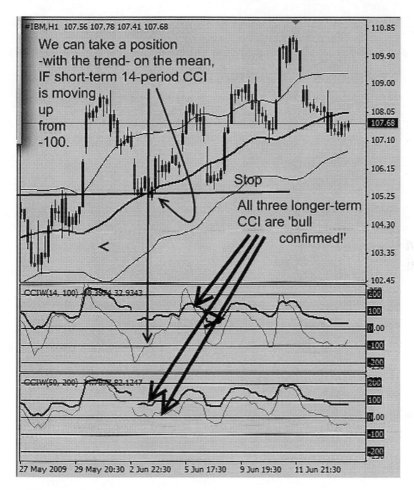

Figure 6.6

Traders seeking to take a position '*with the trend*' can attempt to purchase pullbacks on the mean (yes, Mean Joe Green) if:

1. Longer-term CCI (at least the 200 and 100) are above zero…

2. The 50-period CCI is not below -100.

3. Common sense seems inline.

What you will notice is that if we time our long-entry when the 14-period travels back up from underneath the -100 area, we are using the shorter-term indicator as a sort of 'wrist rocket' to step in just at the right time when momentum is seemingly in our favor. What's more, by taking a position on the mean (while timing such with a 14-period pop back up into the Containment Zone) we have also given ourselves a clear stop loss point, should the market fall apart. We simply place our stops on the opposite side of the mean, knowing a breach will likely have the pair testing the lower end of the Containment Zone…

Please remember: **The first loss is always the best loss.**

Anyway, should the pair pop up into Standard Stan in the 1.25 area… Once we're above the standard deviation level, we can actually use the visual identification of the 'Containment Zone' as our stop to ensure we exit the trade profitably…

Thus, savvy traders needed to only wait until the 14-period CCI '*reloaded*' and crossed (the trigger) back above the -100 oscillator containment area reentry point to implement long positions. What we 're really doing here is using The Four Horsemen to guide our way…

The 100 and 200 are like big burly swordsmen, which are hard to budge without significant force. The 50-period CCI is more like the guy who's fast on his feet, but still tough enough to take on the big dudes… And the 14-period is similar to the scout of the party…

The fastest of the bunch, but also the first to turn-tail at any sign of danger… Basically, when we see the 100 and 200-CCI stay above the 0-line, we can infer there really isn't any reason for them to move out of their range… The 50-period CCI will sometimes venture over the 0-line, before the hefty battlers, just mentioned… However, the 14-period will often venture (quickly) way out into the yonder…and he will always return to tell his pals what he's found. Crossing back over the 100-line, traders can take 'rocket trend reentry' positions (usually on the median); however, we still want to keep an eye on the flighty 14-period CCI character… If he crosses back over the +100 or -100 level he was just scouting, it means the larger weighted CCI lines could soon to follow too, as the whole bunch runs from larger momentum on the way…

Just to mention the opposite situation from what we covered in the two charts above, if the 100-Period CCI were trading below the 0-baseline (meaning the stock, currency, or commodity is likely trading right at the 100-period moving average (mean) as well) and the 14-period CCI spiked above the +100 oscillator level, the trader could look for a short entry, assuming the 100-period CCI had not begun ascending (attacking the 0-baseline), at the same time.

I'd like to mention that aggressively taking positions before CCI lines actually breach the +100/-100 oscillator levels, falling/rising from upper/lower extreme ends of the indicator window is extremely dangerous.

Moreover, as the 1.25 standard deviation representation on the chart shows, movement above +100 and below -100 could indicate a larger spike of momentum to come.

With all of the aforementioned in mind, we will now look at one final aspect of CCI – Identifying Reversals.

IDENTIFYING POTENTIAL REVERSALS WITH CCI

Identifying reversals can be slightly trickier than timing 'with the trend' positions, as anytime we are trying to take a larger contrarian position against the trend, we are truly fighting momentum. However, as in life, all things eventually **-<u>always</u>-** come to an end, trends eventually…stall…and cease too.

Thus, to spot potential larger reversals at hand, we will use the +100 and -100 Containment Zone lines (again), applying the 100-period CCI; however, unlike the above example, we will only use one CCI window, instead of two. What's more, in our single CCI window, we will also draw a 21-period CCI, leaving the 50-period and 200-period CCI's out. I'm making this change for two reasons:

1. At times, we must 'switch up' the lens, which we're observing the market from, especially if we are not seeing markets clearly.

Figure 6.7

2. Using the 21-period gives us a sort of 'middle ground' between the jittery trading action of the 14-period CCI and the more stagnate movement of the 50-period CCI. Basically, if your intuition is telling you a reversal might be on the horizon, but you are not able to see any real signs of such within news, fundamentals, or your charts…you can always switch-up timeframes, or indicators (if even momentarily) just to turn over a few more stones.

We're actually going to use the longer-term 100-period CCI line as inference and confirmation of a potential downside and/or upside reversal, even though the line may be trading above (in the case of a bull trend), or below (in the case of a bear trend) the +100 or -100 Containment Zone lines…

I'm not really a big fan of using the 100-period (or even the 50-period) as an indicator of reversal, through mean convergence from outside the Containment Zone… However, because what I'm now discussing is the 'usual' way CCI is used, I must mention it. Please keep in mind, that when we attempt to identify a reversal with the 100-period appearing as if it is about to cross from above or below the Containment Zone –back into the Containment Zone- the seconds of data that transpire while the 100-period is actually crossing back into the Containment Zone can be (what feels like) and eternity of volatility with the currency, or stock bouncing around, before finally making the move back into the mean. The bottom line is that if we are going to trade reversals back into (and through) the Containment Zone we must be prepared for excess volatility as traders duke out uncertainty.

Anyway, the main rule is this: The 100-period CCI line must be trading well above the +100-line level, or below the -100-line, before even thinking about a reversal.

If the 100-period CCI has just barely traded above the +100-containment line, and then fails, we might assume that simple mean-bound choppy trading is really the name of the game in the near-term, instead of looking for a larger reversal. (That is, unless some sort of fundamental news has surfaced making us think differently.) What I'm saying is if CCI is just "flirting" with the topside +100 oscillator level, but did not make a pronounced move above, implementing a short position would likely be more presumptuous than calculated.

To hammer home my point, when the 100-period CCI line is trading *'almost at'*, or above the -100-Containment Zone line, taking a short position is a low probability scenario, as jittery trading could easily bring about a pop up into the mean, or higher, where we would likely be stopped out.

High probability (overbought) reversals *[meaning the bull-trend could be nearing an end and a sharp downside move could potentially be pending]* generally surface when both short-term (21-period) and long-term (100-period) CCI lines are trading well above the +100 oscillator level, or below the -100 oscillator level.

When the short and long-term CCI lines are at the extreme ends of the oscillator, 'trend capitulation' or *'the fifth wave,'* in terms of Elliot Wave Theory could be in effect.

I would like to mention that several years ago, it seemed like CCI rarely moved above, or below -250, or +250 in the CCI oscillator; however, with more volatility these days…the occurrence is commonplace. Thus, when I mention 'extreme values' within the CCI oscillator window, **we must remember to use common sense**, while also making sure to note that increased volatility in the current market, could push values further above and below +100 and -100 than in recent years.

You may have noticed in Figure 6.7, when the 100-period CCI-line was trading well above the +100 Containment Zone line (not "just flirting" with it), the occurrence foreshadowed a large reversal looming on the hourly chart, which could have provided significant opportunity for savvy traders.

What's more, you will also notice that the 21-Period CCI line crossed BELOW 100-period CCI - while STILL above the +100-Containment Zone line…and then subsequently fell under +100 towards the mean. In essence, we are basically saying "I want to see longer-term momentum *rapped out* with short-term momentum also overheated, before even considering the possibility of looking for a reversal."

It's important to note traders will need to configure their CCI time periods to best fit each chart timeframe traded; however, 21-period and 100-period CCI can be used as initial benchmarks.

Moreover, never ever, ever, ever, ever, ever, ever, ever trade without a stop and never take on more risk your account can handle. When in doubt stay out.

While there a many more examples of CCI trading, everything we've discussed here are a great starting point for traders who are not only seeking to help identify trend – in an effort to increase discipline– but may also help one identify reversals and most importantly…give additional guidance when to 'stay out' of the game, should choppy mean-bound trading seem in the cards over the near term.

With everything that we've covered in Part One of Volatility Illuminated, I'm thrilled to now move into Part Two, where we will really dive into volatility and probability, while also taking a very close look at VWAP and of course WVAV and WAVE • PM.

The information you are about to read –as far as I know - is **<u>nowhere else</u>** readily available for traders within markets, or on the Internet. I have spent hundreds of hours preparing the following pages of Volatility Illuminated.

The information you're about to read is **<u>NOT</u>** a re-hash of someone else's stuff…

What you are about to read came from **REAL trading,** which I discovered **<u>only</u>** after countless hours grinding it out in markets with real money.

Some of the gems you're going to read about were discovered through massive losses (always a great place to discover incredible insights) and some were unearthed through long strings of wins- carving out similar data (outside of traditional market knowledge) to refine and shape in preparation of the information here.

What I'm saying is even if at the end of the book, you're like, '*geez, that sucked, I'd like my money back,*' I'm okay with it, because I plan on using the information here in my own trading –because it was derived from REAL trading– not sitting behind a 'strategy tester' looking back into history.

What you're about to read was uncovered with real cash, in real time and I will continue to use the information with my own real cash, long after you have put the book down. I hope you are able to take a ton away from the following pages, though as always, please remember to trade safely and of course: *common sense is king.*

Even though we're not even close to the end of the book yet, I would like to mention that I appreciate you having purchased this book... Should I swing for the fences [again] trading -when I'm like, 60; you sleep easy knowing you helped pay for my room at the old folks home. *I will do my best to convert the Bingo hall into a trading floor though.*

Anyway, I hope you enjoy Part Two, and please remember to keep an open mind...

PART TWO

VOLATILITY

ILLUMINATED

CHAPTER SEVEN

INFORMATION ACCELERATION IN THE 21ST CENTURY AND THE VOLATILITY PARADIGM

"BELIEVE NOTHING, NO MATTER WHERE
YOU READ IT, OR WHO SAID IT, NO
MATTER IF I HAVE SAID IT, UNLESS IT
AGREES WITH YOUR OWN REASON AND
YOUR OWN COMMON SENSE."

~ HINDU PRINCE

GAUTAMA SIDDHARTA

What if?

What if some of the information we believe is truth…is not…

Rather, please allow me a moment to rephrase…

What if the information we believe -as truth- is valid in some regard, but to us -as traders- is not providing an accurate picture of reality within markets?

In Chapter Three, we already covered how our own memories can play tricks on us, how media can literally recreate our perception of past events (shown in the poison tree example), we even saw how our emotions *can be* cyclically altered through headlines and media.

What we have to understand…is that not all information is incorrect and not information that we have might believe is false…actually is. In reality, there is another variable happening here, which we did not touch on in Chapter Three.

See, the entire paradigm of how we (and markets) receive information has changed dramatically over the past 10, 30, 50 and 100 years.

To understand Volatility Illuminated, we have to look into information –itself- in raw form, as we take it in daily.

I know the aforementioned sounds slightly cryptic, however, as you're about to see, information has changed.

Moreover, the **'speed of information'** has also accelerated, causing the **critical mass** of **'noteworthy distributions'** to alter in look, shape, size, smell, and impact, as well.

As you are about to see, credulous public acceptance of 21st Century information **and** dangerous historical benchmarks are not only causing greater potential fallibility and volatility within Government and markets, but in our reception, digestion and action upon much of the information we receive daily, as well.

In the end, we will never truly understand market volatility if we do not come to a solid understanding that present-day mass-market and public ignorance of the contemporary *'altered information'* paradigm, has created an *'explosive exponent'* within trading, politics, economics, and even sociology.

To illuminate the problematic circumstances I have just mentioned, throughout Chapter Seven, we will see how even the major indices may be presenting unclear information, how and why the larger information paradigm has changed, and how all of the aforesaid is impacting markets, trading and volatility overall.

After Chapter Seven, you should:

1. See why we must question the larger paradigm of the distribution and reception of information by market participants, affiliates and media overall.

2. Understand that often, extensive market volatility is the product of the masses not understanding the true reality of the information they are presented, misleading packaging of the information from the start, and overall, a significant –unrecognized- change in the larger light-speed information paradigm…over the past 100 years.

3. See how information and markets have changed in recent years, thus, clearly recognize why understanding volatility and probability within today's trading environment is absolutely critical to navigating markets profitably.

4. Come away with firm clarity and understanding that those who trade purely from technicals and/or fundamentals (retail, or institutional), without attempting to understand the volatility paradigm surfacing in modern markets, are setting themselves up for eventual failure.

See, populations, investors and even politicians often move in herds, sometimes completely disregarding new and challenging information, should the information require a change in belief structure and/or defy comfortability, career, wealth, or socio-economic standing and status. What I've just mentioned means when there is a dirty truth hanging over markets, the masses usually ignore the occurrence for as long as possible. However, when the larger potentially damaging situation can no longer be ignored, the masses will again move '*en masse*', with fierce vigor. What we're talking about is panic...

To separate ourselves from the crowd in life and trading, we must take the time to understand why and how the information paradigm has changed. In the end, it is not enough to simply understand volatility through traditional methods such as the Market Volatility Index VIX (a measurement of market fear through option premiums); we **<u>must</u>** also understand the theoretical and philosophical underpinnings of how mass market volatility is created from the start.

PRE-LOADING MAJOR MARKETS FOR VOLATILITY

First in our discussion, I would like to take a moment to introduce you to what you likely already know as a reliable benchmark of markets: The Dow Jones Industrial Average (DJIA). As most are likely aware, the Dow is comprised of thirty of the largest major public companies within the United States. In essence, the DJIA is an 'average' of thirty stocks, all with 'large cap' weighting, meaning their respective markets caps generally exceed $5 to $10 billion.

As the Figure 7.1 shows, the DJIA is comprised of large name companies most would recognize in a heartbeat.

Figure 7.1

On first glance, it makes sense to trust the Dow Jones Industrial Average as a valid benchmark to track the U.S. economy and the sentiment of investors through the daily buying and selling of the index. Moreover, it is also likely fair to say that then the Dow moves up, investors feel good about the economy and when the Dow falls, investors feel the economy is in trouble.

NAME	SYM	MASS	PRICE
IBM	IBM	10.02	$102
Exxon Mobil Corp.	XOM	6.88	$70
Chevron Corp.	CVX	6.82	$69
McDonald's Corp.	MCD	5.58	$57
3M Co.	MMM	5.23	$53
Johnson & Johnson	JNJ	5.07	$51
Wal-Mart Stores Inc.	WMT	4.99	$51
Procter & Gamble Co.	PG	4.85	$49
United Technologies	UTX	4.66	$47
Coca-Cola Co.	KO	4.43	$45
Boeing Co.	BA	3.86	$39
Hewlett-Packard Co.	HPQ	3.39	$34
JPMorgan Chase & Co.	JPM	3.23	$33
Caterpillar Inc.	CAT	3.20	$33
Verizon Comm.	VZ	3.16	$32
E.I. DuPont de Nemou	DD	2.61	$26
Merck & Co. Inc.	MRK	2.59	$26
AT&T Inc.	T	2.57	$26
Home Depot Inc.	HD	2.55	$26
Kraft Foods Inc. Cl A	KFT	2.20	$22
Walt Disney Co.	DIS	1.96	$20
Microsoft Corp.	MSFT	1.94	$20
American Express Co.	AXP	1.86	$19
Intel Corp.	INTC	1.57	$16
Pfizer Inc.	PFE	1.33	$14
General Electric Co.	GE	1.12	$11
Bank of America Corp	BAC	0.94	$10
Alcoa Inc.	AA	0.87	$9
Citigroup Inc.	C	0.30	$3
General Motors Corp.	GM	0.20	$2
TOTAL		99.99	

Not so fast though, there's something else happening here that savvy traders will likely want to be aware of.

Some argue that measuring the 'average' of thirty stocks is not a true snapshot of the *whole* economy and thus, does not accurately measure the present-day health of all sectors and business within the United States.

However, in our never-ending pursuit of truth - and the true underpinnings of volatility - we brush off the typical arguments both for and against the DJIA in exchange for greater understanding of a perhaps larger (hushed) problem looming under the surface.

The problematic issue with the DJIA actually has nothing to do with the 'total amount' of companies that make up the index... Rather, the knotty concern with the DJIA is really in the way the index calculated from the start.

Did you know there are <u>basically</u> five methods used to calculate indices?[30]

They are:

- Market Capitalization Weighted Indices
- Modified Market Capitalization Weighted Indices
- Price Weighted Indices
- Fundamentally Based Stock Indices
- Attribute Weighted Indices

Can you guess which of the previous five methods is used to calculate the Dow Jones Industrial Average? If you guessed 'price weighted', you guessed correctly.

Traditionally, price weighted indexes are calculated by summing the prices of all components and then dividing by the total. When the Dow kicked off way back in 1896, there were only 12 initial components. Charles Dow added up the prices of all the companies and then divided by 12.

Figure 7.2

Company 1	$30
Company 2	$20
Company 3	$40
Company 4	$50
Company 5	$100
Company 6	$30
Company 7	$20
Company 8	$30
Company 9	$20
Company 10	$15
Sum	$355
Divided by total	$10
Index Value	35.5

That's it, nothing to it!

Over the years, 18 more companies were added to develop the present total of thirty components. There's more to the story though…

The real meat to this tale is in the math behind how the Dow is calculated…

Let's take an example where we have 10 companies in an index:

Looking at the Figure 7.2, we see that the total of all prices equals $355. Moreover, by taking the sum and then dividing by the total (10), we end up with an average price of $35.5, which would be the 'index value'.

But let me ask you a question, what happens one of the stocks split in the index? Would it change the index value?

You bet it would.

Figure 7.3

Moreover, given that the more expensive a stock becomes, the more likely it is to split, unless of course, it's Berkshire Hathaway.

For the sake of example, let us assume the most expensive stock in our list, Company 5, splits. Instead of calculating the index value with the previous $100, if we made no other adjustments, we would use the post split price of $50 in our sum of all the prices.

Company 1	$30
Company 2	$20
Company 3	$40
Company 4	$50
Company 5 (spilt)	$50
Company 6	$30
Company 7	$20
Company 8	$30
Company 9	$20
Company 10	$15
Sum	$305

The new sum of $305 divided by the total (10), would give us a new index value of 30.5, versus the pre-split index value of 35.5.

Because of the split, the index value is now 14% lower than it was before the split, however, nothing fundamentally changed in the stock and really, not a single share was sold in the whole process.

To overcome the loss in index value should a split occur, the Dow Jones Company instituted the use of a divisor.

Figure 7. 4

Company 1	$30
Company 2	$20
Company 3	$40
Company 4	$50
Company 5 (spilt)	$50
Company 6	$30
Company 7	$20
Company 8	$30
Company 9	$20
Company 10	$15
Sum	$305

The divisor is calculated by taking the post spilt total of the prices and then dividing by the original value.

For example, if we had 10 $100 stocks and one component split, the divisor calculation would be simply to divide $950 by the original $1000, which would give us a divisor of 0.95.

Then, to calculate the actual index, the post split sum of all stock prices is divided by the divisor, which provides a more accurate price of the index.

In the case of our previous example, if we utilize a divisor we would divide the post-split sum of prices ($305) by the new divisor (0.87), bringing us back to original total of $350. Then dividing by 10, just like in our pre-split example, we would end up with a correct index value of 35.5.

Thus, the divisor brings the sum of all prices (reflecting splits) back to the correct *pre-split* summed value of prices…for us to then divide by the total components in the index.

The methodology I have just shown is a *Price Weighted Index*.

Sounds reasonable correct?

Not so fast. There is an inherent issue with this method.

Foremost, as time passes and more companies within the index split, the divisor becomes smaller and smaller...

Normally small numbers aren't too scary right? Wrong.

Every time a stock splits in the Dow, the divisor becomes more minute, thus creating even more volatility within the index.

Did I just use the word volatility? Yes I did. Volatility is in fact created within the Dow Jones Industrial Average because of the way it is calculated.

Let me explain... As of June 9, 2009, the Dow Jones Company announced:[31]

The Dow Jones Industrial Average will be calculated with a new divisor **prior to the open of trading on Monday, June 8, 2009.** The divisor for the **Dow Jones Industrial Average changes to 0.132319125** (from 0.125552709) as a result of the following actions:

• General Motors Corp. (Pink Sheet: GMGMQ) is to be deleted from the Dow Jones Industrial Average.

• Cisco Systems Inc. (NASDAQ: CSCO) is to be added to the Dow Jones Industrial Average.

• Citigroup Inc. (NYSE: C) is to be deleted from the Dow Jones Industrial Average.

• Travelers Cos. Inc. (NYSE: TRV) is to be added to the Dow Jones Industrial Average.

After 113 years, so many stocks have split in the Dow Jones Industrial Average, the divisor is now at an extremely low 0.132319125.

What does this mean to you?

Think about it for a moment, if a stock moves up $3 in a single day, the occurrence would add 22.7 points to the DJIA closing value for that day. ($3 / 0.132319125 = 22.7)

Let's take a moment and step back from the situation though…to consider the 'common sense' behind what's happening. If you have a $10 stock that moves $3 in one day, the stock would have individually gained 30% in the session. However, if you have a $100 stock that moved $3 in one day, the stock would have gained 3% in one session.

Which is more likely- a stock gaining 30% in one session, or a stock gaining 3% in one session?

The common sense answer is obviously that it is more likely that a $100 stock will move $3, over a $10 stock. Thus, because of the way the Dow Jones Industrial Average is calculated, higher price stocks within in the index have greater influence in the total value of the index. What's more, the higher stocks move (within the index), the more rapidly the index value climbs…or falls.

To gain the upper hand on the Dow, one could theoretically track the top ten most expensive stocks on a daily basis for greater guidance into the indexes' potential movement, versus just tracking the index by itself.

Why?

Think about it for a moment… If higher price stocks have greater probability of larger price swings, and **prices** really have the greatest impact on the index value, it would makes sense that we would more closely watch the stocks that see greater day-to-day price swings, over the lesser price components.

I will explain this in detail in a moment, first though, please note that as of June 18, 2009, the components (and respective prices) of the DJIA were:

Figure 7.5

Components of Dow Jones Industrial Average

COMPANY NAME	TICKER	PRICE
3M Co.	MMM	59.37
Alcoa Inc.	AA	11
American Express Co.	AXP	24.64
AT&T Inc.	T	24.04
Bank of America Corp.	BAC	13.22
Boeing Co.	BA	48.44
Caterpillar Inc.	CAT	33.65
Chevron Corp.	CVX	68.06
Cisco Systems Inc.	CSCO	18.92
Coca-Cola Co.	KO	48.81
E.I. DuPont	DD	24.97
Exxon Mobil Corp.	XOM	71.05
General Electric Co.	GE	12.1
Hewlett-Packard Co.	HPQ	38.35
Home Depot Inc.	HD	23.52
Intel Corp.	INTC	16.01
Intl Business Machines	IBM	105.89
Johnson & Johnson	JNJ	56.09
JPMorgan Chase & Co.	JPM	35
Kraft Foods Inc. Cl A	KFT	25.41
McDonald's Corp.	MCD	58.17
Merck & Co. Inc.	MRK	25.91
Microsoft Corp.	MSFT	24.07
Pfizer Inc.	PFE	15
Procter & Gamble Co.	PG	50.64
Travelers Cos. Inc.	TRV	42.08
United Technologies Corp.	UTX	54.2
Verizon Communications Inc.	VZ	29.66
Wal-Mart Stores Inc.	WMT	48.17
Walt Disney Co.	DIS	23.53

Index Value on June 19, 2009   8,539.73

Now, in Figure 7.6, please note the 'total impact on index value' of a one-day 1.5% gain in the top 10 most expensive stocks, over the top 20 least expensive components (Figure 7.7).

Figure 7.6

Top 10 (Most Expensive) Dow Stocks

Company	Stock Price	One-Day 1.5% Gain	Pt. Impact on Index
Intl Business Machines	105.89	1.58835	12.00
Exxon Mobil Corp.	71.05	1.06575	8.05
Chevron Corp.	68.06	1.0209	7.72
3M Co.	59.37	0.89055	6.73
McDonald's Corp.	58.17	0.87255	6.59
Johnson & Johnson	56.09	0.84135	6.36
United Technologies	54.2	0.813	6.14
Procter & Gamble Co.	50.64	0.7596	5.74
Coca-Cola Co.	48.81	0.73215	5.53
Boeing Co.	48.44	0.7266	5.49
		Total	**+70.37**

All things being equal, a 1.5% move up in every stock in the Dow Jones Industrial Average would equate to a +128-point gain in the total index closing value.

Of the +128-point gain, the top 10 most expensive stocks would have contributed to 54.93% of the gain, while the bottom 20 would have contributed to 45.07% of the gain. Ironically, the top 10 stocks moved the exact same percentage as the bottom 20 and yet have greater 'weight' on the total index value.

Figure 7.7

Bottom 20 (Least Expensive) Dow Stocks

Company	Stock Price	One-Day 1.5% Gain	Pt. Impact on Index
Wal-Mart Stores	48.17	0.72255	5.46
Travelers Cos.	42.08	0.6312	4.77
Hewlett-Packard	38.35	0.57525	4.35
JPMorgan Chase	35.00	0.525	3.97
Caterpillar Inc.	33.65	0.50475	3.81
Verizon	29.66	0.4449	3.36
Merck & Co. Inc.	25.91	0.38865	2.94
Kraft Foods	25.41	0.38115	2.88
E.I. DuPont	24.97	0.37455	2.83
American Express Co.	24.64	0.3696	2.79
Microsoft Corp.	24.07	0.36105	2.73
AT&T Inc.	24.04	0.3606	2.73
Walt Disney Co.	23.53	0.35295	2.67
Home Depot Inc.	23.52	0.3528	2.67
Cisco Systems	18.92	0.2838	2.14
Intel Corp.	16.01	0.24015	1.81
Pfizer Inc.	15.0	0.225	1.70
Bank of America	13.22	0.1983	1.50
General Elec.	12.1	0.1815	1.37
Alcoa Inc.	11.0	0.165	1.25
		Total	**+57.73**

What we're talking about here is an index that is preloaded for volatility, especially if old market adage of *higher prices over the long haul* holds true. Fact is, as the prices of the individual components in the DJIA climb, the more volatile the index becomes, given the present price/divisor paradigm.

With the aforementioned in mind, we can assume that the higher the DJIA moves:

1. In terms of point swings, the daily moves will be greater.

2. Media hype will only increase in years to come, as 200, 300, 400 and 600 point swings begin to surface -daily- in the index.

3. The index has been 'artificially pre-loaded' to gain-ground.

Point number three in my last statement *hopefully* caused a few readers to raise their eyebrows… I did -in fact- say *'artificially pre-loaded to gain ground.'*

Please allow me a moment to clarify… In the fall of 2007, the Dow Jones Industrial Average hit an all time high of 14,198.10, obviously before U.S. mortgage markets fell through the floor, and before the entire financial crisis really unfolded. By June of 2009, the DJIA was down about 40% from the 2007 high.

Funny thing though…if you remember the divisor announcement a few pages ago, we also know in June of 2009, two stocks were removed from the index, and were replaced by two new companies.

The announcement read:

- General Motors Corp. (Pink Sheet: GMGMQ) is to be deleted from the Dow Jones Industrial Average.

- Cisco Systems Inc. (NASDAQ: CSCO) is to be added to the Dow Jones Industrial Average.

- Citigroup Inc. (NYSE: C) is to be deleted from the Dow Jones Industrial Average.

- Travelers Cos. Inc. (NYSE: TRV) is to be added to the Dow Jones Industrial Average.

Let's take a moment to consider the reality of the situation here... In October of 2007, General Motors posted a relative high of $41.93, while Citigroup tagged a high of $45.09 in the same month...

By June of 2009, General Motor's stock was trading at $1.75, while Citigroup was trading at $3.17.

In all, from October of 2007 to June of 2009, General Motor's stock lost 40 points (-95.8%), while Citigroup had peeled off 42 points (-93%). Here's the thing though, if you remember our discussion a moment ago about the DJIA being *'price weighted'*, using the pre-June 9, 2009 divisor of 0.125552709, the total point declines of General Motors and Citigroup contributed to 653 points of the 5,658.37 points lost in the DJIA, since the October 2007 highs.

So how would the Dow ever climb back to a level where media and investors would ever pay close attention to the index again, if Citigroup and General Motors stocks are likely to stay under $10 for a long, long time? *What do you think the solution is?*

General Motors and Citigroup were '*black eyes*' for the Dow, and considering it is much, much tougher for a $40 stock to add $10, versus a $100 stock, both stocks were poised to remain as major drags on the index for years.

What I'm saying is if a few of the stocks in the index have been beat up considerably (like fallen under $10), wouldn't the occurrence make it much harder for the Dow to ever post new highs again, with the cheaper stocks weighing heavily on the total index value?

You know it.

Dump the losers and replace them with stocks that have a better chance of gaining ground. The higher the new stocks climb, the more points they will add to the total index value.

Bingo! General Motors and Citigroup were kicked to the curb and replaced by Cisco and Travelers.

Fact is, as of June 9, 2009, because Citigroup and General Motors were booted from the Dow, the index now stands a greater chance of recouping losses (and eventually making new highs) than if the flailing bank and auto manufacturer were still a part of the benchmark index.

When the Dow eventually climbs back to new highs, media will likely tout '***the bull is back***' or something like '***you can't keep the Dow down***' (or whatever), however, media will likely **forget to mention** the mega-money center bank that was replaced by a property & casualty insurance company and the '*American as apple pie*' auto-manufacturer that was replaced by a network and communication devices company.

What's more, when considering that there's no longer any auto-manufacturers in the Dow now, it seems awkward to assume the index truly reflects a fair breadth of products used in the calculation of consumption and GDP growth – in America.

At the end of the day, if every time the Dow pulls back in an economic hiccup, 'beat-down' stocks are replaced by others that hold greater potential to ascend, the event really means the index will likely make new highs –again- in the years to come, but not truly reflect the American economy, as it is said too.

Analysts will continue to tout 'the investor who bought Dow stocks and held them over the past fifty years has seen his portfolio continually climb, even with the crash of 1987, the dot.com bomb and the financial crisis.'

But what they won't tell you is **part** *of the reason the Dow is able to keep making new highs* –decade after decade– is the lesser performing components are dumped like a bad date, any time the kitchen gets hot.

Eventually, the Dow will hit new highs and day-to-day volatility (in terms of price swings) will be greater than ever. Really, we're talking about preloading volatility into markets.

In a few years, when the Dow is back at highs… Citigroup and General Motors will likely still be in the gutter trying to recover.

There's even more to the story though…the volatility story, I mean… As I've just pointed out, the way the DJIA is calculated –and preloaded- is all geared to help the index constantly make new highs over time. New highs mean new press and new press means more exposure. It's about maintaining 'benchmark status', while keeping investors interested in…investing. However, much like our memories are easily influenced by media (in recollection of historical events) the Dow example is another instance of 'important information' completely passing by the general public. Given the larger financial crisis, political events of the day and everything else one must constantly worry about, why would the calculation of an index ever even be important to take note of? What we're really talking about is the total mass of information required for investors to truly stop and mark as important. In the 21st Century information paradigm, unless an event has enough 'sauce' to spark significant fear (loss) or exuberance (greed) within individuals, the information passes like a shooting star on a cloudy night. Eventually, the DJIA will likely hit new highs and media will again gawk and squawk about the event, thus sucking investors into the poison tree –yet again- and of course, eventually the economic cycle will take a downward turn and those same investors will see their wealth decrease, as major indices take another nosedive.

I'm not saying that we shouldn't invest…after all, now that the DJIA has been 'reloaded' for possible upside, the present day actually appears to be a decent time to buy…at least if the U.S. Dollar doesn't plummet in the near future, due to the loss of credit quality of U.S. Treasuries, based on excessive spending by the Government…*but that's another conversation.*

The point, however, is we can certainly invest in markets and indices, so long as we are fully cognizant of the volatility paradigm. Moreover, we must also recognize that the larger problematic issues behind how the delivery and reception of 'information' has changed in the 21st Century, while actively seeking out information that could present future volatility – ahead of time.

As many readers may still be a little unclear about the larger shift in the 'information delivery and reception' paradigm I keep mentioning, we will now cover 'why' and 'how' the aforementioned has changed and what it all means to markets and volatility.

Over the next section, we're going examine **Einstein's Theory of Special Relativity** to see how information has changed and at the same time, how such impacts markets.

However, please do not feel that you need to work through the math; really, the most important part is to simply just make sure to take the time to understand the philosophical and theoretical underpinnings (as pertaining to markets and volatility) behind the physics.

MARKET VOLATILITY THROUGH EINSTEIN'S THEORY OF SPECIAL RELATIVITY

I'm sure many readers are wondering how Einstein is relevant to markets and volatility... Moreover, those who aren't too fond of math likely already have their fingers into the next chapter, ready to skip over the following pages at the first sign of big brainwork. However, please know what we're about to cover is very important in the larger understanding of macro market volatility and how individuals, professionals and markets collectively receive and act on (or discard) critical information.

As we are about to see, information actually does have 'mass' and with the technological innovations of the past few decades, the overall formula behind the *energy of information* moving markets has changed.

What I'm saying is because information is now moving at the speed of light, **market volatility is increasing (_and will likely continue to swell_)**, as the larger populous is progressively more inundated with *even more* information... Moreover, as the masses continually become exceptionally trusting of, and more dependent on media, while at the same time (and unfortunately), gradually more neglectful of taking the time to personally seek out *'real information'* about to impact their lives...

As you're about to see, the 'postmodernism' of market moving information is a troublesome condition of *'see no evil, hear no evil, don't want to deal with any evil'*, causing markets (especially Forex) to present more and more volatility (seemingly out of the blue) every day. Moreover, because the masses prefer to turn their heads at information containing real warnings within markets, when bad news can no longer be ignored, markets tumble...fast.

Don't be discouraged though...because as long as you're willing to see information and markets clearly, you're one of the few...now *'in the know.'*

We will begin our discussion of physics and the larger *'light speed information'* paradigm with Einstein's <u>Theory of Special Relativity</u>, taking special notice of Mass Energy Equivalence ($E = mc^2$) and Length Contraction.

As a quick side note, $E = mc^2$ is not *'the'* Theory of Relativity, as many believe...

In reality, $E = mc^2$ stands for Mass-Energy Equivalence and is one of four derivatives from Einstein's 1905 paper: *Zur Elektrodunamik bewegter Körper (On the Electrodynamics of Moving Bodies)*.[32]

The aforementioned paper attempted to define the structure of spacetime, via Special Relativity.

Spacetime –as a loose definition- is a mathematical model, or theory attempting to mold space and time into one continuum.[33]

While $E = mc^2$ is not the core concept I am presenting here, the theory of Mass-Energy Equivalence and Special Relativity do have a few points we should note in terms of information in the 21st Century, financial markets and volatility.

Just as a quick primer, within the Theory of Special Relativity, we find four major consequences:[34]

$\longrightarrow$ **Relativity of Simultaneity:** Two events, simultaneous for two observers, may not be simultaneous for the observers, if the observers are in relative motion.

$\longrightarrow$ **Time Dilation:** Moving clocks should theoretically, tick more slowly…than an observer's "stationary" clock.

$\longrightarrow$ **Length Contraction:** Objects in motion, as measured in relative width from the stance of an observer, will shorten…in the direction they are moving with respect to the observer.

$\longrightarrow$ **Mass-Energy Equivalence:** $E = mc^2$, energy and mass are equivalent and transmutable.

Quickly walking through each of the four points of Special Relativity:

1. When examining **Relativity of Simultaneity**, at some level the theory holds true within markets, as the overall concept tells us that simultaneity is not absolute, rather is dependent on the observer's position.

2. Time Dilation means the faster something moves, the more time slows down for the thing in motion. If you were standing on earth and you could see a spacecraft moving on the other side of the universe - and it was/is moving at the speed of light…

In fifty years of your life, the spacecraft might cover 30 percent of your visible sky.

However, for the people in the spacecraft, because they are moving at the speed of light, in the same fifty years, they would have aged significantly less. What the theory is saying is time is relative to the location of the clock; in other words, time is relative to frame of reference.

What the theory is also implying is without another reference point, time will remain constant. The issue here (with the way the Dow is calculated too), is we **do** actually have a constant frame of reference, by which we base time off of, derived from the simple fact that none of is moving - or has moved- at the speed of light (or even remotely close to it) anytime in the past 100- years. *(And likely since the beginning of time, unless there's something I'm missing.)*

Here's something to consider though… In 1909, a devastating press release sometimes took days -even weeks- to reach the investing masses, given the lack of mass communication, as seen today. Let's say, for example, it's 1909 and in your previous life, you were JP Bigwig…and you controlled a massive position in coal all across America, especially in the Appalachians.

While you're in Canada fishing, a freak earthquake hits your largest coal investments, devastating production.

Because it is 1909 –and you're in the woods fishing, your team can't exactly call you on your cell…

See what I'm saying?

In modern markets though, information travels exponentially quicker (and more efficiently) via fiber optic cable, satellites, television, cell phones, and Internet…

The speed of information has increased, though time is still the same as it was in 1909. Consider what's really happening…information is –literally- now traveling close to 300,000 kilometers every second. How fast is that? If I were light, I could circle the globe seven times in one second; or about 28 times, in the four seconds (by my estimate) it is taking you to read this sentence.

In 1909, information often traveled at the speed of old Jeb and his sidekick in the wire-house. Jeb got the wire and then told some kid to run around and tell others. The kid's name was Flash.

Humor aside, what we have to understand, is because the information has increased in speed, while time remains constant, the occurrence has changed the 'mass' element of market moving information, and thus, is causing increased volatility within markets. A few physicists might argue with me, but they don't trade with real cash every day, watching how events impact markets every second… From the laboratory of the trading floor, the empirical evidence shows information is moving so fast, most slips by unnoticed, until the mass is just too big to ignore.

As I am about to show, the theory of Length Contraction will provide us with some proof that that 'mass' of information has changed. Then, later in the chapter, I will show how volatility (through the mass and speed of information) has increased overall, by examining major historical moves in the Dow Jones Industrial Average over the past 100 years.

Again, what we have to understand is because information is now moving at the speed of light, another variable within relativity absolutely must have changed. The variable I am speaking of is the larger ignorance and passivity of society, through complete inundation of information, whereby information is ignored until the total mass of such threatens critical impact, either through fear, or exuberance.

Figure 7.8

3. Length Contraction means the faster something moves, the more it compresses in relation to the observation of a stationary viewer.

Figure 7.9

Take a moment to glance at the image of Mr. Stick Trader (Figure 7.9), though please don't laugh at my artwork! In the theory of Length Contraction, the faster an item moves in relation to the observer, the more it will compress.

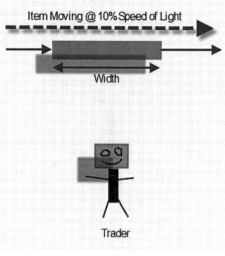

In context: For a stationary individual or securities trader for example, the little black box moving from left to right (in the image above) is slightly more than three times the width of the stick figure's head.

Now, look at Figure 7.10 on the following page...

If the little black box accelerates to 85% of the speed of light, the box would appear only about one and a half times wider than the head of Mr. Stickman Trader.

Here's where the story gets interesting... Consider that perhaps the 'thing' is information.

In the early 1900's, when the Dow Jones Industrial Average was just getting off the ground, information really only traveled by wire and/or telephone. For example, in 1906, the telephone industry put in a record-breaking achievement completing the first-ever long-distance underground line call, totaling 90-miles from New York City to Philadelphia.[35]

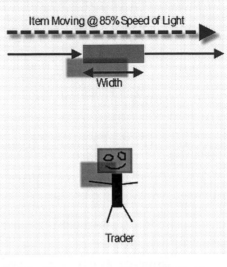

Figure 7.10

Today, however, information moves much, much faster… Case in point, information virtually moves at the speed of light through fiber optic cable.[36] Fact is, in our world, information travels 40,000 miles into space and back creating, *"a pause of about half a second between speaking on a transatlantic phone call or live television link and your voice reaching the listener."*[37]

Because the speed of information has accelerated dramatically over the years (traveling at the speed of light today), in context of Length Contraction, the increase in speed of information means the total breadth (mass) of information has shrunk.

Let me rephrase that, because information is passing by so quickly each day, the amount of time we pay attention to information (because the mass of passing information has compressed) has decreased. What I'm saying is with more information passing through our perceptions daily, information is here today and gone tomorrow, with the public quickly forgetting whatever just passed by our consciousness. We quickly forget, or simply fail to take notice of information –until– the information has so much mass, the game changer can no longer be ignored.

Again, if you are still standing in the same place and information has accelerated, what is it that has changed?

Mass changed…

CRITICAL MASS AND CONSCIOUS UNAWARENESS

For the public to take notice of any information as 'significant', the information must have substantially greater mass today, than in historic years of the markets. In reality, what has changed is the total deterioration of the general public's memory of yesterday, active cognizance of today and even more worrisome, any thought of tomorrow, based on the speed of information in today's Internet world.

In plain language, with information moving so much faster today, whatever the 'take notice' event is, it unfortunately must be a whopper- to stick. Unless the information contains some sort consequence to our immediate life, the information is quickly forgotten (or ignored) all together.

Though I believe your memory is better than most, please simply state what you ate for lunch one week ago from today? *[Don't worry, I can't remember either.]*

I will cover the larger populous-oblivious paradigm in detail in the next chapter. Moreover, I will show exactly why and how the speed of information is not only causing the average individual to become less aware of social veracity within business, politics, and community, but also why and how the occurrence has triggered an epidemic of volatility within financial markets.

What we must understand for now though...is perhaps the global financial crisis has less to do with credit, mortgages, and lack of regulation, than most believe.

In essence, the ugly economic matters at hand are truly about rapidly passing information overlooked by the public daily. Furthermore, with major media constantly promoting fear and gloom (such was true before the financial crisis too) most individuals protect their sanity by simply disregarding negativity.

The problem though, is as a society, we have manufactured a condition where all warnings of pending disaster (to the global economy based on the non-existence of credit swap regulation, for example) are completely ignored unless the walls totally start crumbling.

Concerning the present financial crisis, in the years just before the entire debacle began, the public acted just as it should, turning cheek to the potential global credit clutter looming, to protect the fragile emotional state of modern acceptance-based socio-economic egocentricity, all fueled by the increased speed of information within today's reality.

What I'm saying is this: *Who cares about some credit issue a thousand miles away when we work 10 to 12 hours a day, only to then run around all evening in a frenzied state of chic productivity too?*

Think about it, with so much information to take in each day, how would the average Joe even have known to take notice of the credit-based warnings surfacing from tenured professionals (prior to the entire global financial meltdown) anyway?

Because the average Joe and Josie are as busy as heck and completely bombed with information all day, there is simply no way he or she can even take in all of the information presented in the first place. And, because modern media attempts to make every single little story a huge ' bombshell', the average person has virtually no way to distinguish the really important information they should be taking notice of, over the constant media fear and exuberance clutter. Therefore, he (or she) picks what matters most…

*We pay attention to **<u>now</u>** and **<u>five minutes from now</u>**...at least...until a cataclysmic bolt from the blue completely rocks all of our lives collectively.*

It's important to also note Newton's Laws of Motion apply as well, specifically in relation to force. As measured by Newton's Second Law of Motion, *force = mass * acceleration*.

What this means is we will also need to measure 'acceleration' in terms of the verve of information within today's marketplace.

As you are about to see, we can theoretically model **Einstein's** theory of **Mass-Energy Equivalence** ($E = mc^2$), deriving some semblance of energy needed to account for 'acceleration' within the force required to move markets.

In understanding the theories here, readers are about to gain some incredible insights into the truths behind volatility, social passivity, information purpose/deployment, speed and financial market reactions to global events and media... Truths many may have never even thought possible.

4. $E = m\,c^2$

E = the energy

m = mass

c = the <u>speed of light</u> in a vacuum (<u>*celeritas*</u>), (about 3×10^8 m/s)

In terms of Joules: $1J = 1\ kg * m^2 * s^{-2}$

Just in case you're wondering:

```
Walking speed - 15 mph
Bicycling speed - 23 mph
Airliner cruising speed - 625 mph
Speed of sound (at sea level) - 761 mph
Speed of light - 670,616,629 mph
```

However, because information has increased in speed, are we now in a state where:

$E = m((\Delta s_i + \Delta k_i)/c)^2$

Where...

E= Energy (Volume)

m = Market Cap

ΔSi = (S_i) Change in the Speed of Information

ΔKi = Fear/Acceptance of Information Presented (Measured through option premiums, or the

Market Volatility Index VIX)

c = the speed of light in a vacuum (*celeritas*), (about 3×10^8 m/s)

While the above formula is not meant to be a precise model of physics, the theory behind what I am saying is:

Volatility is -in essence- a measurement of energy, in relation to mass and speed, in terms of information.

It is arguable then, that the greater an item's mass, the more energy it takes to create and sustain speed, in a circumstance where resistance prevails. In the case of any financial product, there's an old cliché that we can use to help understand volatility a little more…

"No one ever has to buy, but they do have to sell…sometime."

What we're really talking about here is the amount of energy needed to keep a stock, currency, option, or futures contract at any given level. With the absence of buying incentive/pressure, all instruments would eventually fall to zero.

Again, Newton's three laws are:[38]

1. Every object will remain at rest or in uniform motion in a straight line unless compelled to change its state by the action of an external force.

2. Forces produce accelerations that are in proportion to the mass of a body ($F=ma$).[39]

3. Every action of a force produces an equal and opposite reaction.

For the purposes of this book, what we're rally examining in terms of volatility rests within law #2, whereby we know Force equals mass times acceleration.

Simply put, the heavier an object is, the more force one must exert to 'start the ball rolling', or stop the boulder from tumbling.

Like the major indices were putting in all time highs in 2007 (as the general public just stood by and ignored the totality of the dangerous credit situation growing, which was also seemingly *'implausible'* by mainstream media that was clucking about, while touting new highs daily), when the larger 'mass' of the global credit hydrogen bomb could no longer be ignored, the same media and public all panicked at the same time (October of 2007) and en masse, tumbled markets over a cliff.

Even the credit rating agencies played there part too, as seen in Moody's downgrade of AIG on October 3, 2007, precisely the 'panic' catalyst required to sweep the legs out from underneath the Dow and drag the index under critical support of 10,000.[40]

What we're talking about is the point of unsustainable information (mass), where even media, credit ratings agencies and investors must finally come to grips with the reality at hand.

Henceforth, buying energy (in relation to exuberance and/or conscious ignorance by the larger public to truly understand economic circumstances) is more difficult to sustain than selling, based on the logic that investors have to sell sometime, but they never truly have to buy.

What we have is a 'gravitational effect', which tugs hard on stocks, currencies, options, or futures the higher they travel in a defined timeline. In addition, much like it is much more difficult to push a boulder up a hill, than down, the larger the boulder, the greater the possibility of excess volatility when the mass becomes too heavy to hold up, or the general public is no longer able to coherently understand the information at hand.

Remember our conversation about consumer sentiment and inflation in Chapter Three. It's no wonder the average Joe wouldn't even know to be on the lookout for inflation, as he or she, likely hadn't studied the saturation principles of money supply and were really only basing their opinions on the junk media was touting at the time...

Moreover, in December of 2008 and January of 2009, mainstream media were more focused on deflation, than inflation.

In terms of our previous discussion of Length Contraction, the little snippets of information (the clues to upcoming rallies, or pending panics) pass by seemingly unnoticed because information is now moving at the speed of light. However, when a piece of information finally passes by that is **so large** that it can no longer be ignored, the masses, media, analysts, politicians and credit ratings agencies act on the information in one large herd of lemmings…over a cliff…

THE TIPPING POINT OF INFORMATION MASS

As stocks, currencies, options and even futures rip through the roof, all are (as a metaphor) traveling into the atmosphere, like a rocket. The further the rocket moves from the earth, the less gravity 'weighing' it down and thus, the acceleration becomes more torrid. (Have you ever noticed the fifth wave in Elliot Wave Theory is generally always the steepest?) A stock can never totally escape the forces of gravity, though we can admit that momentum begets momentum. Much like the upper echelons of our atmosphere, even though gravity eases as the object seemingly 'breaks free' (almost *mass-free* from the perception of investors), other factors begin to come into play.

For instance, the higher a financial instrument travels, the greater the 'risk premium' in terms of fair valuation, seen through financial ratios.

Eventually, once the last fool is in, buyers mysteriously dissipate, seemingly overnight. However, in the final stage of 'rocket gains' just before the stock runs out of fuel, media hype and investor exuberance was likely at its greatest.

Really, no fuel contains as much octane and/or potential horsepower as exuberance. Much like nitrous fueling a hot rod in a street race though, the power unleashed often tears apart the motor at the same time.

When the last bull realizes he's nothing more than a sucker, suddenly the 'mass-free' paradigm shifts and investors suddenly see the situation in true light for the first time... Where mass was previously ignored, suddenly it is apparent that the moon is seemingly crashing through the atmosphere...but investors have nowhere to hide. The object now colliding with reality is too big.

When the 'rocket like run' is out of fuel – media yells fire in a crowded movie theatre and the masses pile on top of one another in an attempt to all escape at the same time.

There's another factor that plays in here too:

Conversion.

A few moments ago, I said the greater the mass of an object, the more energy required to 'get the ball rolling.'

There's a conversion factor here we have to consider. As we know, most financial instruments do not start out as large, or mega-cap companies. Metaphorically, small cap stocks are like baseballs, while large cap companies are like bowling balls.

Image this: I hand you a baseball and a bowling ball and ask you to throw each as far as you can. Which would you be able to toss further? A baseball of course. What if;

however, the baseball was actually 'magical' and as it was in the air, shifted shapes- into a bowling ball?

In reality, baseballs and bowling balls are static matter; however, financial instruments are not. The higher a stock, currency, option, or futures contract travels, the more it expands, adding mass. In the case of a stock, we can measure mass accumulation through market cap growth. If shares outstanding remain the same, as market cap grows, so must price.

There is an equilibrium point though, where the stock (via earnings per share) can no longer sustain itself, and thus plummets back to earth, like a rocket with no fuel (the absence of buyers.)

Where all of this leads us to is simply a question of energy required to sustain altitude, like a satellite. The issue is that unlike a satellite orbiting earth, stocks can never escape the gravity of earnings expectations, the reality of returns, and of course, larger economic cycles.

Currencies are bound to GDP and expectations for GDP growth, inflation and of course: interest rates.

Should a currency travel too high, the occurrence could negatively influence a country's trade balance, whereby an overvalued currency will eventually trigger a trade deficit and thus, negatively affect GDP.

What's more, when trade deficits drag out for significant periods, not only will the occurrence hinder GDP growth, but often lead to increased national debt.

The conversion tipping point of a currency is when the country's national debt is seen as 'unsustainable' by foreign lenders, and thus the currency plummets, as credit quality deteriorates.

Central banks supposedly act as a mechanic/driver to currencies, adding or subtracting fuel (via interest rates and other open market operations); much like a balloon-driver does propane to a hot air balloon.

However, what if the balloon driver was either an idiot from the start, or is/was really taking orders from someone who would profit from the balloon plummeting?

Either way, the absence of competent, honest, reality cognizant balloon drivers (non-lobbyist/media influenced, not seeking personal prosperity, beyond ego-driven and/or not disgustingly greedy individuals, policymakers, politicians and corporate executives) means the whole experience is going to be one hell of a rough ride (volatility.)

Think of the occurrence as an equilibrium point within Forex markets, where a central bank must know how to apply heat to keep the balloon from sinking too low (or rising too high), while also understanding that when used incorrectly, the flame could catch the entire balloon on fire.

If the balloon driver were competent from the start, the balloon wouldn't be on fire right now.

Examining another instrument, options, on the other hand, can be measured in terms of *'expectations of volatility'*, as seen through option premiums.

Option floor traders are very, very smart fellows – and in my option, are some of the savviest of all traders (of course with the futures guys too), as they understand profitability is more about buying and selling volatility, than tumbling in on the directional hype bandwagon of fear, or exuberance.

Option traders *get it*…that trading is about volatility, not directional fear, or greed.

Option traders profit by selling the probability of credulous investors feasting on poisonous fruit…over and over and over.

So where am I going with all of the aforementioned?

Foremost, to truly profit within equity markets, options, Forex, commodities and futures as individual investors we need to <u>*wake the hell up*</u>, stop buying into media hype (because they don't really know anyway), stop ignoring smaller snippets of critical information passing by at light speed, and above all, start looking at markets in terms of volatility and probability.

We must start looking at markets in terms of speed (information), mass (distributions), and acceleration (expectations).

The Dow Jones Industrial Average stands a much greater chance of recovery today, now that the two worst performing stocks have been replaced with seemingly healthier components.

But has anything really changed within the economy?

No.

However, as the Dow gains ground again, media will tout recovery. But the index didn't really wait patiently for the recovery of the two worst performing components, rather, General Motors and Citigroup were just replaced like burnt fuses in the index.

What we're talking about is pre-loading markets for volatility, by sweeping the ugly dust under a rug.

But the dust is still there and so are Citigroup and General Motors, which collectively employ over 500,000 people.

If *-and when-* the Dow rallies again, most investors will plop cash into markets (while media touts recovery), **completely unaware of the fact that all of the index components didn't really 'recover'.**

Fact is, two companies that are STILL thought of major U.S. economic contributors (though potentially holding index down in the future) were quietly discarded in the night, like a mobster does a dead body.

None of the aforementioned means we can't profit handsomely from markets in the future, we just have to be aware of the situation unfolding now.

We have to understand that because information **does** have a tipping point (as do markets), and because most information surfacing through **media is most often wrong,** (with the real market-moving catalysts ignored), we must stop paying attention to media hype and start paying attention to volatility and probability. In the end, by waking up to the true mass-credulous, media-suckered paradigm of today, while also paying attention to volatility and probability, we can finally transcend the larger *'mass-populace ignorant of light speed information'* paradigm now facing investors in the 21st Century.

Now, please take a moment and look at Figure 7.11, which shows the three largest declines in the Dow Jones Industrial Average from 1896 to 1909… As readers will likely immediately recognize, the index experienced some whopper declines during the previously mentioned period.

Figure 7.11

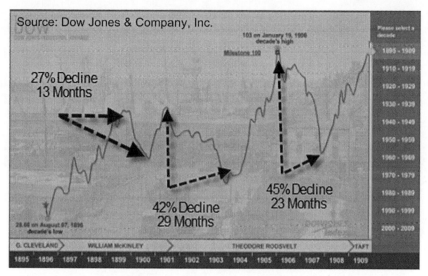

If we take note of the major declines at the start of the 19th Century, there are a few major points we can learn from. First, big drops in the Dow (and market) aren't new... **Selloffs happen.**

They happened when the Dow first began trading and they happen now. The second point; however, will need a little more explanation.

Figure 7.12

DATE OF HIGH	HIGH PRICE	DATE OF LOW	LOW PRICE	POINT LOSS	PERCENT LOSS	MONTHS OF LOSS	AVG LOSS %	AVG TIME
7/1/1901	77.08	12/1/1903	44.35	32.73	42.46%	29.00		
1/19/1906	103	11/1/1907	57.56	45.44	44.12%	22.00		
10/1/1912	93.9	12/24/1914	53.17	40.73	43.38%	26.00		
10/23/1929	381.2	2/2/1932	41.22	339.95	89.19%	28.00	54.79%	26.25
5/1/1940	147.7	4/28/1942	92.92	54.78	37.09%	23.00		
5/29/1946	212	10/1/1946	172	40	18.87%	5.00		
8/1/1956	534	11/1/1957	418	116	21.72%	15.00		
12/1/1961	728.8	6/26/1962	535.75	193.05	26.49%	6.00	26.04%	12.25
2/9/1966	995	12/1/1966	789.95	205.05	20.61%	10.00		
5/1/1969	949	7/1/1970	687	262	27.61%	14.00		
1/11/1973	1051	12/6/1974	577.6	473.4	45.04%	23.00		
7/1/1976	994	3/1/1978	743	251	25.25%	20.00		
4/1/1981	1014	7/1/1982	803.00	211	20.81%	15.00	27.86%	18.00
10/1/1987	2639	12/1/1987	1842	797	30.20%	2.00		
5/1/1998	9147	10/1/1998	7632	1515	16.56%	5.00		
12/31/1999	11497	10/1/2002	7398	4099	35.65%	34.00		
10/1/2008	14198	2/1/2009	6470	7728.2	54.43%	4.00	31.53%	11.25

Source: Dow Jones & Company, Inc.
Dow Jones Industrial Average Major Declines 1901 to 2008

* I've included 1946 and 1998, which showed similar characteristics of typical historical bear market selloffs

Readers may have also noticed that I annotated the 'total time of selling' for each relevant decline. Please also now take a moment to glance over the next table I've prepared (Figure 7.12), which shows every major decline in the history of the Dow Jones Industrial Average, which exceeded 20%.*

Over the past 100-years of the Dow, we can break trading action up into four periods, each with their own 'characteristic' paradigms:

1896 to 1929: Industrial Revolution economy.

1929 to 1961: Post Great Depression American economic growth market, characterized by "middle game" industrial development and The Securities Act of 1933.

1961 to 1981: Baby Boomer's come into their own entering colleges and taking positions in workplace. Era characterized by mass acceptance/distribution of televisions, and thus, the initial birth of the *'light speed information'* paradigm, as noted in 600 million American's having watched Neil Armstrong become the first man to walk on the moon, on July 21, 1969.[41] Era also included the invention of the personal calculator (1966) and the release of the first consumer computers (Scelbi & Mark-8 Altair and IBM 5100 in 1974 and 1975).

1981 to Present: *Technology Explosion Market.*

In the popular Website How Stuff Works, writer Marshall Brain lists 12 major technologies of the 1980's as:[42]

- Personal computers
- Graphical user interface
- CDs
- Walkmans
- VCRs
- Camcorders
- Video game consoles
- Cable television

- Answering machines
- Cell phones
- Portable phones
- Fax machines

Here's some interesting information not readily in the minds of most…

In my second book, Trade with Passion and Purpose (Wiley, 2006), I had the wonderful experience of interviewing Joe Ritchie, whom some may recognize from New Market Wizards, by Jack Schwager. I won't ever forget the time I spent interviewing Ritchie, which was really a series of conversations over about two months. Ritchie is truly one of the greatest market innovators of all time, as one of the very first to computerize option valuation and merge the information into his firm's trading on the floor of the CBOT. During the 1980's and 1990's, Ritchie's firm Chicago Research and Trading (CRT) took over $1 billion in trading profits out of markets.

I also interviewed Ritchie for my column in Trader Monthly Magazine, which unfortunately, has gone out of business with the global financial crisis.

In my interview with Ritchie, he referred to traders on the floor of the CBOT (in 1977) with programmable calculators, as instantly becoming, "a one-eyed man in the land of the blind."

With everything mentioned in over the past few pages in mind, my point is that while technology has indeed progressed over the past 100-years, so has Wall Street's ability to act on, and react on information…

However, traders and firms who are now **truly** technology to benefit in day-day-day market activity are rare. Though the average investor believes he, or she has 'greater insights' into markets with their supercharged trading platforms, I believe the exact opposite is really the case. Really, average investors of today are less savvy than 100-years ago, while really, having just become nothing more than media induced volatility-conditioned chimps. I'm even talking about intraday retail Forex traders who *think* they're savvy chartists.

Case in point, remember our recent discussion on CCI? In one of my recent Webinars, I asked the room of traders (about 40-people) what CCI indicated… The ONLY answer I received was 'overbought' and 'oversold' above or below +100 and   -100, respectively. Not ONE of the supposed serious traders knew what CCI really was. I don't mean to be rude and I hope I don't sound like I'm attempting to be.

However, what I'm saying is, '*what the heck are overbought and oversold*' anyway?

I'll tell you what they are…Overbought and oversold are the explanations of CCI presented to the masses by 99% of market-information Websites out there…

Chimpanzees beget chimpanzees.

To break this devastating trend, we must look beyond the commonplace explanations of indicators and trading served to the public daily.

Moving on, to the below table of major declines in the Dow Jones Industrial Average (shown again), I would like readers to take serious note of final column on the right labeled '*Avg Time*'.

Figure 7.13

Source: Dow Jones & Company, Inc.
Dow Jones Industrial Average Major Declines 1901 to 2008

DATE OF HIGH	HIGH PRICE	DATE OF LOW	LOW PRICE	POINT LOSS	PERCENT LOSS	MONTHS OF LOSS	AVG LOSS %	AVG TIME
7/1/1901	77.08	12/1/1903	44.35	32.73	42.46%	29.00		
1/19/1906	103	11/1/1907	57.56	45.44	44.12%	22.00		
10/1/1912	93.9	12/24/1914	53.17	40.73	43.38%	26.00		
10/23/1929	381.2	2/2/1932	41.22	339.95	89.19%	28.00	54.79%	26.25
5/1/1940	147.7	4/28/1942	92.92	54.78	37.09%	23.00		
5/29/1946	212	10/1/1946	172	40	18.87%	5.00		
8/1/1956	534	11/1/1957	418	116	21.72%	15.00		
12/1/1961	728.8	6/26/1962	535.75	193.05	26.49%	6.00	26.04%	12.25
2/9/1966	995	12/1/1966	789.95	205.05	20.61%	10.00		
5/1/1969	949	7/1/1970	687	262	27.61%	14.00		
1/11/1973	1051	12/6/1974	577.6	473.4	45.04%	23.00		
7/1/1976	994	3/1/1978	743	251	25.25%	20.00		
4/1/1981	1014	7/1/1982	803.00	211	20.81%	15.00	27.86%	18.00
10/1/1987	2639	12/1/1987	1842	797	30.20%	2.00		
5/1/1998	9147	10/1/1998	7632	1515	16.56%	5.00		
12/31/1999	11497	10/1/2002	7398	4099	35.65%	34.00		
10/1/2008	14198	2/1/2009	6470	7728.2	54.43%	4.00	31.53%	11.25

What I would like to point out is that the average duration of bear markets has decreased by nearly 60% since the 1901 to 1929 market. What's more, if we take out the larger total bear market from 1999 to 2002, bear markets in the past 20 years have only lasted about a quarter of the time that they did in the past 47 years.$

$ -Note- The historical average PE ratio for the Dow Jones Industrial Average is 15.5 (since 1929). In early 2002, despite dot.com bomb selling, the index still had a PE of 25, thus overvaluation contributed to the longer than usual bear market. Index changes in 2009 instantly lowered DJIA trailing PE from 21.21 to 11.41, while also dropping forward PE from 18.06 to 12.80, thus setting the index for a future run into (approx) 11,700, or a 15.5 historical PE.

What we can assume –over all- is bear markets, though totaling *'about the same'* in terms of percentage loss, are accelerating in duration.

Why?

Because fundamentals improve quicker today, over 75 years ago? No…

Duration of sell offs has decreased in total time, because through the acceleration of information, collectively, investors have a much narrower memory of yesterday, with media constantly pumping exuberance through television, Internet and radio the second the economy shows signs of recovery.

What's more, take into consideration the fact that the Dow Jones Industrial Average has now been 'reloaded' for volatility, the second the index fires over 10,000 again; the occurrence will become headline news… **Guaranteed.**

Will you buy into the volatility?

Information has accelerated, and thus our memory of yesterday has declined, while at the same time, the collective public's ability (and desire/effort) to take notice of important micro-information (that could have major impact on the future) has decreased.

What I'm saying is… Not only have markets become more volatile (as noted in the increase in total time of DJIA bear markets); but speed and volatility of intraday and longer-term market changes are only going to increase even more in the years to come…

The fact that 99% of the investing public has no idea of events like the DJIA having been re-loaded for gains is proof of the pudding of the general public's micro-information mass ignorance, with your old pal 'media' doing nothing to bring you the real truth behind the events of today… At least, until some sort of underlying hum within markets can no longer be ignored, and the major indices are crushed once again…

Perhaps something like the United States' National Debt of $11 trillion (FYI, foreign investors owned $3.47 trillion of public debt, at the time of printing), the potential pending deterioration of credit quality in U.S. Treasury notes…and the implosion of the greenback.

CHAPTER EIGHT

VOLATILITY AND PROBABILITY THROUGH THE MOVEMENT OF DISTRIBUTIONS

Over the following pages, we will focus on volatility and probability in terms of Forex markets; however, the concepts also apply to equities, options, commodities, and futures. As many traders are already aware, Forex markets often display significant volatility catching many participants by surprise. However, with a simple understanding of descriptive statistics, traders could soon find themselves ahead of the curve.

"In other words, 'How can we perceive volatility before it occurs?' Over the following pages, I will attempt to explain how using principals of descriptive statistics can help to identify trending and reversals, while also foreseeing volatility within almost any charting timeframe.

In the end, we will break through market volatility with a greater understanding of the dynamic movements of subset distributions, while also utilizing common probability within descriptive statistics to capitalize on potential market action."

Many traders – both new and experienced – often find themselves at a loss attempting to understand why Forex markets tend to experience extended volatility both intraday and over the long haul. In simple terms, much of the seemingly erratic moves are really the product of institutional order flow, causing larger movements within markets. While the aforementioned explanation is almost infuriating simple, we must understand, *large money* is really the pure catalyst behind extended movements within markets, not at-home investors. We can argue that by acting in unison on common technical signals, the mass army retail investors do indeed add to the issue of erratic volatility within markets. However, volatility caused by the retail community is 'quick-*shot*' volatility at, or near areas where commonplace technical signals (like Stochastics rolling under +80, for example) unfold. What's more, quick-shot volatility caused by retail traders is not 'trend sustaining', as really, institutions are the only entities with enough buying or selling power to prolong trends.

Moreover, the individual investor is often set up for failure from the start, because not only is he or she not able to 'see' institutional order flow (imagine the ticker tape in equities), but because traditional 'pre-loaded' information he/she is receiving is often 'missing' critical components, all at the same time.

The question is then, how can traders transcend failing technicals, increasing volatility and jaded information- to achieve greater insights and perceptions into serrated movements within Forex.

In other words, *"How can we perceive volatility before it occurs?"* Over the following pages, I will attempt to explain how using principals of descriptive statistics can help identify trending and reversals, while also foreseeing volatility within almost any charting timeframe.

In the end, we will break through market volatility with a greater understanding of the dynamic movements of subset distributions, while also utilizing common probability within descriptive statistics to capitalize on market action.

It is important to note that even when traders embody substantial technical and fundamental knowledge, risk prevails without the proper understanding of the larger probability and volatility paradigm behind currency trading.

Here, traders are encouraged to boldly challenge typical pre-conceived notions of technical and fundamental analysis, in an effort to see beyond 'the accepted standard' retail traders are told to believe daily. The 'accepted standard' does not presently uphold volatility and probability as important aspects of markets or trading. However, given that 80% to 95% (depending on who you talk to) of retail Forex traders lose, while many retail brokerages actually take the opposite side of their trades, perhaps the at-home trader isn't *supposed* to know anything more than the 'accepted standard'.

Traders who understand descriptive statistics though, will find greater clarity and perception of volatility within intraday and longer-term movements unfolding in markets.

WORDS OF CAUTION

- Within Forex and trading, there is no holy grail; thus, please do not read the following with the firm belief that you will never again be faced with confusion, unclear volatility, or losses in markets. What you are about to learn is an incredibly effective guidance tool helping identify trending, volatility and at times, reversals; however, even the concepts here must be used with prudence and common sense.

- You are about to read about descriptive statistics, which within itself has many different approaches, methodologies and studies. I will not delve into the *justification of math* underneath most statistical concepts here. Instead, I am presenting descriptive statistics from a simple, <u>conceptual</u> framework. However, there are many resources available to explain the empiricism of descriptive statistics on the Internet and in your local library; you will also find plenty of recommended reading in the bibliography at the end of the book, should you chose to learn more about the subject (which I highly recommend).

- Never forget that economics and fundamentals rule all...at least, over the long haul. Traders who do not take the time to properly uncover the true economic paradigm within markets –and the future possibilities of such– will likely often find themselves on the wrong side of the trade, especially those who hold positions during longer timeframes. While the concepts presented within Volatility Illuminated are designed to specifically help traders navigate intraday movements and volatility within markets, we have no excuse to ever slack on our fundamental research. Please take time to do the proper research every day.

TRANSCENDING MARKETS THROUGH VOLATILITY AND PROBABILITY

Almost all financial markets display relentless volatility for traders attempting to capitalize on trading within shorter-term timeframes. Intraday uncertainty and volatility are just **facts of trading** in virtually every market. Moreover, because of the inherent underlying "volatility paradigms", many traders (both new and seasoned) stand significant risk of unforeseen losses, almost any moment their positions move against intraday order flow.

In Addition, while order flow may not seem like a reasonably transparent variable in Forex, in reality, through descriptive statistics, we may not only predict when and where institutional order flow could commence, but where such could end as well.

In the end, through volatility and probability, savvy traders will learn to **'ride the waves'** of order flow within markets.

At some level, I expect these concepts to be met with resistance, as traders find difficulty in leaving '*the old notions*' of technical analysis behind.

By this I mean, often when 'the accepted standards' are challenged, some have trouble letting go of the information that has been taught as reliable for so long, even if it's flawed. However, reiterating Henrik Ibsen's famous statement from the 1882 play *An Enemy of the People*, "the majority is always wrong."

From the shoes of most retail traders, many likely find themselves continually frustrated from confusing signals from technicals, which often seem completely misleading in real time. For some strange reason though, many retail traders continue to believe (or perhaps *want to believe*) in their 'accepted standard' technicals, despite the losses surfacing in their accounts.

Really, technical analysis is only true so long as enough people are acting on the same information at the same time. However, as we saw in Chapter Two, technicals are actually failing in today's market, because too many people are acting on the same 'pre-set' information at the same time.

Here's where we start to level the playing field…

We will no longer look at charts as instruments of trading… producing 'signals', which we trade from.

Instead, we will look beyond the charts.

We will firmly resolve **to understand** that by looking at charts whatsoever, we are viewing **data** and the **translation of data and nothing more**…

We will also resolve to stop looking at **magical technical patterns** (hyped, invalidated signals some schmooze is selling), or bogus Expert Advisors (EAs) that do not and/or cannot justify their existence from some sort of understandable framework of descriptive statistics, mathematics, or physics.

In addition, while I've already touched on the aspect of price action as 'data', the concept must be revisited briefly… just in case.

The 'data' is so much more than just <u>price action</u>, in reality, 'the data' is screaming aloud… begging us to stop and pay attention for a moment…

The data is saying, "If you take a moment to truly look into me, I provide significant insights into probability/volatility, order flow and fundamental underpinnings…truly moving markets."

Fact is, technicals generally only perceive events in the past… Traditional technical analysis' *predictive worth* is nothing more than hope that an event that occurred yesterday, will happen again.

Really, technical analysis is the study of information that has already occurred, **<u>without any regard to the</u> <u>probability</u>** of what could truly transpire in the future.

In essence, technical analysis is nothing more than the study repetitive pretty pictures throughout history.

Unfortunately, there are those who will continue to argue traditional technical analysis can predict tomorrow… Concerning most signals though, when the technician is asked *'why will it work again?'* most explanations will sound like:

"Because it worked in the past..."

> "How did I miss such an obvious signal like that one?" Chances are that you did not miss the signal; it may not have been presented when you were considering the trade. Many traders suspect that signals may have appeared differently to them in real time, but few really take the time to explore the character of the indicators from which they trade."
>
> Constance Brown
> Technical Analysis for the
> Trading Professional

Humbug.

Technicals work perfectly when studying historical charts; I agree. *Nevertheless, the one time you attempt to trade from one of the supposed super-signals... I can assure you, will be the one time the signal will fail.*

Have you ever entered a trade based on an overbought or oversold indicator, only to see the trade move against you?

In the amazing book Technical Analysis for the Trading Professional, author Constance Brown inquires, ***"How did I miss such an obvious signal like that one?"***

How many traders ever **really** look into 'why' what is happening - is actually happening?

Repeatedly, I see traders completely disregard the philosophical, fundamental, mathematical and common sense reasoning behind the charts they trade from.

I can assure you that when these traders and investors grow sick and tired of losing money, they will finally either quit, or start putting in the time. Regardless, trading purely off technicals is similar to looking for Braille in the drive-thru.

Using our earlier discussion of CCI as an example, when (for example) the EUR/USD begins ascending and CCI travels above +100, traders who have based their understanding of the indicator on 99% of the commonplace explanations available, one would believe the EUR/USD is now entering 'overbought' territory.

In reality, the EUR/USD (on whatever timeframe being viewed) is simply moving outside of (about) the 1st standard deviation mark, which really means '*distribution potentially on the move.*'

The same logic applies to **expectant** fundamentals, in that enough people **have** to believe in a future outcome for the actual trading action to mimic the "perceived outcome" by those same people.

Even more devastating though, when fundamentals shift, often, many technical traders are not even aware that the occurrence has taken place and thus, find themselves not only on the wrong side of the trade, but often stopped out at exact high and low prints of the relative range too.

When we begin to understand descriptive statistics not only allow us to intuitively 'feel' the true fundamental sentiment behind the market, while also overstepping the simple 'hope', which too often comes from traditional charting, we begin to see that both technical and fundamental perceptions of the larger market are actually transparent within the data unfolding before our very eyes.

Descriptive statistics are defined as:[43]

[1]Descriptive Statistics are used to describe the basic features of the data gathered from an experimental study in various ways. They provide simple summaries about the sample and the measures. Together with simple graphics analysis, they form the basis of virtually every quantitative analysis of data. It is necessary to be familiar with primary methods of describing data in order to understand phenomena and make intelligent decisions.

Various techniques that are commonly used are classified as:

• Graphical displays of the data in which graphs summarize the data or facilitate comparisons.

• Tabular description in which tables of numbers summarize the data.

• Summary statistics (single numbers) which summarize the data.

I ask, *"How can anyone make an intelligent decision in markets, without understanding the data at hand?"*

See, so many traders use technical analysis to decipher their entry and exits without *truly* evaluating the logical validity of the technical signals surfacing.

What's more, tack on complete oversight of the common sense economic fundamentals and truly, it's no wonder retail traders are often stopped out at the top, or bottom…or just plain wrong altogether.

The aforementioned aside, let's discuss how technical analysis also completely overlooks vital *"real data"* traders need most.

Principally, we know technical analysis is a "lagging event," meaning the action unfolding on charts can **only** exist insofar as **another event** has already occurred.

In short, an equity, index, option, commodity, futures contract, or even currency must have already witnessed a trade 'print', before the data ever even shows up on a chart.

Which came first, the chicken, or the egg? In the world of trading, a transaction MUST always take place before the instance shows up on a chart.

(To split hairs, one might argue the two events are simultaneous. however, a transaction can take place without the existence of a price chart, but a chart cannot exist without a transaction, or series of.)

Really, the true wealth in technical analysis is the identifiable and/or representative display of empirical data unfolding, otherwise known as *descriptive statistics*.

When we change the way we *think about* what we are seeing on charts, we change our total understanding of technical analysis, especially *'hocus pocus hope indicators'* and/or methodologies built for failure from the start.

When we begin to understand that by viewing and analyzing the data displayed on charts, from a stance of descriptive statistics, we will begin to see that we can completely discard the mainstream technical crap foolishly embraced as the *'accepted standard,'* and instead start measuring and utilizing volatility and probability as tools for profitability.

I hope that readers understand why I'm beating a dead horse… We **must** understand that the accepted standards of trading tools presented to the retail crowd…are flawed.

So how do we overcome the issue through volatility and probability? First, we must also understand that all data, all price action we empirically see on our charts is:

1. Data coming forward tick by tick.

2. When summed, creates a series of smaller subset distributions, within larger distributions.

3. No different, or more complex, than any other data measured by statisticians.

How is it we can predict weather patterns, and yet, mainstream media and general populace investors can't see the Dow tumbling downward through 10,000 one week in advance?

Anyway, in our discussion of descriptive statistics, we really only going to focus on the concept of 'normal' (bell shaped) distributions…

The application of normal distributions applies to trading insomuch as the data we are measuring is constantly moving with the periods we are studying.

What I'm saying is because a subset distribution's mean (seen through a moving average, for example) is constantly in motion, as prices rise and fall, the 'data' (prices) will never stay skewed on one side of the mean, or another.

When studying smaller subset distributions, _eventually_ **the data** **will** **cross back over the mean** (moving average); because within markets, our means are **never** totally stagnate.

The 'traveling factor' behind a moving mean proves that the data we are measuring **will eventually** return to the mean, perhaps even crossing above, or below, possibly even extending significantly in the opposite direction.

It is the concept of the **mobile mean** (where old data is replaced – i.e. the newest day of a 50-period Simple Moving Average forcing the 51st day to drop off) that justifies measuring volatility through standard deviations under the premise of a normal Gaussian curve. (Really, we're talking about the Central Limit Theorem.)

What's more, as John Bollinger points out in his book *Bollinger on Bollinger Bands*, the Central Limit Theorem tells us that even when **long-term** data is not normally distributed (as is the case with virtually every financial instrument, including Forex), "*a random sampling will produce a normally distributed subset for which the statistical rules will hold.*"[44]

In short, smaller samples within the market will not produce the kurtosis of the larger data set.[45]

GAUSSIAN CURVE REVISITED

Within descriptive and inferential statistics, we will use a random normal distribution (Gaussian Curve) to measure volatility via standard deviations. In terms of the Gaussian

Curve, we are looking at a normalized distribution, where the sum of all values of x, are meant to equal 1.

The previously mentioned means if we are measuring price movement within 21-periods on a 5-minute chart (for example), the result should equal a probability of 1.

In other words, the sum of all values that have transpired in the measured period should present a probability of 1 (**an empirical absolute**) that the events have happened. What we're referring to here is a probably of 1 that all of the data presented will rest within our chart, regardless of where the data is within the chart. As long as the data **exists**, we're in business on a probability basis.

Figure 8. 3

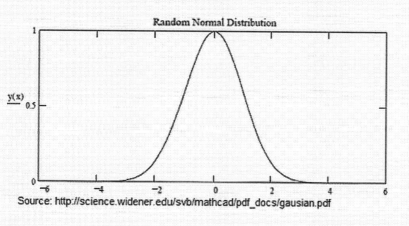

Source: http://science.widener.edu/svb/mathcad/pdf_docs/gausian.pdf

Moreover, by using historically measured occurrences of data, we can statistically infer the probability of future events.

I need to clarify a question a few readers might have lurking in their heads... In my previous attack on traditional technical analysis, I pointed out that if one were to ask a technician *why most traditional technical signals were valid,* he or she, would often be stuck without a proper response, other than that of the signal having shown to work in the past.

So why, for heaven's sake, is this statistical junk any better? As I already mentioned, I'm not going to write a novel showing the mathematical justification for volatility/probability; however, I believe some explanation is required for peace of mind.

In statistics, the concept of authenticating data is known as classical test theory, predictive, or concurrent validity.[46]

Concurrent Validity is, "*An index of criterion-related validity used to predict performance in a real-life situation given at about the same time as the test or procedure; the extent to which the index from one test correlates with that of a nonidentical test or index; e.g., how well a score on an aptitude test correlates with the score on an intelligence test.*"[47]

What we're looking for is the theoretical outcome (on paper) to return a high correlation value (correlation coefficient) to the real world information presented daily.

How will we do all of this?

As you are likely already aware, data within a Gaussian Curve is measured via 'standard deviations' from the mean.

The arithmetic mean, of course, is the average of all prices recorded in the period we are studying. Thus, by being able to calculate the average prices for a particular period, we can also measure probability of movement away from the mean through standard deviations (confidence intervals) and thus, the probability of all data truly resting within our distribution, validating our previous concept that all of our data (in the timeframe measured) should total 1.

If you remember your old statistics days, you may also recollect that the majority of all data occurrence probability falls within three standard deviations of either side of the mean. What we know is that 49.86% of all the data should rest within three standard deviations of each side of the mean.

In translation, measuring three standard deviations on both sides of the mean, equates to 99.72% of the data within the period measured.

In other words, there is a 99.72% probability that all of the data will fall within three standard deviations of the mean.

Breaking the standard deviations down, there is a 34.13% probability our data should rest on one side (above, or below) of the mean. Moving out a little further, there is a 47.72% probably that all of the data will sit within two standard deviations of one side of the mean, and a 49.86% probability that all of the data will rest within three standard deviations of one side of the mean.

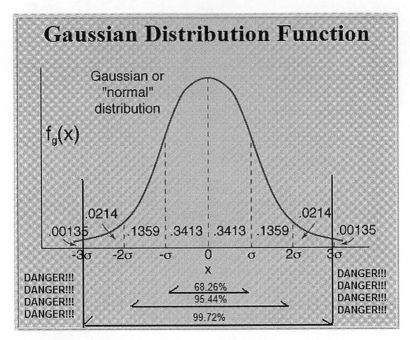

Figure 8.4

However, while there is one standard deviation to the left of the mean (above a moving average, in the case of trading charts), there is also one standard deviation to the right (below), and thus, we know to multiply all of our probabilities by two, compensating for data on both sides of the mean, not just one.

There is a 68.26% probability all of the data will sit within one standard deviation of either side of the mean, a 95.44% probability all of the data will rest within two standard deviations, and a 99.72% probability of all data in our period measured will reside within three standard deviations of either side of the mean.

In terms of measuring the 'mean' for this chapter, we will only be using Simple Moving Averages and not Exponential Moving Averages (which put more weight on near-term price data, over the latter.) It's true Exponential Moving Averages track price action more closely, however, we're keeping things simple here...

I think John Bollinger presents a great argument for using Simple Moving Averages in his book Bollinger on Bollinger Bands, asserting that we are simply adding one more variable to an already complicated scenario, by using Exponential Moving Averages.

I'm not saying that you shouldn't use EMA's, but for these pages (at least for now), we're going to keep things clean and simple.

As many likely already know, a Simple Moving Average (SMA) is created by summing the data (close prices, for example) for any given period and then dividing by the total number of periods aggregated.

For example, on a five-minute chart, a 20-period SMA will present the arithmetic mean (average) of all closing prices for the past twenty 5-minute bars at the location of the mean, on the current bar.

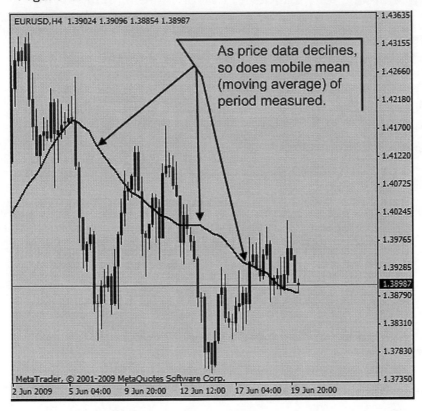

Figure 8.5

As price data declines, so does mobile mean (moving average) of period measured.

The Simple Moving Average, is thus, the 'mobile mean', which we are basing our standard deviations *(confidence intervals)* from, attempting to measure total 'probability' of breadth, or 'wingspan' of the data unfolding on a chart.

As Figure 8.5 shows that we are seeing *'more than just a moving average'*, rather, we are seeing a visual representation of the "mean data range" over the past 20-periods, where we will uncover key statistical data to volatility and probability.

In essence, we are able visually map the middle point of our data curve, by charting a Simple Moving Average.

With the mean identified, we must now identify benchmarks (confidence intervals), in an effort to validate our probability distributions, as accurate and usable within trading. We're really talking about mapping the 'distribution' of data through standard deviations.

Moreover, we are also mapping the actual distributions to be able to answer the question of _why_ implementing probability not only accurately reflects the past, but is also incredibly useful in attempting to perceive the future, over standard technicals.

In essence, the distribution is really a sort of teeter-totter (unfolding around the mean), where we are able to actually see **how** the data is unfolding on our chart.

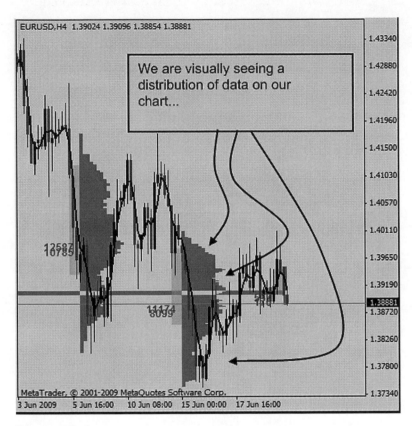

Figure 8. 6

In terms of inferential statistics, we also know there *should be* a 99.7% probability that all of the data (in the period measured) will rest within three standard deviations of the mean…

As the below chart shows, other than two small blips outside of the lower 3rd standard deviation, almost all (99.7%) of the data does indeed rest within 3-standard deviations of the mean.

Figure 8. 7

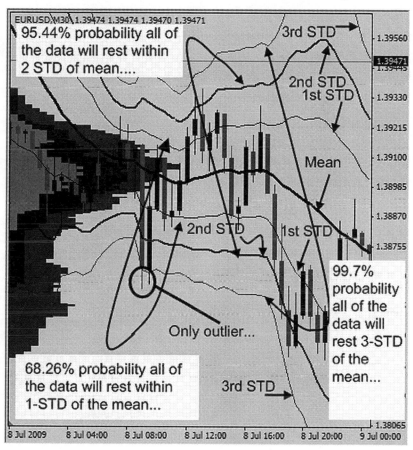

Just incase Figure 8.7 was a little confusing, Figure 8.8 (on the following page) shows a clearer picture of Gaussian Curve concept on an actual chart.

Please note that I used a 20-period Simple Moving Average (SMA) to measure the Gaussian Curve in Figure 8.7.

Looking at Figure 8.8, traders will notice that when we simply overlay three representative curves (denoting the 1st, 2nd an 3rd standard deviations) with the mean being the 20-SMA, we see how the Gaussian Curve looks when mapping actual data.

Now though, let us think of the Gaussian Curve in another format… Let us imagine the curve as an actual "teeter-totter" like scale, which will shift higher and lower on the left and right sides, as the data moves from side to side.

The question is how we will measure, or map the data shifting from side to side on the teeter-totter? To provide any insight into ascending, or descending prices, we must have some way to map distribution data shifting, thus prompting the teeter-totter to lean in one direction, over the other.

As a solution, we will simply map a shorter-term subset distribution within a longer-term distribution. As the shorter-term distribution moves from right to left on the larger teeter-totter, the result **should be** for the larger teeter-totter to fall to the left, as the bulk of data begins to add pressure, thus denoting trending…

Think of it like this... Suppose we're standing in a part looking at a big teeter-totter called the *'50-period seesaw'*, which is for the most part, well balanced. Now imagine I walk up to it with a box of bricks labeled *'20-period stones'* and dump the load on the far left side of the teeter-totter, what would happen to the larger 50-period seesaw?

Figure 8.8

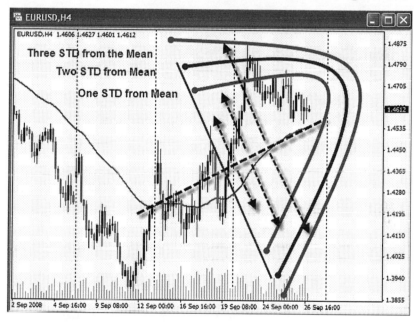

It's a no-brainer of course, the larger teeter-totter would lean to the left...

With a little shameless marketing in mind, I'm going to call the teeter-totter the Whistler Trending Scale (WTS). Moreover, just to make sure the point of moving subset distributions is absolutely clear, please again imagine a larger teeter-totter sitting idle in a park, with both sides suspended in mid-air equally…

We can generally assume all things are relatively calm (or normal) in that one side is not dramatically higher, or lower than the other.

However, if I were to set my neighbor's super big chunky ice-cream kid on the left side of the totter, what would happen?

Everything you own in a box to the left. Now, if you imagine the larger teeter-totter is 50-periods of data, what happens when I slide 20-periods of data to the left?

The key point to note in the WTS, is simply that when the shorter-term data (measured by a 20-SMA) moves to the left of the 50-SMA (longer-term mean), the scale should tip down to the left, thus denoting a *bull trend*.

- Data to the left: bull.

- Data to the right: bear.

- Data significantly flanking either side, but headed back to the center: Mean reversion.

Figure 8.9

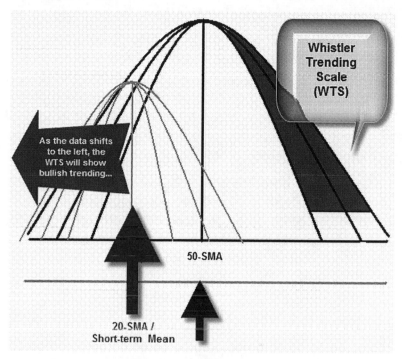

Historically, the instance of a short-term distribution sliding from one side of the totter to the other is known as a "moving average crossover". In effect, Moving Average Convergence Divergence (MACD), comprised of 12 and 26-day moving averages is an example of a short-term distribution mean sliding back and forth across a longer-term average.

However, it is important to note that what we are not doing here is simply looking for instances of a short-term distribution crossing over a longer-term mean for a trade signal.

Again, what we are **not doing** in our study of volatility and probability is simply using mean (moving average) crossovers for signals. Not only would the signal be lagging, but likely constantly setting us up for failure as our traders were stopped out on pullbacks surfacing almost immediately after taking a position.

Instead, we will be using distributions (and the outliers of distribution width) to measure potential future volatility probability and current 'acceleration' volatility/probability within the short and long-term mass (distributions), we are measuring.

Moreover, we will use the outliers of distribution width (total mass width), by means of standard deviations, to identify trend entries and exits for trending and/or potential consolidation to come.

(Note: The areas shaded more darkly in Figure 8.9 are simply to point out the second and third standard deviation outliers of the 50-period distribution.)

If you are having trouble with the larger concept of sliding distributions, please take a look at Figure 8.10, where I have rotated the WTS 90 degrees to the left. The image again shows how when a shorter-term distribution slides to the left of the mean, whatever instrument we are measuring…is taking on a *'bullish bias'*, and vice versa for distributions sliding to the right. Again, we are not looking for 'moving average crossovers' here at all, we simply taking note of the occurrence of sliding distributions.

Moreover, instead of eying the precise traveling of the moving averages, our trading clues will come from the expansion and contraction of the standard deviations framing the various distributions.

Figure 8. 10

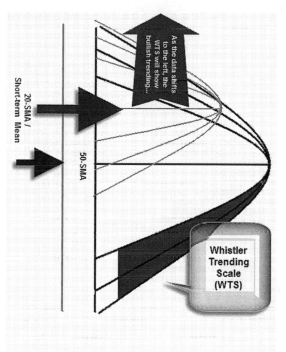

How do we map standard deviations?

As you may have already guessed from Figure 8.7, we can simply apply Bollinger Bands (the actual application of standard deviations on a chart); however, we will not be using the typical settings commonly pre-loaded within charting packages.

If you are not aware, Bollinger Bands are really the 'application' of the standard deviation formula to charting.

I sometimes think many retail traders never truly understand how powerful Bollinger Bands really are, simply because the name is slightly misleading...

Don't get me wrong, John Bollinger is a <u>genius</u> and one of my greatest market inspirations, however, what we're really seeing is a probability distribution measured through the actual expansion and contraction of standard deviations. For the sake of keeping our terms clear, over the following pages, we will call Bollinger Bands 'volatility bands'. Again though I believe Mr. Bollinger is nothing less than a market genius, however, like so much information surfacing in markets today, many investors are missing the power of indicator (based on probability theory and statistics) as most explanations of the tool are incredibly misleading.

Here's an example:

One major Website defines Bollinger Bands as:

"A technical analysis technique in which lines are plotted two standard deviations above and below a moving average, and at the moving average itself. Because standard deviation measures volatility, these bands will be wider during increased volatility and narrower during decreased volatility. Some technical analysts consider a market which approaches the upper band to be overbought, and a market which approaches the lower band to be oversold."[48]

There we are with our two favorite words again: overbought and oversold. Whoever wrote the above definition has obviously never traded with real money... Foremost, Bollinger Bands (volatility bands) expand and contract because of the squaring of the exponent in the standard deviation formula, which causes a 'multiplier effect' in the bands. What's more, even remotely inferring that when price touches the upper, or lower bands means 'overbought' or 'oversold' is fairly incorrect, at least as presented to average Joe-Q-investing public. Obviously, a 7-period distribution will have significantly less mass than a 50-period distribution; thus, usually when price touches the second standard deviation of a 7-period distribution, price is likely just starting to near the 1st-standard deviation of a 50-period distribution.

Do you see what I'm saying? The concept of 'overbought' and 'oversold' is relative to the period measured… I hate to pick on details, but the little snippet of information the mainstream investment education Website left out…is pretty darn important.

Geesh…

I'm not kidding, this stuff keeps me up at night…

With the previously mentioned in mind, I would like to note that the WTS is literally a scale of common sense, showing that when we add weight to one side, the occurrence creates motion whereby the scale shifts. What I'm saying is the tag of the second standard deviation on a short-term distribution does not mean price is oversold, the occurrence likely means the lesser distribution (in terms of periods measured) is shifting on the scale and price is moving…

To clarify the actual movement of a distribution, as seen in price action, in Figure 8.11, you will notice I have drawn a 20-period moving average and a 50-period moving average, the former with volatility bands at 3.2 standard deviations, and the latter at 1.2 standard deviations. (It is important to note that when drawing volatility bands on charts, we must always set our standard deviations slightly above where we normally would, to account for data loss in the electronic application of the formula. By this I mean, we want to set the 1st-standard deviation at 1.2, the second at 2.2 and so on.)

In terms of the WTS concept, we immediately see the 20-period distribution is now above the 50-period mean, obviously denoting the teeter-totter has leaned to the left, or in other words, the EUR/USD is experiencing bullish trading action. There's more to the story though... Remember the previous discussion of data probability (in relation to the mean), measured through standard deviations?

Figure 8.11

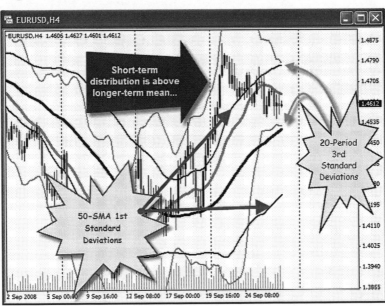

Looking at Figure 8.11, we know through probability 99.7% of all our data should theoretically rest within 3-standard deviations of the mean. In the case of our 20-period distribution, if a sharp selloff were to occur in the next bar, where do you think the selling action would likely pause, at least temporarily?

Probability tells us…likely on the lower 3rd-standard deviation of the 20-period distribution, which is coincidentally sitting almost precisely at the mean of the 50-period distribution.

However, as witnessed in the chart, just a short while ago, price actually tagged the upper 3rd-standard deviation of the shorter-term distribution, before commencing the present consolidation… The event of price hitting the third standard deviation did not mean the EUR/USD was oversold, rather, the occurrence just meant fierce buying was attempting to push the shorter-term distribution into a new range… Now, with the 20-period lower third standard deviation still above the 50-period mean, the occurrence of consolidation could simply be allowing both distributions a moment to 'breathe' and potentially store energy for another move higher…

The aforementioned is just a quick example of the great power measuring standard deviations (and the movement of distributions) within markets… You will soon see that we can also identify when trending is about to begin, when 'true trending' is in effect and also when trending has ceased and consolidation is about to commence.

Using concepts of descriptive and inferential statistics, and specifically standard deviations, we can time our entries to capitalize on volatility induced breakouts and breakdowns, taking positions when probability of order flow is truly in our favor.

Moreover, we will also know when the probability of continued trending has ceased, thus telling us to close our directional positions and switch gears to lateral trading strategies...

It's all probability and volatility, seen through the expansion and compression of standard deviations and distributions on our charts...

THE EXPANSION AND COMPRESSION OF SUBSET DISTRIBUTIONS

Jumping right in, Figure 8.12 (below) shows the EUR/USD on a 4-hour chart... We are again looking at a 50-SMA, with our volatility bands set at 1.2-standard deviations. We've also included a 20-SMA with volatility bands set at 3.2-standard deviations.

Within the longer-term distribution (the 50-period), we are using utilizing the 1st-standard deviation to derive the smallest portion of probability (in terms of descriptive statistics), that would infer potential follow through of price away from the mean (divergence).

We know there is a 68.4% probability that all of the data should rest within 1-standard deviation of the mean.

It's also important to note that when measuring 1-standard deviation from the mean, the occurrence of price moving away from the mean, through the 1st-standard deviation would line up with 50-period CCI traveling above +100, or below -100. Again, while the rest of the retail herd is thinking the event is showing the currency as 'overbought' or 'oversold', because you are more educated and much more savvy now, you will know that really, the instance just means the distribution is 'on the move.'

Don't you just feel bad for all those other traders attempting to navigate markets with <u>flawed information</u>.

They've been set up for failure, unlike you...

What the above is telling us is when a currency, stock, or other trading instrument moves above, or below a **<u>longer-term</u>** 1st-standard deviation, the instance is NOT screaming overbought, or oversold, rather, the instance may instead be saying three things:

1. A fundamental event or coincidental news occurrence has prompted traders to take action, and is creating a move away from the mean. In essence, there is a reason the bricks (prices) are sliding to one side of the teeter-totter.

2. If the move is real (not just a 'quick pop' anomaly), the short-term distribution should 'confirm' the fundamental mindset shift, by sliding over the mean of the longer-term distribution and then hold reasonable ground during the initial pullback(s), after the breakout.

3. Short term volatility (measured through standard deviation) will lead price, an inherent luxury of squaring of the exponent in the standard deviation formula, when electronically applied to price action on charts. (I will explain this in greater detail in just a moment.)

Figure 8.12

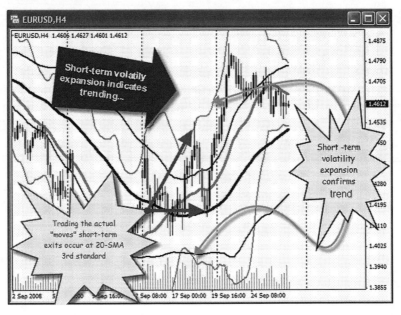

If short-term volatility, as denoted by the 20-SMA 3rd-standard deviation spikes above long-term volatility, as denoted by the 50-SMA 1st-standard deviation, the breakout is "confirmed."

Why?

What we are seeing is an instance of short-term volatility leading price…

Please allow me a moment to pause and explain a very, very important concept…

If we were simply measuring **total distribution mass** through probability (standard deviations), conceptually, we're talking about the total 'wingspan' of the distribution…or in other words, how *'wide'* the distribution is…

If all things were **equal,** meaning *normal and calm in markets…and* we were measuring 50-periods of data and 20-periods of data…*and* we were measuring total 'width' (mass) of both distributions…*and* we were doing so by mapping the **3rd-standard deviations of each,** would the 20-period 3rd-standard deviations be inside, or outside of the 3rd-standard deviations, of the 50-period distribution?

Think about it for a moment…

If all things were equal, meaning prices were in a **'normal state',** like *not trending,* just calmly traveling sideways, would the total mass (width) of the 20-period distribution be greater, or lesser than that of the 50-period distribution?

Clearly, the 20-period mass would be lesser (narrower) than the 50-period distribution.

Why?

We're simply measuring less data. In short, there is greater probability of higher and lower prices in 50-periods of data, than 20-periods of data, when 'all things are equal', or prices are in a 'normal state'.

However, when volatility increases, because we're measuring less data in the 20-period distribution, the distribution mass would expand quicker than the 50-period distribution.

The rule holds true when measuring 50-periods at 2.2-standard deviations and 20-periods at 3.2 standard deviations as well, though there is slightly more room for trader error.

Figure 8.13

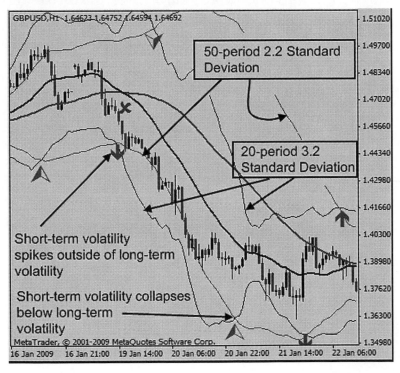

Really though, what we're talking about is the empirical state where short-term distribution **width** will always expand quicker than longer-term distribution width, based on the fact that the shorter-term distribution has **less mass** overall.

Remember our previous discussion of Newtonian Motion and the equation of force? Force = Mass * Acceleration. The lesser the mass, the greater the possibility of acceleration and thus, more force to move our distributions. As the Figure 8.13 shows, when short-term volatility spiked outside of long-term volatility, a significant downside move in the GBP/USD occurred on the hourly chart.

Figure 8.14 – Repeated

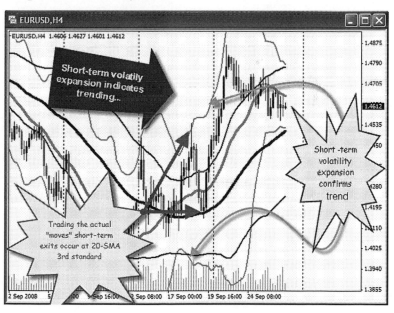

There is even more to the story here though...

Back on our original chart of the EUR/USD (Figure 8.14), readers will notice when the EUR/USD touched the topside 3rd-standard deviation of the 20-SMA, the pair quickly fell back to the 50-SMA mean, before resuming the ascending trend.

The longer the period measured, the greater the probability prices will fail at the 3rd-standard deviation. What's more, in shorter-term periods, prices tagging the 3rd-standard deviation denotes three events occurring:

1. Short-term volatility has accelerated to a point where prices are tagging statistical 'outlier' variables.

2. Trending will likely ensue.

3. Before trending ensues, a pullback to the mean, or 1st standard deviation is highly probable.

See, we know statistically, there is a 99.7% probability that all of the data will sit within 3-standard deviations of the mean. Thus, on a short-term basis, if we have bought a currency pair in a **bull-trend** and the pair strikes the shorter-term 3rd standard deviation (on the topside volatility band), we may want to consider taking profits.

It is important to note that price touching the 3rd-standard deviation does not mean the trend is over, rather, simply that a pullback to the mean may perhaps, be in the cards… Then, we can attempt to re-buy the pair on the mean, if we believe the trend is still intact.

Moreover, if price has just hit the third standard deviation *and* short-term volatility **is** collapsing back below long-term volatility, we can rest assured price **is indeed** about to consolidate, or reverse. Why? Simply put, price cannot move up, or down if short-term volatility is compressing. Because of the squaring of the exponent in the standard deviation formula, the application of standard deviations to price data creates a '**multiplier effect**' in the lines representing the standard deviations.

What I have just mentioned is the reason volatility bands expand and contract, providing us with key information regarding the release of energy within price action and thus, the expansion and compression of distributions.

It doesn't matter if you're looking at a 5-minute chart or a weekly chart, if short-term volatility is expanding, prices are trending in the period measured. Moreover, if short-term volatility is compressing, prices are consolidating.

Figure 8.15 shows precisely what I'm talking about…

As you can see, when short-term volatility (measured through the 20-period 3.2 standard deviation) compresses, in every occurrence, prices travel laterally until short-term volatility begins expanding again.

Moreover, as you will also notice, both times when short-term topside volatility attacked long-term volatility and compressed back below, the occurrences were almost precisely where the EUR/USD stalled on the upside.

Why?

Again, price simply **<u>cannot</u>** continue trending if short-term volatility is compressing. Short-term distribution width (mass) as measured through the 3.2-standard deviation, otherwise known as topside volatility, **must** be traveling upward for bullish action to continue.

Why?

If short-term volatility is compressing, the occurrence means the distribution is 'compressing' and a distribution must **<u>release energy to move</u>**, not vice versa. Short-term distribution width (mass) as measured through the 3.2 standard deviation, otherwise known as volatility, must be expanding for directional action to continue.

See, price movement in markets is about order flow, which is really about the expansion and compression of energy in subset distributions. Logically, short-term distributions must release energy first, thus stimulating the same occurrence in longer-term distributions.

You will read more about the 'release of energy' in the following chapters so if you're having trouble fully comprehending, or believing, this 'energy expansion and compression' thing, don't worry...

Figure 8.15

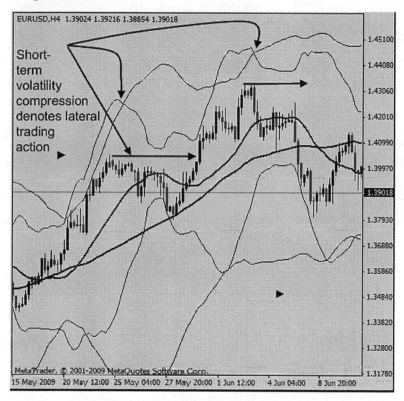

You will see the exact same occurrence in Figure 8.16, with short-term volatility expanding outside of long-term volatility on the downside, prior to the EUR/USD plummeting on the 4-hour chart.

As short-term volatility remains outside of long-term volatility, trending continues. Then, just like clockwork, when short-term volatility compresses back below long-term volatility, the move is over and lateral trading ensues.

One more time, when short-term volatility is outside of long-term volatility, we will likely want to use trending strategies. Conversely, when short-term volatility collapses below long-term volatility, we will likely want to start using short-term term channel trading strategies, while continually eyeing a possible longer-term *"trade with the trend"* entry.

Figure 8.16

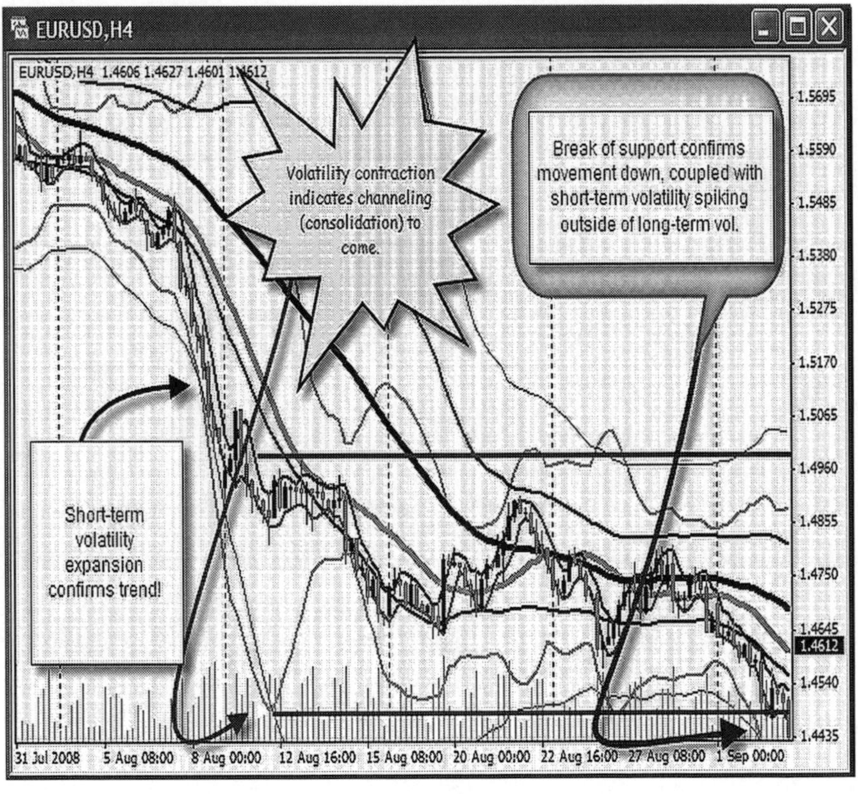

If we were able to close a position when short-term volatility collapses below long-term volatility and then open the position back up when short-term volatility begins to expand, we are -in essence- putting significant probability in our favor- to ride a larger wave of market action, otherwise known as energy expansion, or trending.

Of note, when traders begin to apply all of the aforementioned to their own charts, there will be instances of short-term volatility expanding (with price moving), however, just at the time short-term volatility actually moves outside of longer-term volatility, the price reverses. Why? Because the longer-term distribution had too much mass to start with.

Please remember: Force = Mass * Acceleration.

It doesn't matter how hard you try... You (the person reading this book right now) cannot push a dump truck full of lead up a mountain. The dump truck has too much mass. So how do we measure mass in terms of trading and price distributions?

We can measure mass two ways:

1. Visually, you can look at the total width of the longer-term distribution and gauge (with common sense) whether the distribution is too wide to begin (or continue) trending, or...

2. You can use the indicator I have developed and supplied with this book titled: Whistler Active Volatility Energy • Price Mass (WAVE • PM). I will explain WAVE • PM in Chapter Twelve.

For now, another problem likely persists for traders… How to denote trending?

In the Figure 8.17, I have inserted a 50-SMA 1.2-STD, a 50-SMA 3.2-STD, and a 20-period 3.2-STD, while also adding two 3-period SMA's (the darker two black lines closely tracking price), one measuring highs and one measuring lows.

Working from left to right in Figure 8.17, we see trending was confirmed when short-term volatility spiked outside of long-term volatility, as denoted with the 20-SMA 3.2-STD spiking outside of the 50-SMA 3.2-STD. What's more, the EUR/USD also fell below the 50-period 1.2-standard deviation, indicating the larger distribution was on the move. The instance of the EUR/USD falling below the 50-period 1.2-standard deviation would have shown up on most CCI windows with the 50-period CCI falling below -100, which clearly did not mean 'oversold', rather, the occurrence was shouting 'distribution on the move'.

Figure 8.17

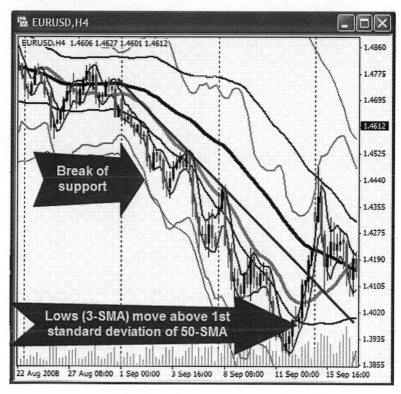

As the chart shows, the downside move stalled when the 20-SMA 3.2-STD collapsed back below the 50-SMA 3.2-STD.

For those who were thinking there was more downside to come (at least immediately, anyway), volatility/probability traders knew the move was over and mean-regression (at the very least) was in effect.

What I've just mentioned was clearly noted not only when short-term volatility collapsed back below long-term volatility, but also when the 3-SMA lows crossed back over the 50-SMA 1.2 STD, implying downside order flow was no longer in effect and shorts would be squeezed.

Using short-term highs and lows of the 3-SMA (traders who prefer a little more 'wiggle room' can use 10-period SMA's off highs and lows) we are able to quickly identify when the highs and lows of the immediate range fail support and resistance. What's more, because we are measuring 3-periods of data, it will take more than one freak candle of upside, or downside volatility to truly change our directional bias.

By using the 3-SMA for confirmation, we are able to further isolate head-fake moves, from true trending.

You will notice that while the EUR/USD was channeling, **both** the 3-SMA highs and lows never moved above, or below the 50-SMA 1.2-STD. Again though, the actual instance of trending was not confirmed until short-term volatility spiked outside of long-term volatility.

What's more, as the chart shows, the WTS would have moved violently to the right, thus inferring trending to come, as the short-term (20-period) distribution moved to the right side of the long-term (50-period) teeter-totter.

Shown in Figure 8.17, recognizing volatility spikes can yield big moves, as noted in the almost 300-PIP drop in the EUR/USD.

It's important to note that in the framework of the information here –as always- common sense is required.

As you may have noticed, in the above chart, short-term volatility did not constantly stay outside of long-term volatility…

The instances of short-term volatility compressing are marked with price moving back to the 20-SMA, but did not fully reverse. Every extended move in markets **<u>will</u>** see pullbacks as volatility reloads for another move...

Figure 8.17

Figure 8.17

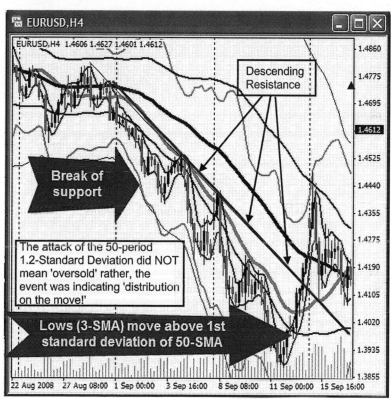

In the above chart, we also know the EUR/USD never violated descending resistance of the relative range, until the trend completed itself. Using the 3-SMA (lows); however, would have absolutely closed the trade before descending resistance was violated, thus perhaps saving a few PIPs of profit.

What's more, in one instance (a little over halfway through the move) the EUR/USD struck the 3rd-standard deviation of the 20-period distribution. Savvy traders may have inferred it was time to take profits; thus setting themselves to re-enter -with the trend- at the 20-SMA mean (which was precisely at descending resistance as well.)

In addition, as previously noted, because the 3-SMA lows never moved above the 1.2-standard deviation of the 50-period distribution, taking a long-position **any time** during the decline would have been foolish.

Regardless, it is important to note that when trending ensues, we should always attempt to understand *why* the move is occurring in the first place, on a fundamental basis. However, with a little common sense understanding of descriptive and inferential statistics, distributions and probability, all of the information here should help traders identify trending, channeling and reversals.

Again though, common sense is king, and if you're not sure why what's happening is happening…as a rule of thumb, *"when in doubt, get out."*

We have just covered volatility and probability (in terms of mobile subset distributions), based on 'price action' alone.

It's important to note what we did not cover is volume/dollar volatility/probability as well. Price action is reliable when we understand that it is…

…purely price action.

Looking towards volume/dollar trading action as well, we will now jump into Chapter Nine, were we will discuss VWAP (Volume Weighted Average Price), thus adding another variable for aggressive intraday traders seeking to capitalize on volatility…

After our introduction of VWAP, we will enter into a more detailed discussion of 'institutional order flow' and then tie everything together through Whistle Active Energy Volatility • Price Mass (WAVE • PM).

CHAPTER NINE

VOLUME WEIGHTED AVERAGE PRICE (VWAP)

In currency trading, many retail traders can lose fortunes, before ever even hearing about VWAP. It's an odd occurrence really, that so many self proclaimed 'high-tech' at home traders navigate markets daily without even having the faintest clue about institutional trading performance benchmarks, like the one I have just mentioned. Clearly, the simple fact that so many retail traders have no clue about VWAP simply proves success continues to rest within the hands of those controlling the bulk of order flow.

VWAP (Volume Weighted Average Price) is really a moving average of price, weighted for the amount of shares that are traded over the duration of the period measured.

For institutional traders running order flow, VWAP is used as a major benchmark of performance for those seeking passivity in order execution. In other words, trading to VWAP is a type of dollar cost averaging during the session, as measured by the volume/dollar average of the session, or whatever period measured.

VWAP is calculated using the following formula:

$$P_{\text{VWAP}} = \frac{\sum_j P_j \cdot Q_j}{\sum_j Q_j}$$

Where:

P_{VWAP} = Volume Weighted Average Price

P_j = price of trade j

Q_j = quantity of trade j

j = each individual trade that takes place over the defined period, excluding cross trades and basket cross trades.

In terms of execution, there are two type methods, which most institutions use:

1. Guaranteed Execution

2. Target Execution

Guaranteed Execution is where a broker explicitly *'guarantees VWAP, or better'* for clients, meaning the broker guarantees the VWAP price, or better, or usually, the trade is free. What this means is that in a rapidly ascending market, the broker's computer(s) will likely buy boldly on dips, to ensure the 'guarantee' of VWAP, or better holds, as prices rise into the day.

Target Execution is usually a less expensive commission process for clients, as unlike guaranteed execution, target leaves more discretion to traders, while also requiring more price dispersion…

What this means is there is usually greater 'spread' in total execution price, in relation to VWAP.

Let's break VWAP down to more simple terms… VWAP is the total dollar average of the shares traded in a day, or in a given period…

VWAP differs from a basic moving average in that the calculation takes into account the dollar volume of the instrument (measured through volume) traded in any given time period. Conversely, moving averages simply calculate the 'average price' over a given time period, without recognition of volume.

Don't worry if the aforementioned sounds a little foreign, or confusing right now; it may take a little while for the concept to sink in. (Especially why keeping an eye on VWAP is so important!)

In reality, VWAP is a definitely a 'paradigm shift' for most retail traders...

Why?

Retail traders seek to make money when a stock, currency, commodities, or futures price moves up or down. In essence, the retail trader has been conditioned to believe his sole 'opinion' about price action in markets, should be to know whether prices are moving up, or down. Retail traders believe the better the trader you are, the more you will know whether prices are about to ascend, or descend. Little does the retail trader know, intraday action is more about risk and fill, over the up, or down *'opinion'* of prices.

For the institutional traders attempting to *'work orderflow'* he or she knows trading is really about risk, in relation to benchmark performance.

<u>At the end of the day, institutional traders simply seek to achieve the best possible prices possible for their clients.</u>

In terms of institutional trading, large orders are broken down into smaller orders, which are then *'worked'* (via trader, or computer, or both) over a given period.

The phenomenon of breaking large orders into small orders and then working the little orders over a period of time is called *'iceberging'* and is intended to lower the overall cost of the transaction, while keeping the large order out of the sight of other market participants.

Please take a moment to observe the below table... In column two 'Price' we can see over a given period (it could be 1-minute, 5-minutes, 1-day, whatever...) there were two transactions: One buy at $24.50 and one sell at $24.00.

Figure 9.2

Volume		Price	Total	
Bought	1000000	*$24.50*	24500000	
Sold	500000	*$24.00*	12000000	
Volume	1500000	$48.50	36500000	
Moving Avg→	$24.25	$24.33	← VWAP	
Bought	300000	$23.30	6990000	
Sold	200000	$22.50	4500000	
Volume	500000	$45.80	11490000	
	2000000	$94.30	47990000	
Moving Avg→	$22.90	$24.00	← VWAP	

If we were using a simple moving average, the actual line on the chart would be marked at $24.25, which is the average of the two prices.

However, if we were to incorporate the volume traded in the same period, the moving average line would instead be marked at $24.33.

Why?

As the below image shows, when we calculate VWAP, we are actually multiplying volume by price, summing the calculation and then dividing by the total volume in the given period...

For our price of $24.33, the math would be:

[(1,000,000 * $24.50) + (500,000 * $24.00)] = 24,500,00

Then we would divide 24,500,000 by 15,000,000 (the total volume traded in the period) to get the VWAP of $24.33.

What's so important to understand is that while a simple moving average provides the average (middle, mean, or mid) price of the period measured, VWAP actually takes into account the fact that more shares were traded at the higher price, versus the lower, thus giving us a more accurate indication of whether there are more buyers, or sellers in any given period.

Figure 9.3

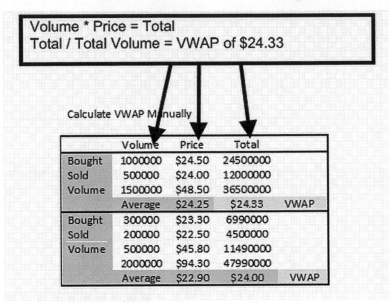

Calculate VWAP Manually

	Volume	Price	Total	
Bought	1000000	$24.50	24500000	
Sold	500000	$24.00	12000000	
Volume	1500000	$48.50	36500000	
	Average	$24.25	$24.33	VWAP
Bought	300000	$23.30	6990000	
Sold	200000	$22.50	4500000	
Volume	500000	$45.80	11490000	
	2000000	$94.30	47990000	
	Average	$22.90	$24.00	VWAP

Do you see the implications here?

A simple moving average is nothing more than present a line with a 50/50 guess of whether buyers or sellers were present. However, VWAP actually provides greater insight into the actual buying and selling that occurred in any given period.

Can you see why price action technical analysis can often set retail traders up for failure from the start?

The aforementioned **does not** mean we can't use moving averages, or price action only technicals, we simply **must** understand moving averages and other technicals do not take volume into account.

We must understand that price action is a derivative of volume and that without volume (the actual instance of a transaction), price cannot exist.

Again, price action moving averages are not *totally* misleading… After all, we are measuring the average of prices (and nothing more), over a given period.

Used in conjunction with VWAP (in terms of volatility/probability, as mentioned in the previous chapter), moving averages are a great identifier of 'average distribution' price movement.

In terms of VWAP, here's what readers must understand…

What we're talking about is a **benchmark of price**, which institutional traders are measured by, in terms of commission structure and performance.

If you're an institutional trader and you receive a buy order for $40 billion EUR/USD, your client needs some sort of way to measure whether you've done a good job of filling his order in relation to the prices of the day… Thus, if you receive a $40 billion order for whatever, chance are, you're not going to be able to fill the whole order in one shot, without creating a stampede. Thus, you need to fill the order slowly over time, whereby your client will then measure your overall performance with some sort of benchmark of average prices throughout the session.

Benchmarks include VWAP, TWAP (Time Weighted Average Price), LHOC (Low, High, Open, Close [average]), just to name a few.

The bottom line is, if you are an institutional trader and you are able to consistently fill your clients orders at prices better than VWAP (or other benchmarks), everyone will likely be very happy. What's more, in some cases, traders are even paid bonuses for achieving better fills over time. While there are many benchmarks institutional traders are gauged by, the most widely coveted is VWAP...

With this in mind, please look at the following two charts, Figures 9.4 and 9.5.

In Figure 9.4, we are seeing 14-period, 21-period and a 50-period regular Simple Moving Averages. What I would like you to immediately take notice of is the fact that if we were looking at shorter-term moving averages, like the 14-period and the 21-period, the (on the 5-minute chart) the EUR/USD pierced the moving averages three times, once in the beginning of the rally and then twice towards the end. For the at home trader, this price action likely just looks like "*volatility.*"

Figure 9.4

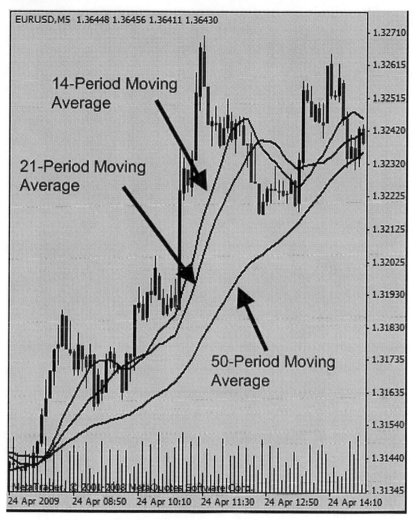

Figure 9.5

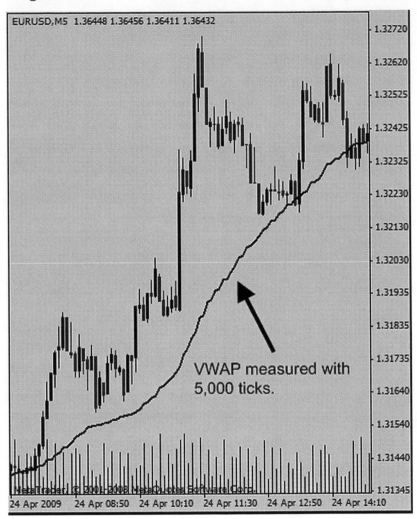

VWAP measured with 5,000 ticks.

Now, if we look at the Figure 9.5, however, we see that the EUR/USD attacked 5,000-tick VWAP twice, which it stalled at almost precisely...

In Figure 9.4, the 50-period SMA is the only technical moving average that comes close, but still, the EUR/USD did not actually 'touch' the indicator.

So what's happening here?

Foremost, we must remember that price action –only– moving averages are nothing more than technical indicators of 'average price'.

It's important that you understand this concept. Moving averages, at least in-terms of providing accurate trading signals, are nothing more than indicators that only hold **if** enough people act on the same information at the same time.

VWAP is similar, except that the 'people' acting on the information are institutional traders, who control the bulk of the order flow. Do you see how important this paradigm shift for retail traders is?

If you want to know where order flow is, than it's important to watch an indicator that shows what and where institutional traders are looking at... Not just a simple technical tool that is only relevant from time to time, most often by luck and luck alone...

If we want to use moving averages, than we need to understand that they should be used as, 'benchmarks for volatility distributions' and not fancy technical analysis trading signals, with no real explanation...

Figure 9.6

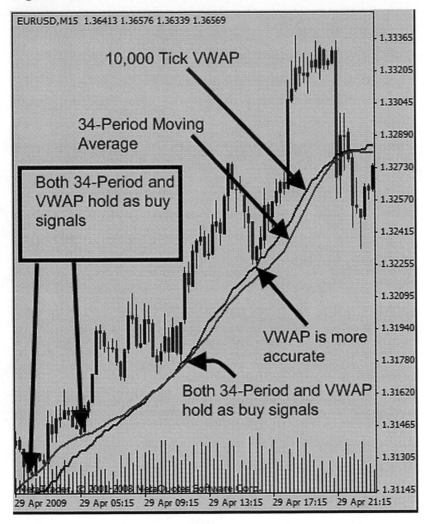

EURUSD,M15 1.36413 1.36576 1.36339 1.36569

10,000 Tick VWAP

34-Period Moving
Average

Both 34-Period and
VWAP hold as buy
signals

VWAP is more
accurate

Both 34-Period and VWAP
hold as buy signals

MetaTrader (c) 2001-2008 MetaQuotes Software Corp.

29 Apr 2009   29 Apr 05:15   29 Apr 09:15   29 Apr 13:15   29 Apr 17:15   29 Apr 21:15

When distributions move above and below one another (like a 14-period moving average crossing under a 21-period moving average, for example) we should be thinking: *On a price action basis alone, the shorter-term volatility distribution just moved under the longer-term distribution...*

What we should **not** be thinking is: *The red line crossed under the blue line and that's a **definite** sell signal.*

Now, if we take a look at the next chart, you will notice I have drawn two more lines, a 34-period Simple Moving Average and 10,000 tick VWAP.

It is important to note that I added the 34-period only after '*trying*' to make several moving averages fit VWAP.

In the case of the 15-minute chart, the 34-period was the closest benchmark moving average I could find.

Unlike the 34-SMA, the 10,000 tick VWAP is a constant value that traders can use (at least for the time being...remembering that everything eventually changes within markets) when attempting to wiggle into the mindset of institutional traders.

What is so important to understand here (reiterated again) is the 34-period is nothing more than a technical indicator of average distribution price action.

However, VWAP is an *actual* institutional benchmark that many of those who are working BIG orders, are likely watching to time their trades.

Figure 9.7

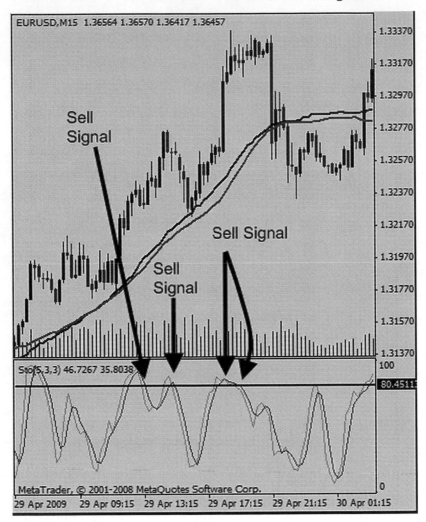

If you had $40 billion in orders to work, would you buy as close to VWAP as possible, or way above it, like many at-home technical breakout traders?

Of course you would buy **into** VWAP, knowing that if the EUR/USD were to then begin rallying again, your buy would be under VWAP, **as VWAP continued to ascend.**

Again, In the shoes of the institutional trader, he would want to buy a pullback **into VWAP**, if the trend looked like it was going to stay intact, knowing that another leg up would move VWAP higher, and thus, provide the trader a better fill than VWAP for the day.

If the EUR/USD were to break below VWAP, the trader would likely sell inventory, knowing he would likely be able to buy lower, as selling tapered later on.

The 34-period held as a buy signal (with the trend) in the first leg of the up move, but VWAP was more accurate in the final instance of '*test*' before the last wave up.

Why?

Foremost, because if a trend is truly to stay intact, institutional traders will buy into VWAP, attempting to time their trades as close to the benchmark as possible. Institutional traders don't look at other technicals like MACD, or goofy awkward period moving averages.

Unfortunately, because the at-home trader hardly has any real information, and was likely inferring a sell signal when his 14-period and 21-period moving averages were breached, or other momentum indicators were showing signs of being *overbought*, the retail trader likely got short, while the institutional trader was buying exactly into VWAP...

As the Figure 9.7 shows, three times during the uptrend, retail traders were given sell signals by stochastics (*using the common preset variables of 5,3,3*).

Do you get it?

Do you see it?

Please tell me you see how conventional indicators completely set retail traders up for failure!

I'm not joking about this stuff...

Most of the technical indicators retail traders look at are nothing more than pretty lines on a chart...

Retail traders who were watching the 15-minute chart and stochastics (Figure 9.7), were likely scratching their heads saying '*geez Forex is volatile*'; however, the savvy trader who understands VWAP and volatility/probability knows there's more to the picture... Savvy traders know trading profitably is more about the minds of those working institutional order flow than a few dim-witted lines on a chart.

<u>This is Volatility Illuminated</u> .

Figure 9.8

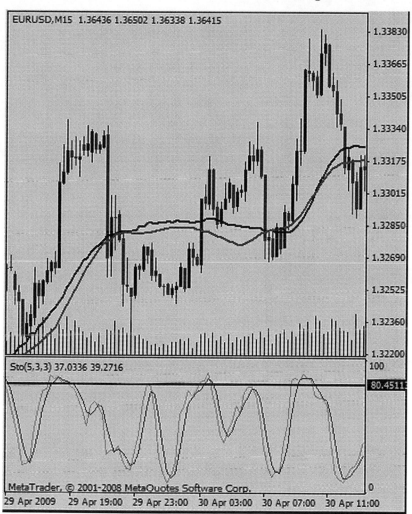

Okay…I hope you're asking if there's a downside to VWAP?

If you are, you get a gold star.

Just like any indicator, VWAP will not illuminate *everything* that is happening within the market, *all* the time.

When a currency crosses over VWAP, the occurrence does **NOT** always mean a reversal is pending…

In fact, Forex markets sometimes move all over VWAP, providing virtually no insight into the institutional mindset.

If you look at Figure 9.8, you will notice that when the ascending trend ended (or at least, slowed), the EUR/USD traded all over the place (above and below) both VWAP and the 34-period moving average. The at- home trader was likely taking some serious licks during this time… And the institutional trader may have been too.

The aforementioned is why I am coming forward with WVAV and WAVE • PM which will help both institutional and retail traders solve some of the problems mentioned above.

(Please note that the WVAV strategy was built for institutional trading. In fact, WVAV could very well even save institutional traders working billions in order flow - piles of commission cash - by knowing when lateral markets are about to ensue, and when trending is truly in effect.)

As we move forward into our discussion on WVAV, we need to remember:

VWAP is a glimpse into what the institutional trader is thinking in identifiable situations of trending.

VWAP by itself isn't enough.

However, when we add VWAP together with volatility bands (WVAV) and WAVE • PM (price distribution mass) we will have an edge many traders never do.

The true gem behind WVAV is the indicator is almost a sort of artificial intelligence in and of itself, as the methodology provides guidance into when markets are about to (and will continue to) move sideways, and when volatility is foreshadowing and/or sustained trending.

In effect, with what I'm about to show, traders will know when to use lateral 'channel trading' techniques and when to buy pullbacks, with the trend.

CHAPTER TEN

- WVAV -

WHISTLER VOLUME
ADJUSTED VOLATILITY

We're finally here… The explanation of WVAV. Before I jump in, I would like to provide readers with a little background of some of the events over the past year, which helped bring WVAV to life.

In the fall of 2008, I traveled all the way to Dalian, China to speak at the amazing Global Chinese Financial Forum, hosted by ChinaWorldNet.com.

I then journeyed to Guangzhou, China (75 miles outside of Hong Kong) to work with traders and programmers from ECTrader.net, to breathe life into the concepts at hand.

I would also like to mention the WVAV (as you are about to read about here) is not a 'cut and dry red line crosses blue line signal system.'

Instead, WVAV is part of a larger *methodology*, helping to derive trending and consolidation, while also providing some insight into potential institutional mindset. Furthermore, using the information in the following pages will require some common sense. If you're looking for a 'red line crosses blue line' signal, this is not it. However, with some rational analysis of the situation at hand, I think you will find WVAV an extremely powerful tool like no other - readily available- without spending thousands of dollars.

We will now begin our discussion of what WVAV is and how the indicator assists in understanding order flow and institutional motivations, and why such is both important and valid.

WHAT IS WVAV?

WVAV is really three pieces combined to sum the whole. WVAV consists of:

- Two indicators of VWAP in the same period, but measuring different data.
- Two sets of VWAP volatility bands.
- Two normalized measurements of price distribution 'energy', otherwise known as 'mass', also known as WAVE • PM.

In the end, over ten years of research went into the 'theoretical makeup' behind WVAV and WAVE • PM.

Really, the philosophy and theory behind WVAV and WAVE • PM are why the indicators are novel within today's *'light speed information'* markets.

In essence, we are approaching markets from a stance of physics, while also incorporating volatility and probability within the movement of distributions...

MEASURING MASS AND ENERGY

There are a few simple guidelines of theory readers must understand about WVAV and WAVE • PM ...

Foremost, we are talking about the movement of mass and the energy required to move whatever mass we are measuring. Understanding the concepts here, we will need to put effort into reshaping the way we think about price movements in markets...

Movements in markets are not purely about directional price action...

Movement in markets is about the expansion and compression of energy.

As an analogy, please think about markets as a big rubber ball... When all things are neutral, the ball is round and centered... However, because money is involved, markets (currencies, equities, options, commodities, futures, whatever...) NEVER stay completely neutral, or round.

Why?

Again, **because money is involved.**

Individual speculators, corporations, funds, Governments, brokerages and a variety of other players are constantly trying to make money on movements within markets...

Figure 10.1

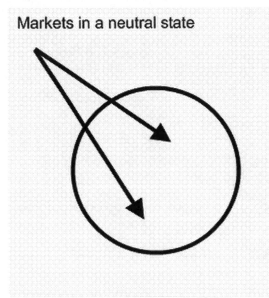

Markets in a neutral state

Movement is based on the perceived value of the financial instrument *today and* the expected value *of tomorrow.*

Thus, because the news of today is always shadowed by the unknown of tomorrow, participants are constantly buying and selling positions in an effort to profit from the expected movement of any moment beyond now.

The aforementioned is partially why regular technical indicators fail... Typical technicals only present data that has already occurred, without guidance into tomorrow, other than some type of expected -reoccurring- similarity to what happened yesterday.

However, tomorrow is never exactly like yesterday or even today, which is why technical indicators constantly seem to provide false signals, with every new day that passes.

What's more, it's important to understand one more very important concept…

Really, in terms of volume, we have again arrived at the chicken before the egg, or the egg before the chicken argument.

Does price action appear before volume, or does volume appear before price action?

The answer is volume precedes price.

One must first effect a transaction (meaning a certain dollar amount must not only be tendered to buy, or sell, but accepted, as well), before a price can *print* on a chart.

What this means is all technical analysis is a *derivative* of price action, which is a *derivative* of volume.

Thus, we can use price action in determining volatility and probability (and/or other indictors) only so long as **we understand** the reality of the situation unfolding.

When we use technicals based off price action alone, without direct reference to volume (dollars put into action) in markets, we are missing the 'origination' of the larger picture: volume.

Do we drive without a gas gauge? No way.

We have to know how much fuel is in the tank, before embarking on a trip. If we have no idea what's going into the engine (or how much is in the tank at all); how far will we make it?

No very far at all.

Volume buying, or selling at any given level is our gas gauge. If price is moving up and hardly any buying volume occurs, the gas going into the engine is weak, and will likely cause a sputtering breakdown.

What's more, without a 'gauge' of the '*effectiveness*' of the gas and/or a gauge of how much gas is in the tank, we are trading two-fold blind.

Thus, technicals (that do not take volume into account) are a measurement of output and not the '*fuel*' going into the engine. Anyone can look back and measure total miles traveled in a trip, but it takes a more savvy driver to calculate how many miles are feasible, based on the gas in the tank, and the quality and impact of, in terms of miles per gallon, as we look towards a trip ahead.

Traders who solely use 'price action *derivative* indicators' are attempting to use historical trips, as a measurement of future possible miles. The problem is that the upcoming trip very likely has much different terrain, than the previous drive.

Here's what I mean:

Did you know that driving at an elevation above 10,000 feet can cause your car's engine to have 34% less power output, "*due to a combination of lowered oxygen levels, and a significant reduction in atmospheric pressure.*"[49]

Metaphorically, when a stock, currency, or other financial instrument rallies heavily at '*high altitude*', the event likely infers traders *'stepping on the gas'*, given the emotion and intensity of the situation. However, just like automobiles at high altitude, more gas is required to compensate for the loss of power...

Traders *'step on it'* causing a fierce rally (like the steep 5th wave upward in Elliot Theory.) However, the higher the altitude, the greater the likelihood of the engine breaking down and possibly running out of gas too, based on the lead-foot overcompensation taking place.

While the aforementioned might seem like overkill, the point is we must know what's going into the engine and how the fuel is not only affecting, but interacting with the motor, if we expect to truly see high-performance.

Utilizing volume within trading is *'foresight'*, using 'price action' technicals **alone**, is hindsight.

Back to the round ball explanation...

The ball is basically a distribution of market action showing trending, or consolidation. What's more, because information is moving at the speed of light today, markets hardly ever stand still.

Thus, we need to understand the theory behind 'compression' (consolidation) and 'expansion' (trending) of the energy moving distributions within markets.

Figure 10. 2

Now, please look at Figure 10.2. What's happening to our ball?

You guessed it… The 'ball' compressed! Well, maybe you didn't guess it, I really don't know.

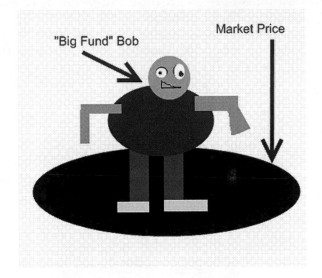

The point is that when pressure is applied to the ball, we see 'compression', or lateral trading.

Also, please note that the compression is being caused by '*Big Fund Bob*' sitting on the market (*please don't laugh at my artwork again!*)

Here's where some understanding of volume really comes into play, for the retail trader. See, most at-home traders believe that volume is required for a '*surge*', but really…this is not always the case.

Often, the volume is really from 'Big Fund Bob' sitting on the market, because he can't make up his mind. When markets travel sideways, we are really seeing big players slugging out order flow, without guidance to future direction. In essence, the large players are lacking insight, just like the little guy. During this time of 'lateral trading', 'consolidation', or 'storing of energy', markets travel sideways, while participants struggle to find information to motivate a larger move up, or down. I know this is contrary to what most retail traders believe, thus, please take a moment to look over the below chart...

In following hourly chart of the EUR/USD (Figure 10.3), readers will notice the currency pair witnessed a fierce upward rally on March 18th and 19th of 2009.

The rally really only lasted a little over a day...

Figure 10.3

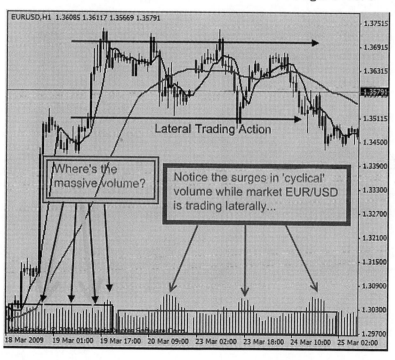

However, the following seven days (the 26th and 27th are not visible) witnessed lateral trading.

What's more, during the 20th to the 27th, the EUR/USD experienced seven (three visible) volume surges before taking out support in the 1.3418 area.

See, what we have to understand is volume isn't always the *sole motivator* of rallies and/or breakdowns; rather 'volume' can be *Big Fund Bob* sitting on a currency, stock (or whatever), both ways.

Big Fund Bob isn't sure what the outcome is going to be either, and so a sort of trading tug-of-war takes place, while bigger players '*jockey for position.*'

What's more, in sideways markets, volatility and hedge players step in to take advantage of the situation too.

Figure 10.4

Fact is, energy is stored in markets (seen through volume and compression of price distributions) when Big Fund Bob is sitting on the ball, meaning the larger players are stifling directional movement, fueling lateral trading action.

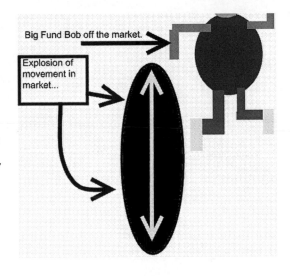

Without clear news, or information that presents greater and more transparent expectations of tomorrow, than today; markets will travel sideways, thus 'storing energy'.

So what happens when Big Fund Bob 'gets off' the bid and/or ask? An explosion of movement occurs...

In the case of the EUR/USD, the lateral trading action was partially motivated from *Big Fund Bob* keeping the pair from traveling higher.

What's more, when the EUR/USD took out support, other funds, institutions and retail traders were prompted to dump positions, hence the extended 'pullback.'

Figure 10.5

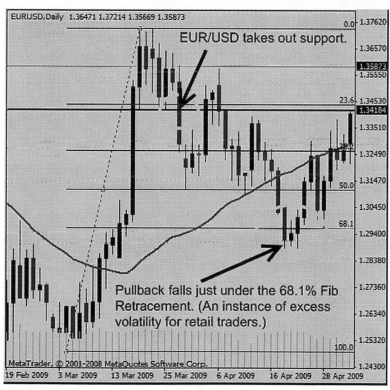

Another point to quickly mention, as Figure 10.5 shows, the pullback pierced the 61.8% Retracement slightly, before attempting to resume an ascending move… Retail traders who took long positions right on the key Retracement were likely stopped out in the 'volatility pop', only to watch the EUR/USD reverse and move higher later on.

Over the past year, I've been receiving increasing amounts of email from retail traders complaining of excess volatility and indicator failure… This example should **again** serve as proof of the pudding that 'excess volatility' (in terms of common indicators failing slightly and/or entirely) is readily present in today's market. Because we now have an entire army of retail traders who are acting on the same information, at the same time, with the same pre-set technical indicator inputs, short-term 'quick pop' volatility is increasing.

When the technicals fail, like a herd of lemmings, the retail traders rush to cover, or are electronically stopped out, causing an excess 'pop.' Retail volume is not enough to keep a trend intact, which is why the 'pops' usually occur at key technical levels and then reverse.

Overall the critical concepts to understand here are:

1. Market movements are about the expansion and compression of distributions.

2. Volume doesn't always have to persist for a torrid trend to ensue. Often, heavy volume causes sideways trading, a point many retail traders are unaware of.

3. The longer an instrument compresses (stores energy) the greater the likelihood the expansion period will be fierce.

4. Stock technical indicators rely on price action alone and are devoid of critical dollar/volume data needed to trade successfully on a short-term basis. We can (and will) use technical indicators that rely on price action alone, but we must **understand** that the indicator relies on price action alone.

5. If we can map the expansion and compression of energy within markets, we really are measuring the probability of volatility (measured in total width of distribution) where big money will step up, or fade.

6. The physics mumbo jumbo I discussed in Chapter Seven is extremely important as market movements (seen through *volume/dollar/price action,* derived from the expectations of market participants) are about order flow, seen through energy and mass, not technical analysis.

ADDITIONAL NOTE:

Before moving forward, I would like to take a moment to reiterate a few facts again from Chapter Two - Why Indicators are Failing in the Current Market.

According to the Bank for International Settlements' Triennial Central Bank Survey (Foreign exchange and derivatives market activity in 2007), Bank for International Settlements' Triennial Central Bank Survey (Foreign exchange and derivatives market activity in 2007), "the median share of electronic execution is 17% for non-financial customers."[50] The point here is retail traders do not move markets over the long haul.

However, according to the Wall Street Journal, "Volumes on dbFX, the online retail trading platform from Deutsche Bank, increased 37% in the first quarter of 2009, from the same period a year earlier."[51]

More retail traders have entered the game.

What we're talking about is a fresh wave of neo-volatility from a whole *new* set of traders (*now at the table*) who might not really know what they're doing.

New traders use preloaded technical analysis variables, which as I've mentioned, increases the 'mass army' of at-home traders doing the same thing at the same time, on information that really isn't that great in the first place.

What I'm saying is: expect even more '*quick pop*' volatility -directly at key price action technical levels- in the weeks, months and years to come.

The problem is only going to get worse...

MASS AND ENERGY THROUGH STANDARD DEVIATIONS

Coming back to our discussion from Chapter Eight, we can measure energy through volatility, also known as the total width of distributions, a critical component of mass.

When a distribution is wide (meaning a ton of mass) the more volume (buying or selling) required to continue the trend (or distribution expansion.)

The more mass an object has, the more energy required to move it.

We will now move directly into our discussion of Whistler Volume Adjusted Volatility (WVAV), in terms of volatility/energy. Then, in Chapter Twelve, we will cover Whistler Active Volatility Energy • Price Mass (WAVE • PM).

The overall concept, as you're about to see, is fairly simple... Again, the theoretical underpinning was the difficult part to unearth; the coding (with ECTrader.net in China) was less of a struggle, once the ball was rolling.

At the core of WVAV, we are using Bollinger Bands (volatility bands) to measure price trending, and/or consolidation.

By the way, I would like to again reiterate that I believe
Bollinger's application of standard deviations to price action,
was perhaps one of the greatest trading breakthroughs, seen
in modern times.

Figure 10. 6

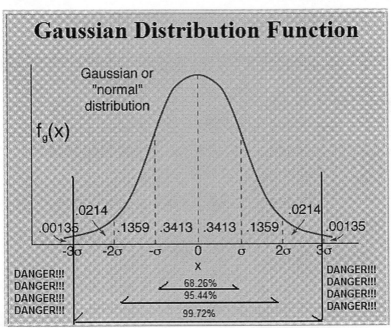

So how does volatility come into play with WVAV and
Bollinger Bands (volatility bands)?

As previously mentioned, volatility bands are a
measurement of total potential distribution wingspan
(mass), through the total potential 'width' the standard
deviations are displaying on our charts. As mentioned in
Chapter Eight, when we map a distribution, we seek to

measure probability from the mean, by one, two and three standard deviations.

Figure 10.6 again shows, there is a 68.3% probability that all of the data will fall within 1-standard deviation of the mean, a 95.4% probability all of the data will rest within 2-standard deviations and a 99.7% probability all of the data will be parked within 3-standard deviations of the mean.

(Please note again that actual Bollinger Band settings need to be 1.2, 2.2, or 3.2 standard deviations and __not__ whole numbers, accounting for data loss in the conversion of standard deviation formula – into electronic format on charts.)

Again, the brilliance of Bollinger Bands (volatility bands), is simply the incredible fact that the squaring of the exponent in the standard deviation formula (when your computer calculates the bands) creates a type of *'multiplier effect'*, causing the bands to expand and contract with volatility. When prices consolidate the bands compress and when prices trend, the bands expand.

While this may sound lowbrow, hold your horses for a moment, before passing judgment.

WHAT THE *MULTIPLIER EFFECT* MEANS TO US

When we overlay two or more sets of Bollinger Bands, we are actually seeing two different sets of volatility.

Here's the best part of all…

If I were to ask you whether the total range of the EUR/USD would theoretically be wider over an entire year, or over one week, what would your answer be?

One year of course.

Over the duration of an entire year, the EUR/USD would simply have more time to trade up and down and would likely have a greater total range than just one week of trading action.

The above concept implies, when all things are constant and markets are *relatively* stable, short-term volatility should rest WITHIN long-term volatility.

In non-technical language, if you have two sets of volatility bands on a chart, a 50-period and 14-period, for example, regardless of whether you are looking at one, two, or three standard deviations, when looking at the same standard deviation setting for 14-period volatility bands, against the same standard deviation setting for 50-period volatility bands, the 14-period standard deviation volatility bands should rest inside of the 50-period volatility bands. (*Again, only if markets are 'normal', or 'stable.'*)

When volatility picks up though, which of the two bands will spike first?

The 14-period volatility bands will spike quicker than the 50-period volatility bands, simply because there's less mass to move.

Do you see what I'm saying?

We're talking about volatility leading mass. The less mass an object has, the quicker it can move. In terms of regular moving averages, a 14-period moving average is, or at least *should be*, much more volatile than a 100-period.

Image this: You're standing in a Field in Kansas watching a herd of hippos graze in the luscious grass... Suddenly an old truck drives by and *backfires,* startling the hippos into a stampede.

Which of the hippos is likely going to be in the front of the pack, as the group starts moving...

Most likely, the ones that prefer to graze on *slim fast grass*, over their big fat hippo-colleagues.

Anyway, the point is when volatility is about to pick up and prices are about to move, shorter-term volatility will likely start to bolt first, before the counterparts with greater mass.

WHY DO WE LOOK FOR VOLATILITY SPIKES?

When short-term VWAP volatility begins to spike outside of long-term VWAP volatility, we should be on *red alert* that quick institutional money is *'on the move.'*

The quick money, the guys, or computers, who are sharp, recognize a move is about to ensue, and are putting their money to work. We can recognize this occurrence by using volatility bands (Bollinger Bands) in conjunction with VWAP, to measure volatility with dollar volume, instead of just price action (though we will use price action in just a moment too.)

Remember our previous discussion about Newton's Second Law of Motion, where Force = Mass * Acceleration and Einstein's Mass-Energy Equivalence where $E = mc^2$?

Don't worry about the math, just understand the theory…

For trending to ensue, there must be enough force to push the actual price distribution to move beyond the present lateral range (support and resistance).

If a distribution has compressed, there is less mass to move, right? Right.

What we can then imply, is when a longer-term distribution has significantly compressed (meaning mass is low/light) and short-term volatility spikes outside of long-term volatility, we are seeing acceleration in action. Moreover, because the longer-term distribution has shed mass (consolidated) the spike in short-term volatility has greater probability of moving the longer-term volatility (and mass) with it.

We can restate Newton's formula as:

Mass = Force / Acceleration

Then, in terms of $E = mc^2$, the energy required to keep a distribution in motion is the mass times the speed of light (in a vacuum), squared.

The above math is not the most important point here... The critical component is simply in understanding that the greater the spike of short-term volatility, outside of long-term volatility, the greater the speed, or 'force' of the upcoming potential move, assuming the longer-term distribution doesn't have too much mass already.

If you're a physicist, you may be thinking I'm confusing terms, however, for the at home trader who does not have thousands to spend on coding, or technology, and/or the time, or desire to study quantum physics, the concepts of force, acceleration, speed and energy are interchangeable for our purposes here.

Simply put, **the _mass of a distribution_ cannot move without force**. Moreover, there is greater probability of force, when a distribution has less mass, over a bulky counterpart.

In one of my conversations with Alvin Yu the CEO of ECTrader.net while I was in China, I explained the above theory in markets...expecting questions.

Yu, a market genius and great friend, responded (to paraphrase), "Mark what you're talking about is power."

I replied, "What?"

Yu added, "Have you ever heard of Bruce Lee?"

"Of course, everyone in America has," I replied.

Yu suddenly popped his fist towards my face (yes, I flinched). When my heart stopped palpitating, Yu's arm was extended straight outward, inches from my nose. Yu asked, "What's wrong with this picture?"

"You're nuts?" I inquired.

"No," Yu said, "How can I hurt you now, with my fist totally extended?"

Alvin was right... Kung Fu and the market go hand in hand (in more ways than one), as when one's arm is tight to their body, the greater the potential force that he, or she can strike with. As the punch (arm) grows more and more extended, the less power retained. There might be considerable force in during the extension process, but as one's fist moves away from the body, the reality of the situation is that the hand can only go so far. The distribution is in the process of extension (expansion) and there comes a point where a fist can only go so far from one's body.

What the heck does all this mean?

Much like Kung Fu, when throwing a punch, one must eventually retract his or her fist to regain power for another strike... Furthermore, while skinny people might be able to punch quicker, most of the time, the larger dudes usually do more damage. What I'm saying is short-term volatility strikes quicker, but when long-term volatility is on the move, the blow will likely be greater.

No matter whether the puncher is big or little, skinny or tubby, guy or gal, eventually the striker **must** pull back their fist...to reload.

Did I just say 'pullback'?

Yes I did. A pullback is a reload of power. In a moment, I'm going to show you how to perceive a punch coming before you're upended on the chin by markets, and how to tell when the striker has lost power and must reload. I will even show how to distinguish when a counterblow has been served, causing a reversal of edge.

Again, what we're talking about is *mass and force* in terms of volatility, derived from dollar/volume and price action.

So now, let's put the first part of the methodology into action... WVAV volatility/energy...

WVAV
VOLATILITY/ENERGY

I've supplied the code for WVAV, WAVE • PM and Two-CCI (making up Quad CCI in two windows) at the end of the book. I have also supplied a template file *(only on the Website though)* for WVAV, as well. To download the MetaEditor files, please visit:

www.fxVolatility.com/volatility-illuminated-indicator-templates.html

In the following section, we will use WVAV volatility/energy opened *twice* on the same chart. By this, I mean we will overlay two sets of VWAP volatility bands on one chart.

The settings for the first set of WVAV volatility/energy (in MetaTrader) are:

WVAV (Energy)

10,000 ticks:

MA_Ticks	= 10,000
MA_Shift	= 0
MA_Start	= 500
aa	= ********
MidBandVisible	= true
Bands Period	= 21
Bands Shift	= 0
Bands Deviation	= 3.2
Color	= Red

1 = Dark Golden Rod

2 = Black

3 = Black

4 = Black

Overlaying a second set of WVAV volatility bands, please input the following parameters:

WVAV (Energy)

5,000 ticks:

MA_Ticks	= 5,000
MA_Shift	= 0
MA_Start	= 21
aa	= ********
MidBandVisible	= false
Bands Period	= 10
Bands Shift	= 0
Bands Deviation	= 3.2
Color	= Red
1 = Red	
2 = Red	
3 = Red	
4 = Red	

After you have the files and template installed in the proper folders, and are running MetaTrader, please make sure the above settings are correct, while also checking to be certain the indicator parameters are selected as well.

Also:

1. In the **Visualization** tab of the indicator, please make sure: "All Timeframes" and "Show in the Data Window" are checked for both VWAP's.

2. In addition, in the **Common** tab, please make sure the "Allow DLL Imports" and "Allow External Expert Imports" boxes are checked for both, as well.

3. Finally, in please right click on your chart and then select "Properties." When the Chart Properties window comes up, make sure the "Show volumes" box is checked, using any color you prefer.

When finished, your chart should look similar to:

Figure 10. 7

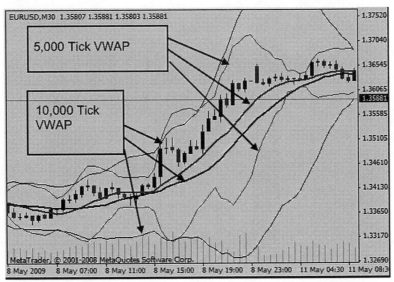

Now, let's take a moment to dig into what we're seeing on the chart.

First, I want to once again remind readers that *what* we are deciphering with WVAV is how, where and why orderflow may be presenting itself (through the measurement of volatility, by way of standard deviations) within currency markets…

What we are **<u>not doing</u>** is simply looking for brainless 'red line crosses blue line' signals.

Figure 10. 8

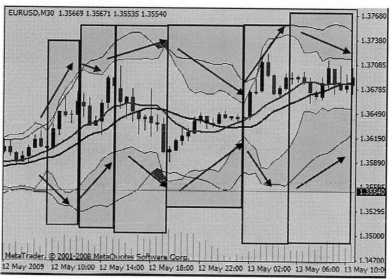

Understanding markets requires some human interaction and common sense. Please apply both liberally.

Figure 10.8 shows the compression and expansion of 5,000-tick VWAP volatility, and 10,000-tick VWAP volatility, as denoted by the arrows I have drawn, following the lighter colored inner section of the chart.

You will immediately notice expansion follows compression, follows expansion, follows compression, follows expansion, etc...

The chart clearly shows that when short-term VWAP (the more jagged, and usually inner, of the two volatility bands) is expanding, we see more directional price action than during moments of compression...

Figure 10.9

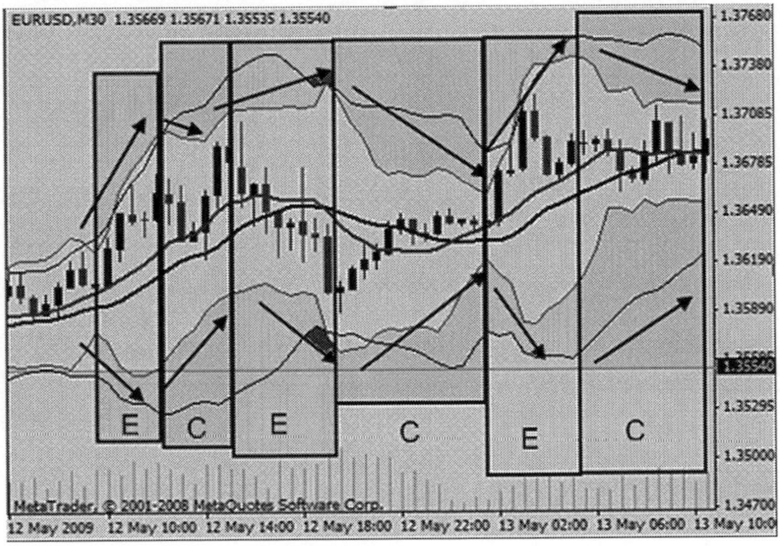

Also, please take special note of the three expansion sections I have marked with an 'E' on the lower portion of the chart and the three frames I have marked with a 'C' for compression.

As you likely see, expansion does not necessarily *always* mean 'breakout', rather, expansion means 'price moving' in the range too.

What's more, please also notice that in the first section (on the far left), 5,000-tick VWAP traded outside of 10,000-tick VWAP, kicking off the first stage of the overall (though mundane) bullish rally.

What's interesting about this first pane, is we clearly see that when 5,000-tick VWAP compressed back under 10,000-tick VWAP on the topside, a quick pullback to the 10,000-tick VWAP mean, immediately ensued.

Can you identify 'compression' and 'expansion' in terms of energy expended and stored? Please take a look at the following 30-minute chart of the EUR/USD and attempt to do so…

Figure 10.10

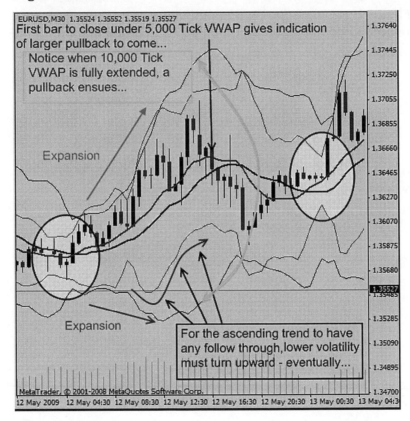

First bar to close under 5,000 Tick VWAP gives indication of larger pullback to come...

Notice when 10,000 Tick VWAP is fully extended, a pullback ensues...

Expansion

Expansion

For the ascending trend to have any follow through, lower volatility must turn upward - eventually...

EURUSD,M30 1.35524 1.35552 1.35519 1.35527

MetaTrader, © 2001-2008 MetaQuotes Software Corp.

12 May 2009   12 May 04:30   12 May 08:30   12 May 12:30   12 May 16:30   12 May 20:30   13 May 00:30   13 May 04:3

What we see is the greatest directional 'bursts' came (coincidentally, *wink - wink*) when 5,000-tick VWAP expanded outside of 10,000-tick VWAP, after a period of compression.

Also coincidentally (or not!) in every occurrence where 5000-tick VWAP volatility compressed back below 10,000-tick VWAP, the EUR/USD experienced a pullback to the mean.

What's more, just a little over the half-way point on the chart (from left to right), you will notice that when the EUR/USD fell below the mean of the 5,000 and 10,000-tick VWAPs (with the 5,000 tick VWAP mean also briefly dropping underneath the 10,000-tick VWAP mean), the EUR/USD never actually 'touched' the 3rd Standard Deviation of the 5,000, or 10,000-tick VWAPs on the downside.

Here's what we know: Through statistics, there is a 99.7% probability will rest within three standard deviations of the mean... We see the aforementioned empirically proved on our charts, as virtually *all* of the data sits within 3-standard deviations of the mean...for both 5,000 and 10,000-tick VWAP.

However, when the EUR/USD tagged the 3rd-standard deviation of the 5,000 tick VWAP, the pair pulled back to the mean. We basically know there will be times when a pair touches the 3rd-standard deviation, but should not trade outside of it for considerable time. What's more, we also know the instance of a pair 'touching' the 3rd-standard deviation is usually followed by a quick pullback to the mean, before the pair travels higher...

We also know when a pair touches the 3rd-standard deviation –once- above, or below the mean (especially on shorter-term periods), the pair most often continues in the direction of the 'touch', after pulling back.

Why?

Because if I am touching the 3rd-standard deviation of a short-term volatility range, I am signaling that price/dollar volume pressure is experiencing 'quick pop' anomalies on the side of the standard deviation touched.

The decline in the EUR/USD under both means – and the lack of the pair's ability to 'touch' the 3rd standard deviation on the downside – signals there just isn't enough volume/dollar pressure to push the pair to a point where it 'touches' a 'distribution outlier', i.e. the 3rd-standard deviation.

What this means to us is that if a pair fails the mean *moving downward*, but then is not able to 'touch' the 3rd-standard deviation on the lower side…and then crosses *back* above the mean in the previous direction, volume/dollars flowing into the currency pair at that particular moment, are clearly bullish.

In the case of the EUR/USD (shown again in Figure 10.11), when the pair failed the mean, there was not enough volume/dollar drive to push the pair into the lower volatility band, and thus, indicated a bullish bias.

Figure 10.11 - Repeated

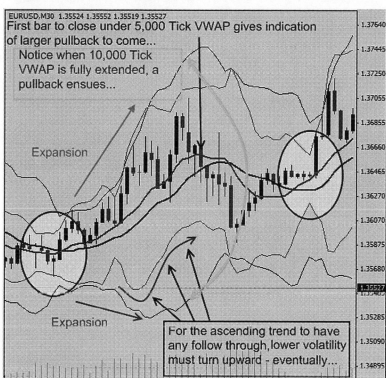

Nothing in *any market* will *ever* travel straight up, or down, so we **HAVE** to expect pullbacks, while also actively seeking to understand why and how they occur.

Figure 10.11 also shows when the 5000-tick VWAP was trading above 10,000-tick VWAP, the instance was telling us short-term dollar/volume was indicating buying momentum, and vice versa for the 5,000-tick VWAP trading below the 10,000-tick VWAP.

Some of the best possible trading opportunities come when 5,000-tick VWAP is trading above 10,000-tick VWAP **and** the 3.2-STD volatility bands have compressed, meaning short-term volatility has contracted underneath long-term volatility...

Then, when the 3.2-STD 5,000-tick volatility bands expand outside of 10,000-tick 3.2-STD volatility, we know we are precisely in the occurrence of short-term volatility *expansion*, whereby price action should follow.

In short, institutional order flow is buying, at least in the near-term. The opposite would be the same for occurrences where 5000-tick VWAP has fallen below 10,000-tick VWAP.

Overall, what we're looking for are high probability instances of institutional order flow showing signs of follow-through, while attempting to eliminate occurrences of taking positions when there is no hope of trending, as seen through short-term volatility compressing.

What I'm saying is when short-term volatility is moving inward, prices simply cannot trend.

Thus, when we see 5,000-tick VWAP **volatility** fall back beneath 10,000-tick VWAP **volatility**, we should be ready for consolidation and/or a potential reversal.

By using WVAV (mapping distribution width/mass outliers), we are able to keep a close eye on volatility expansion and compression, thus taking positions during high probability moments of trending, while also staying out of markets during moments of consolidation. By doing so, we are stepping into the shoes of institutional momentum and letting go of the *old technical indicators* (like stochastics) that really don't work on a short-term basis (consistently) anyway.

With everything that we have just covered, we will now enter into a discussion about what institutional trading is really about, and the theory behind sell side order flow...

Retail traders hardly ever take time to consider the true reality behind what order flow *is* and *why* it occurs in the first place.

CHAPTER ELEVEN

THE PHILOSOPHY OF ORDERFLOW AND MARKETS

I hope the picture surrounding volatility/probability and the mass of distributions is becoming clear... Just in case there are still a few moments of misunderstanding, let's take a moment to go over what's happening.

To start, by watching the compression and expansion of volatility, in relation to intraday trading, we are seeing when and where order flow is picking up and starting to taper. What we want to look for (on 1-minute, 5-minute, 15-minute and 30-minute charts) are instances of *'energy compression'* followed by an attack of the 10,000-tick 3.2-STD by the 3.2-STD 5,000-tick standard deviation.

In terms of volatility/probability, we are really seeing is an instance of distribution *'expansion'*, or a 'punch of force' to get price moving.

We can take positions on a quick pullback of the first attack of the 5,000 -tick VWAP, placing a stop about 20 to 40-PIPs below VWAP. We can then walk our stops up (or down in the opposite case) with higher lows (or lower highs for a descending trend) two bars behind, or a close opposite the 5,000-tick VWAP, or a compression reversal in 5,000-tick 3.2 STD VWAP back under the 10,000-tick 3.2 STD VWAP.

The longer we hold a trade the more willing we should be to give it up if (and when) a compression reversal of 5,000-tick VWAP volatility (reverting) slipping back inside 10,000-tick VWAP volatility occurs.

When the first pullback ensues, if the volatility expansion has truly triggered institutional buying or selling, 5,000-tick VWAP will generally hold the first test. In addition, we should constantly be looking for head fakes, should NO significant volatility expansion occur.

Moreover, when we see a tag of 5,000-tick VWAP, without volatility expansion (meaning there is no energy behind the move), we can think about potentially taking a contrarian position, looking for a mean reversion trade within the channel, or envelope.

However, if the mean reversion position is against a strong trend, it's probably a good idea to stay on the sidelines.

Also, if I am in a winning position and 5,000-tick VWAP compresses back under 10,000-tick VWAP, though I believe there is still reason (fundamentally) to hold the trade, I will seek a close on the opposite side of 10,000-tick VWAP before exiting.

My assumption here is if the move is real, the institutional guys will begin showing up at 10,000-tick VWAP, so as to not miss a 'performance enhancing' fill.

The bottom line here is VWAP volatility/energy expansion denotes high probability of trending to follow, while VWAP volatility/energy compression denotes high probability of consolidation (energy reloading - otherwise known as lateral trading) about to ensue.

There's more to the picture though... As I watch VWAP volatility expand and contract, I'm continually asking myself, *'if I had to work an order for $40 billion right here, would I take the position now, or would I wait?'*

To reiterate, WVAV is NOT a 'red line crosses blue line methodology', what WVAV is showing, however, is some insight into large order flow through dollar volumes moving in and out of markets.

When WVAV volatility/energy is compressing, the instance is indicating a possible reload of energy, also signifying larger players are taking a break to evaluate the situation.

Even major funds aren't sure which way to trade *all* the time, and/or will only buy, or sell in areas where they feel valuation permits such.

In addition, because of the Central Limit Theorem (which means normal distributions should appear in smaller subsets of larger skewed data), we can also infer that because VWAP and regular moving averages are mobile, eventually the currency, stock, commodity, whatever, will revert back to the mean.

The reversion occurrence I've just mentioned is an absolute empirical fact, as the mean is mobile.

What I'm saying is because the mean is following price, eventually the currency (or stock, commodity, etc…) will retrace VWAP. The question is: when?

The more data we're measuring, the longer price can stay away from mean; however, eventually, price will return to the mean, because the mean is following the price.

It's important to note that when trading equities, or other instruments where VWAP resets at the end of each trading day, seeking mean reversion positions (based on VWAP) on a swing trading basis is not always the best idea.

Why?

Because at the end of the day (literally), the mean resets and there is no more reason (in terms of day-to-day VWAP) for the security to revert 'across the mean' than any/all circumstances that caused the initial divergence in the previous session.

In terms of day-to-day VWAP, we're talking about a 'resetting' of mass each session. Thus, for mean reversion on a longer-term basis, either a greater amount of VWAP data must be studied, or another set of data like price action (data without volume), must be taken into accord.

The issue at hand is on a daily basis, there are many various factors affecting a stock, or currency.

(For a moment, we will focus an example on equities.)

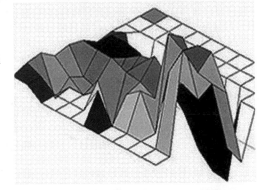

Figure 11. 1

Please take a moment to glance at Figure 11.1, imagining the image as a 'topographic map' of intraday price data (Stock XYX), based on the factors affecting trading action.

Now, please image (for the sake of example) Stock XYZ reported positive earnings today, which have triggered buying in the stock. The darkest regions of the map specifically highlight earnings related buying, while the lighter sections indicate buying due to earnings related news of another (though related) company, which reported yesterday. Both sets of news are positive, shown in the overall upward price action (as denoted in the data *above* the flat plane, which is the previous session's closing price or 'breakeven' for today).

Again, because earnings of the 'related' (highly correlated) other company were positive yesterday, and the earnings of the Stock XYZ are positive today, both sets of news entice investors to buy more than sell.

Clearly, because price is ascending today, VWAP would travel upward during the session as well.

However, what happens if the two previously mentioned companies are tier two stocks (meaning lesser market caps) than the sector leaders. Moreover, what if, a highly correlated *tier-one* company reports significantly negative earnings numbers tomorrow?

Because the tier one company likely has greater pull on the entire sector, the positive news of the two smaller companies could fall victim to sector-wide selling, based on the negative news of the larger, more highly coveted tier-one company.

What we're talking about is the larger gravity (weighting) effect of highly correlated stocks, sector, index, market, or other financial instruments that could influence the outcome of tomorrow's trading, over stock-specific news of today.

In short, because we are resetting the mean (VWAP) each session (in equities) performance of the benchmark must be evaluated by what is taking place *today*, and only *today*.

What I'm saying, is whenever we reset the mean (the same would hold true for a 5,000, or 10,000 tick reset in Forex), we must stop, take notice of the event and reconsider the factors pushing, or pulling on the instrument in question.

To rephrase, when VWAP is reset, the instance of price moving away from the benchmark would not necessarily be a specific derivative of mean divergence, or mean reversion from the previous session. Because VWAP was reset, the occurrence would really be pure divergence, based on the simple fact that the benchmark was just re-set to zero.

The longer VWAP is 'running' however, the greater the probability that price will eventually revert to the mean, based on the concept that the mean is following the price.

Where does all this lead us?

To a much needed discussion of the term 'benchmark.'

MOST RETAIL TRADERS NEVER CONSIDER THE TERM 'BENCHMARK'

To some, it might feel as though the following discussion should have come earlier in the book. And while (arguably) that may be so, I decided to save it for when we were already knee deep in VWAP, as I believe already having the visual picture of what VWAP is (in your mind), will help the following concepts come through more easily.

Over the following pages, impatient traders will likely scoff at the information and quickly breeze over the concepts of *order flow* and benchmark trading.

However, I would like to mention the next few pages might be the most important in this entire book...

We must have a better understanding of who is who in trading (meaning who is buying and selling) and how and why such influences volatility.

The following pages are critical for anyone seeking to move beyond simply being an '*average retail trader,*' to truly finding a greater understanding of intraday volatility.

I've spent many hours attempting to understand why retail traders fight –*tooth and nail*– understanding the larger 'paradigm' behind institutional order flow, versus the cowboy jockey directional '*give me a quick and easy brainless technical indicator*' mentality most at-home traders embrace.

In the fall of 2008, I believe I (partially) found the answer...please allow me a moment to tell you the story...

Over the final few months of 2008, my trading was suffering... I was having trouble diagnosing the issues causing the poor performance, as it seemed the more I looked, the less I came up with in terms of answers.

In the end, I found two main catalysts for the temporary deterioration in my trading.

First, the market had changed and I hadn't.

I was still working on developing new models to compensate for the excess volatility brought on by the financial crisis, while also attempting to compensate for the moment-to-moment excess volatility of retail traders, both of which had begun to surface in July.

I was not really having any trouble perceiving the larger direction of markets, but I constantly found myself losing intraday.

In short, I was developing new volatility models in a rough market and I was paying the price for deploying new concepts in real time, with real money.

My Forex Force trading service on Wall Street Rock Star finished the year up over 1,000-pips, but November and December were brutal.

There's another piece to the story here too...

In late October of 2008, I traveled to one last U.S. speaking engagement, before leaving for China...

During a break, one of the attendees found me outside, and we began to chat... A few minutes into our conversation the chap said, '*this is incredible information (referencing my delivery of common sense fundamentals), but can you just give me something easy I can just make money with today.*'

To date, almost no other comment by any reader, subscriber, or audience participant has ever messed with my head more. I was so up-ended by the comment; I had trouble returning to the room to finish the talk...

It took about three months to figure out why the comment was disturbing... What I've come to realize is:

When it comes to educating others, all my time and effort...years of learning... All of my time preparing a clear, concise, cutting-edge understanding of fundamentals within currency markets is/was a waste.

Wasted because most people do not want to know anyway.

I realized that most retail traders only want 'blue line crosses red line' signals hand delivered, gift wrapped, without ever truly even lifting a finger to learn about markets, or the indicators they're trading from.

From that day, I lost all of the wind in my sails to run the trading service, and while my new models were still suffering in deployment, I had lost the desire to trade too, which was <u>**really**</u> bad, because trading is my bread and butter.

In January of 2009, I shut the service down and I will never spearhead another intraday *'trading specific'* service ever again.

We're planning on launching a new live trading room and a professional trading research service on WallStreetRockStar.com this year, but neither will be an intraday trading service telling people when to buy and sell.

After months of brooding about the audience participant's comment in the Fall of 2008, I realized I needed to let go of the service, because the performance was suffering and I just wasn't into it anymore.

What I also realized was that most retail traders don't want to learn the nuts and bolts of what truly moves markets… When I let go of the comment and concluded that this will likely be my last book…I again found my passion for trading…

What I also come to terms with is an understanding that most retail traders just can't see the value in understanding fundamentals. Moreover, because applying fundamentals to intraday trading takes a significant amount of effort, it's easier to just look for signals from a MACD, or stochastics, or whatever else someone said works well. But regular technicals (without a rock solid understanding of why what's happening is really happening) only sets traders up for failure.

In the end, I ask you to please turn over every stone, including the forthcoming discussion of buy side, sell side, benchmark, etc…

Sometimes the most important –and greatest– nuggets of information are found in the most unassuming places, **like the true foundation of the events occurring**, not in the outcome…the red line crossing blue line technical events.

Also in my drawn out explanation of why most retail traders never really consider what, where and why institutional trading is happening…is simply in the question:

Why would retail traders be motivated to step into the minds of the big guys anyway?

After all, retail traders are trying to make money moving in and out of markets directionally, always with a short or long-term bias.

Institutional traders, however, are thinking *risk* and *performance*.

It's not the retail trader's fault really that he or she has no clue about what's really driving much of intraday action. After all, most of the information provided to traders regarding *what* to look at, *why* to look at it, and *how* to trade it, is generally flawed from the start anyway.

Forex brokers aren't going to tell you, because most often they are in the business of 'broker/dealer' meaning they're taking the other side of your trade...

When we understand that much of intraday trading action volatility has more to do with the term *'benchmark'*, over *'pick a direction'*, we begin to put the odds back on our side.

I believe that if I were to ask 99% of the retail readers what the term *'benchmark'* means, most would say *'index'*, or something similar. Yes, indexes are 'benchmarks', but for our purposes, we're looking for something different, something greater.

Benchmark –as we will use the term here- is the capacity of trading efficacy, by which institutions and institutional traders are both: measured and paid.

What we're talking about is *'buy side'* versus *'sell side'* versus *buying and selling*.

One thing I know for sure is if I were to ask 10 retail traders (*who have never traded or worked for a financial firm professionally*) what the differences between buy side, sell side and buying and selling are, 10 out of 10 would get the answer incorrect.

It just is what it is…

We need to know though, to be the best traders we can be…

BIOVAP MAN AND THE INSANITY OF DR. WATERMELON STUFFER

It is no secret; the business of trading is overcomplicated from the start…

For the retail trader who attempts to dig into understanding of how institutions work, the door is seemingly impenetrable.

Because of such, there is a massive breakdown in the retail community's understanding of what 'buy side', 'sell side', and buying _and_ selling are.

Why should you care?

What we have to understand is that **real trading** is the actual application of expectations to **real markets**.

Analysts analyze; however, traders apply money to reality.

The best analysts in the world often make the worst traders.

Why?

Because while they can perceive an outcome over the long haul, they have no clue how to apply the information in the short-term.

When we truly attempt to understand *how and why* institutional traders are doing what they are, and what they might do next, we're stepping out of the *analyst fairytale world* and into the *real* battlefield of *now*.

The bottom line is, if we expect to succeed in trading we MUST take the time to understand *why* what is happening today…is happening.

Why what is happening this hour, is happening this hour…

Why what is happening this minute, is happening this minute…

We must step beyond simple technical and fundamental indicators and into the minds and motivations of big order flow...to finally see 'beyond the curtain.'

BUY SIDE/SELL SIDE

Briefly, buy side is anyone who is trying to make money on the perceived movement(s) of a financial instrument.

Conversely, sell side is anyone who is trying to make money on the people…who are attempting to make money…on picking the direction of a financial instrument.

Moreover, buying and selling is something anyone who wants to play the game must do…

 Both buy side and sell side…buy and sell.

Perhaps the only people who don't actually buy and sell (in the game of buy side/sell side) are sell side analysts who are merely telling people what to buy and sell, in an attempt to get more people to buy and sell.

Buy side analysts, are often making actual recommendations to buy or sell, which a fund is actually taking action upon.

As Larry Harris notes in the book Trading and Exchanges, "buy side traders are investors, borrowers, hedgers asset exchangers and gamblers."

(I hate to say it, but most retail traders (daytraders and Forex traders specifically) fall more under the 'gamblers' category.

An important distinction differentiating buy side and sell side Harris points out is, "*The Trading industry has a buy side and a sell side. The buy side consists of traders who buy exchange services. Liquidity is the most important of these services. Liquidity is the ability to trade when you want to trade.*"[52]

Buy Side

The portion of the securities business in which institutional orders originate. In most instances, the buy side is limited to institutional buyers such as pension-fund portfolio managers. Individual investors are usually excluded from the buy side because they are not considered formal participants in the securities business.

BusinessDictionary.com

In terms of being 'retail' (a buy side trader, just like a fund trader), you are paying commissions for the ability to guess whether a currency, stock, or commodity is going up, or down.

You are paying for liquidity, which your broker is providing. The broker is 'sell side', as he is providing you with the means to place orders.

Also of important note, Harris points out the concept of *'movement of current income into the future.'*

Buy side traders are really using what they have **now**, in an attempt to realize another value (hopefully greater!) in the future. One cannot trade with more than they have now, as even with margin, once what you have *now* is gone…you have *nothing*.

One of my favorite sayings of all time is from Warren Buffet who states, *"zero times anything is zero."*

For example, as a 'buy side trader', you can leverage $10 into $100 (10:1 margin) in an attempt to make even more money directionally in markets, but if you're wrong, and your original $10 disappears, you have nothing.

In detail, sell side is/are the people/companies providing buy side with liquidity and/or services to effect and/or improve transactions.

In short, institutional traders who are 'moving orderflow' are sell side traders.

Here's what's important to note, sell side traders can both work for a corporation, or remain independent, utilizing the sell-side services of other exchange related companies.

What I mean by this is, some independent traders actually own a seat on an exchange, where they effect transactions to work orders for buy side traders.

However, because they are not their own clearing firm, they must utilize the sell side services of another firm to achieve liquidity.

Basically, when sell side is moving orderflow, buy side individuals or funds are using their services, and are either willing to pay a higher price for their tenured trading ability to work large orders (usually because of long-lasting relationships), or whatever *'edge'* the sell side firm, or trader brings to the table, in terms of helping the buy side achieve a more prosperous fill.

These guys are a type of sell side middle-men, and are acting in a 'broker' capacity, but utilize another firm (a dealer), to clear the actual trades.

Really, sell side means dealer, broker, or *'duel traders.'* It is also important to note, exchanges are in the mix as well, competing with brokerage houses to *'arrange trades.'*

Finally, in our discussion of sell side (and buy side, in terms of definition), it is also important to note (as Harris points out); sell side **ONLY** exists because the buy side is willing to pay for their services.

Sell Side

The portion of the securities business in which orders are transacted. The sell side includes retail brokers, institutional brokers and traders, and research departments. If an institutional portfolio manager changes jobs and becomes a registered representative, he or she has moved from the buy side to the sell side.

BusinessDictionary.com

Now that we've covered buy side and sell side...a few readers may still be inquiring: *Who does the buying and who does the selling...buy side, or sell side?*

Both. Both buy side and sell side...*buy and sell*.

The terms buy side and sell side are simply definitions of the 'capacity' of buying and selling motivation.

The 'capacity' of buy side *buying and selling* is to make money on the movement(s) of financial instruments. The 'capacity' of sell side *buying and selling* is to provide buy side with liquidity, or to create 'price improvement' on large orders.

Easy enough right? Right.

As I write, I'm wondering if readers are now asking what's the larger point of this entire discussion – of buy side and sell side? If you are, I applaud you. The larger picture is exactly within the question itself– the larger picture...is 'the big picture' of why volatility exists within intraday trading in the first place, but it seems to me that almost no retail traders actually '*get it.*'

See, most retail traders consider the 'big picture' to be their monthly charts, or 'those boring fundamentals.'

However, in terms of intraday volatility, the big picture is really within institutional benchmarks. When we understand institutional 'benchmark trading' we will also find a greater understanding of:

1. Why retail technical indicators are built for failure...

2. Why most retail traders lose...

3. How the big guys perceive information differently...

4. Why having an institutional mindset is so important…

5. How we can use volatility, probability and benchmarks (like VWAP) in our own trading to take advantage of potential institutional order flow pending.…

I would like to take a moment to quote John Pinney (JP Morgan) from the book, *Coping with Institutional Orderflow* (Robert A. Schwartz, John Wiley & Sons, 2007) who stated, ***"I will do my best to convey the essence of the research we recently completed on the cost of dynamics associated with institutional orderflow. To a retail trader, the stock exchanges look like a vending machine. An order is placed, the delivery is made and the execution comes back. The broker has completed his or her job, often within seconds."***

Pinney is right, the retail trader DOES believe his, or her platform is nothing more than a vending machine…

Order in, position in, order in, position out.

It is here that we further answer the question of why the retail trader never even knows to consider the mindset of institutional order flow…

Pinney goes on to state, ***"But this is not the case for the institutional trader. As we know, the order size – the 'peg' of institutional trading interest – is much larger than the 'hole' size of the exchange process."***

<u>**PLEASE READ CAREFULLY:**</u>

Take a moment to ponder what Pinney has just described as the concept of *institutional orders being **larger** than the 'hole' of the exchange process…*

If you take one thing away from this entire book…

<u>Please take the following words:</u>

Institutions must constantly break up <u>large orders</u> into smaller chunks; otherwise, they would constantly be attempting to shove a watermelon through a muffler.

Not only would the people around them notice, but also, the event would be both sloppy and ineffective…

In normal circumstances, sell side traders are able to dice the watermelon (large order) and discreetly slip the pieces into the market one-by-one (iceberging).

However, what happens if the car (price) the muffler is attached to…is about to leave the parking lot?

Even institutional traders are sometimes caught off-guard and are forced to start shoving the watermelon through…you know what.

What we're talking about is volatility…derived from big buy side politely asking sell side to insert watermelon into mufflers, all day long.

Sell side is Dr. Watermelon Stuffer and all day long he's receiving orders from Boss Big Bank (buy side).

Moreover, what if he's been told to get the watermelon in the muffler *'or else'* and the car starts to move? You guessed it; he might have to run after the car, trying to shove the whole watermelon (or pieces of) in to the muffler, before the car (price) gets away completely.

What we are talking about is the occurrence where markets begin moving (on low, or high volume) and are seemingly propelled by constant buying, or selling.

Now, assume you are Dr. Watermelon Stuffer for a moment and you're a little smarter than most...

You know the driver is *'just making a delivery,'* and he will actually be back in about 15-minutes... It's a good thing you know too, because you still have half a watermelon to cram into the muffler.

Of course, when the car pulls back into the parking lot...you would start cramming again, before the car pulls out another time. Big Boss Bank is paying you on your performance...based on how much of the watermelon you can get into the muffler, as neatly as possible, before the car pulls out of the lot. If the car pulls out of the lot and you've been able to neatly (and discreetly) dice the entire watermelon and insert it into the muffler, you will be paid handsomely.

But what if you suddenly figured out you'd goofed and crammed all of the little, neatly sliced pieces of watermelon into the wrong car?

It's going to be ugly trying to get the watermelon back out.

What we're talking about is volatility, when the big guys are wrong.

What if, you crammed the whole watermelon into the muffler and it is the not only the wrong car, but the driver just got in?

Roll up your sleeves, because things are about to not only get messy, but frantic, at the same time.

What we're talking about is volatility.

What if you have an absolutely massive watermelon to stuff…but you know the driver's schedule, and thankfully he will be back 30-minutes after each time he leaves to make a delivery…

Each time the car pulls out of the lot, you'd likely just take a seat and wait for him to come back, to begin inserting more of the watermelon into the muffler.

What we're talking about is the occurrence of institutional traders buying at, or near VWAP (or other benchmark) and why they don't often chase price…

Unlike the retail 'breakout' trader, the institutional watermelon stuffer knows the car will be back…

So where is the retail trader trading in this whole event of stuffing watermelons into mufflers?

He's standing over on the curb, waiting for the driver to pull by, to see if he can exchange a couple quarters for a dollar bill…completely oblivious to the whole *stuffing of watermelons thing,* happening just a few feet away.

Fact is, when we understand what's happening on the institutional sell side, we suddenly understand *'why that really weird uptight guy standing behind the car – is always holding a watermelon.'*

However, to see Dr. Watermelon Stuffer, we have to wear special glasses, because there's one thing I forgot to mention… Dr. Watermelon is invisible *most* of the time.

To see him, we have to wear special volatility / probability, VWAP, TWAP, LHOC benchmark glasses.

And we're not always going to be able to see him, even when we think we can, but the longer we wear the glasses, the better we will become at spotting Dr. Watermelon Stuffer, even when he's mostly transparent.

(By the way, these are special cars…that even when the mufflers are crammed with melons, the engines do not cut out… Things just run differently in Financial-Market-Land.)

Here's the thing about almost **all** of the 'other' retail traders though… They're standing around on corners, all with the same quarters, trying to exchange their change for the same dollars…

They're easy to spot too, as they're all wearing the same *fancy pants* and *'blue line crosses red line'* MACD, stochastics, Fibonacci, moving average, relative strength [*whatever*] jackets.

But they're _all_ oblivious to the real game.

The real game isn't even about quarters and dollars, it's about cramming watermelons into mufflers, before the driver leaves with the car in one direction, or another. Fact is, all of the retail traders (in their fancy technical analysis jackets) never even **understood** the real game from the start, which is exactly why they will always be exchanging quarters for dollars on corners.

However, because they're all just standing there, obvious to the world, money in hand…eventually, they all get mugged too.

Many retail traders believe they have an edge though…

They've got a little buddy, who happens to be real fast at math, and can regurgitate _fancy pants signals_ all day long.

He tells the retail traders (_who think they are smarter than the collective whole_) when other retail traders are about to change jackets. Sometimes his _fancy pants signals_ work, but really, he's missed the whole game too.

And eventually, when the driver changes schedules, or routes…or when Dr. Watermelon Stuffer changes his entire outlook on his watermelon stuffing process, or even worse, gets a new tool to stuff watermelons with, the retail trader's little buddy (FYI, his name is EA, for Expert Advisor, but his Mom calls him _Black Box System_) starts to get it wrong… One more time, the retail trader is just stuck there, standing on the corner with his little pal, getting mugged (again!), scratching his head…

See, the whole game is really about the watermelons **_and_** the driver. Concerning the driver, it's about when he's going, why he's going, and where he's going…

While the car is '*price*', the driver's name is '*fundamentals*'.

Let me tell you, since the driver has so much on his mind, he changes his philosophy and outlook daily…

Sometimes though, he gets an idea in his head…and he just keeps on going, until he's out of gas.

In rare occurrences, the retail trader actually really **attempts** to figure out the driver's schedule, but the occurrence is rare.

Regardless, retail traders fail to understand the money (*the real money*) isn't **just** in figuring out the driver's schedule, but **ALSO** in knowing (and seeing) Dr. Watermelon Stuffer's probable plan too.

For the retail trader, the real money is in betting other's (who are watching the car too), when the driver will come and go… Moreover, the intraday trader who has the special x-ray glasses though, knows to only bet when Dr. Watermelon Stuffer is at work behind the car, because when Dr. Watermelon Stuffer is furiously in motion, the car is about to move.

Volatility and probability help determine when the car is about to move, how far it might go, and when it is coming back.

Benchmarks are knowing where Dr. Watermelon Stuffer may begin stuffing, or start retrieving his crushed fruit, or used in conjunction with volatility and probability, where he might just decide to sit the whole game out for awhile.

Fundamentals tie the whole thing together.

Typical technical analysis (used on its own) is a *joke.*

Remember the first chapter about Superman wearing his underpants on the outside?

The retail trader who understands Dr. Watermelon Stuffer is: BIOVAP Man – Benchmark Institutional Orderflow Volatility and Probability Man, and is a superhero for sure…even if he looks a little goofy.

He wears his underpants on the outside, and he sports x-ray glasses.

Dr. Watermelon Stuffer tries to make fun of him, but BIOVAP Man just smiles, nods and replies, *"Whatever melon-boy, just keep on stuffing and everything will be alright…"*

CHAPTER TWELVE

WAVE • PM

Whistler Active Volatility Energy • Price Mass

As we enter Chapter Twelve, there are likely some questions still remaining on how WVAV *and* order-flow come together in the larger picture at hand.

As there should be…

Over the following pages, however, we will begin to tie all of the pieces together in one large cohesive model, for traders to utilize as they navigate markets daily.

With all of the aforementioned in mind, please put any questions on the subject of Dr. Watermelon Stuffer and BIOVAP Man on ice for a few moments, as we cover the final piece of the larger whole: WAVE • PM, or Whistler Active Volatility Energy • Price Mass.

In our previous discussions of mass, we know two things:

1. Mass is a larger component of price movement, via distributions, seen through a Newtonian lens where: Force = Mass * Acceleration, or Mass = Acceleration / Force.

2. The larger the mass, the more difficult an item is to move. Conversely, the less mass an item retains, the easier it is to not only spur into motion, but keep in motion, as well.

With common sense physics in mind, it is easy to begin to understand why unforeseen volatility sometimes surfaces within almost any market, especially in terms of 'head fakes'.

When an equity or currency pair is staging a supposed breakout, but there is simply too much mass to be moved, it *'just makes sense'* that price would fail to **_continue_** upward, or downward…and thus, fall back into the previous range.

What we are really talking about here is the compression and expansion of energy, in terms of *mini distributions.*

If a distribution is already at a point of maximum expansion (too much mass), the likelihood of continuation (trending) into a higher or lower range…is not very likely.

As a picture tells a thousand words, it may be easier to soak up the previously mentioned concept with an actual chart…

Figure 12.1 shows the EUR/USD on an hourly basis, where I have drawn a set of 50-period 3.2 STD volatility bands, to show the 'outlier' points of the distribution.

As you can see, during the recent rally, the 50-period distribution was 'expanding' in width, or in other words...mass. As the EUR/USD traveled into the 1.4030 area, the 50-period mass became too 'heavy' for the pair to continue upward...

Thus, as the consolidation (and compression of the 50-period 3.2 volatility bands) shows, the pair traveled sideways, thus allowing the total mass of the distribution to 'compress' for another move.

The solution to the problem of being able to readily 'see mass' within a stock, currency pair, or commodity? The solution is rather simple; however, like most concepts in Volatility Illuminated, the theory was the most difficult part to unearth...

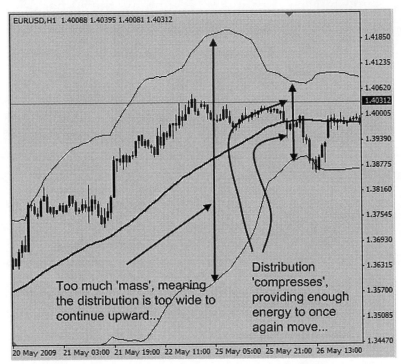

Figure 12. 1

The theory behind measuring the *mass* of subset distributions is simply to visually 'map' or identify the total width of both short and long-term distributions, through a value converting mass into an easily recognizable/understandable format, like an oscillator.

Thus, what we have taken two sets of Bollinger Bands (volatility bands) and simply normalized the total width of each, in range from 0 to 1.

What this means is with our new 'gauge' (imagine an RPM gauge for an engine) we know the closer the oscillator is to 1, the more mass a distribution has, and the less likely the chances of a continued up, or down move, without some sort of consolidation *'cooling'* or *'compression'* of energy first.

In the following image (Figure 12.2), readers will notice I have added the WAVE • PM oscillator in the bottom window…

Please observe that there are two lines in the oscillator, one measuring a 50-period distribution, and one measuring a 14-period distribution.

Obviously, the 14-period line is the more jagged of the two, as we are measuring less data.

Below the 0.5 oscillator level, mass can said to be consolidating, while a move above the 0.5 is generally marked with a period of distribution expansion, or extended price movement.

It is VITAL to note that the **WAVE • PM does NOT give any indication to direction whatsoever**; rather, the oscillator is a gauge of potential energy left within a distribution's expansion cycle…

If price is moving to the downside and WAVE • PM is moving up, the event simply means there is more 'gas' left for an extended move…

Stating the aforementioned another way, if price is moving **downward** and the 14-period WAVE • PM is traveling **upward**; the occurrence indicates the 14-period distribution is widening out, or releasing energy.

Conversely, if price is moving **upward** and the 14-period WAVE • PM (for example) is traveling **upward**, the occurrence indicates the 14-period distribution is widening out, or releasing energy.

It doesn't matter whether price is moving up, or down, if WAVE • PM is moving up, the distribution measured is 'expanding' and/or releasing energy. If WAVE • PM is moving down, the distribution measured is 'compressing', or storing energy.

If price is moving upward and WAVE • PM is moving upward, the event simply means there is more 'gas left' in the move. When WAVE • PM is between 0.7 and 0.9, the event is similar to the RPM gauge on your car showing about 2,800 RPM's, or maximum pull...

Figure 12.2

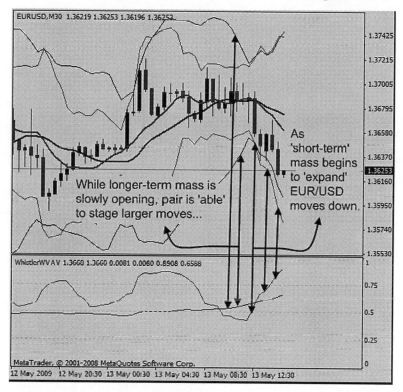

In the above image, you will notice when short-term WAVE • PM is descending; the EUR/USD is in phase of consolidation. Conversely, as noted in the three right-most arrows, when short-term WAVE • PM starts to move above the 0.5 mark, the EUR/USD begins breaking out of the relative range to the downside...

As we've already covered in the book, we know that when short-term volatility is compressing, versus longer-term volatility, the changes of trending a slim. However, when short-term volatility is torridly expanding, the occurrence is telling us prices are on the move and short-term volatility is attempting to push longer-term volatility (or the longer-term distribution) upward, or downward.

Again though, WAVE • PM does not provide an indication of direction, rather, the indicator shows whether a move presents high probability of follow-through, or not, based on how much 'mass' there is to move. It's just common sense that a distribution with less mass is easier to move, than a distribution with a significant amount of mass.

Now, please look at image 12.3, for more insight into the WAVE • PM indicator…

As you will notice, in every instance the short-term WAVE • PM mass line (denoted as the thicker of the two indicator lines) falls, the EUR/USD experiences a period of comparatively lateral trading, or a *pullback* in the relative range. WAVE • PM is visually identifying the 'compression' of the short-term distribution within the larger distribution. Just FYI, we are mapping a 50-period 3.2 STD and the 14-period 3.2 STD in the example here.

However, it really would not matter if were mapping 1.2-standard deviations, or 3.2-standard deviations, as both show the expansion and compression of mass.

What you will also notice is in the first part of the move up, the longer-term distribution was in an 'expansionary' phase, but then started to compress while the EUR/USD *continued* the final phase of the upward movement.

Why?

Because when a trend first begins, the multiplier effect in the standard deviation formula causes both bands to widen out... However, for price to continue in one direction (up, for example) the bottom band must eventually turn around and begin moving upward with the price...

The two bands cannot move away from one another infinitely, as the 'lower' third standard deviation must - eventually- move with the distribution, upward, as noted in the example here. Thus, if a trend is real, the longer-term distribution (again, we're measuring the longer-term distribution via 50-periods of data here), will eventually turn upward and as the lower band pulls up, will show consolidation in the WAVE • PM indicator.

What this means is two things:

1. During the initial expansionary phase of a trend, both long-term and short-term WAVE • PM should witness upward movement.

2. As the top of a trend nears, longer-term WAVE • PM will begin to turn over and 'consolidate.' By the term *'trend'*, I am referring to the *'cycle'* of the relevant trend either up, or down.

Figure 12.3

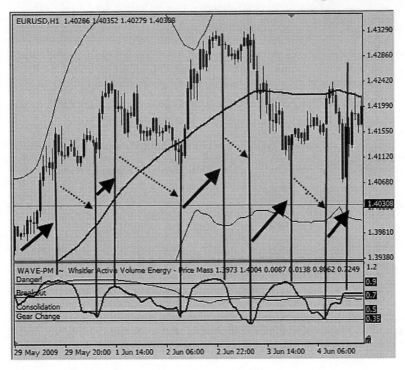

What we know from all of the above is our greatest probability entries (to capitalize on trending) occur when both short and long-term WAVE • PM are below 0.5 and are beginning to move upward.

To active traders, WAVE • PM below 0.50 indicates that energy of both short and long-term distributions has compressed, and we currently are sitting in the greatest possible moment for a potential breakout (or breakdown) to be followed by trending, via energy expansion, because both short and long-term distributions have little mass to move.

Again, the lesser the mass, the greater the probability of seeing 'follow through', once order flow begins pushing...

What's more, as we previously covered in Chapter Ten, once a stock, or currency begins ascending, we can view the event as the 'car' beginning to move out of the parking lot.

If Dr. Watermelon Stuffer did not previously have all of his melon in the muffler, chances are, he's going to get a little messy if he thinks the car is about to pull out of the lot. Henceforth, the instance of 'quick acceleration', often appearing when a pair initially breaks above (or below) a consolidation range, seen through a breach of support, or resistance.

To reiterate some of what we have just covered, when WAVE • PM is declining (especially noted in short-term WAVE • PM falling) the distribution is experiencing consolidation and thus, lateral trending will likely occur.

When WAVE • PM is witnessing a period of expansion (upward movement), the greater the likelihood of continued trending, especially if the WAVE • PM indicator is rising out from underneath the 0.5 area.

WAVE • PM, WVAV AND QUAD CCI

Now, pulling everything together, we will see the 'perfect setup', which well-informed currency traders (and even stock, commodities and futures, etc…) will want to look for… The following example shows a downward move; however, such is precisely what we look for in an up-move, as well…

In the following image of the EUR/USD, traders will notice the pair had consolidated near the 1.4080 to 1.4120 area, and was threatening a break…

Most important, traders will notice both the 50-period and 14-period WAVE • PM lines were trading just below 0.5, as the EUR/USD first broke support in the 1.4044 area. Confirming a potential down-move, 100-period CCI was just falling into the 'Containment Zone', meaning that it was falling back below the 1.25 standard deviation area, on the way back to the mean. Next, traders will also notice 50-period CCI had already also broken into the Containment Zone, while short-term 5,000-tick VWAP 3.2-STD volatility bands (dashed lines) were expanding outside of long-term volatility, as measured by 10,000-tick VWAP 3.2-STD (solid black lines) in the price portion of the chart.

The chart was telling us, '*short-term volatility is spiking outside of long-term volatility*', while also indicating mass had 'compressed' enough that probability of trending was high. In other words, price distribution mass had compressed to a point where a burst of downside trading action could easily get the ball rolling... And it did...

The EUR/USD quickly fell over 100-PIPs, before the WAVE • PM 14-period line turned over to 'compress.'

At the same time, short-term VWAP volatility pulled back inside of long-term volatility, thus giving us further indication that the EUR/USD was about to enter a period of 'pullback', or consolidation.

During this time of consolidation, not one of our CCI's really gave us much indication of the pullback happening, other than the 14-period, which rallied from below -100 almost into the 0-line, before failing again.

Why?

Because CCI only measures prices outside of the 1.25 standard deviation area. However, price consolidation on shorter-term time periods can occur, without longer-term CCI breaking back below the 1st-standard deviation. The occurrence really indicates the longer-term distribution is still on the move, however, in the short-term, a pullback to the mean is in store.

The savvy volatility/probability trader, however, was cognizant of the pullback, as noted in the 14-period WAVE • PM falling short of the 0.9 line, declining down into the 0.55 area...

Because short-term mass had compressed, smart volatility traders would have begin looking for another leg down in the move.

Coincidentally (or not), during the pullback, the EUR/USD rallied right up into 5,000 and 10,000-tick VWAP, where it again failed.

Why the failure at VWAP?

Because if a move is for real, the benchmarks are precisely where Dr. Watermelon Stuffer will begin 'cramming his watermelons into the muffler', to achieve the best possible benchmark performance fills, for the day. The institutional trader knows that should the EUR/USD drop again (which it did), he needs to execute his orders 'better than' VWAP (which he did), as VWAP drops with sustained selling. As VWAP declines later in the session, his previous fills into VWAP will then show 'better than VWAP' performance.

Do you see how everything we have covered comes together?

What we're really talking about is watching 'mass' for 'viability' of a sustained move, and then watching for the precise points during the move where Dr. Watermelon Stuffer must begin wading into markets in order to achieve the best fills possible–where his performance will be measured- in relation to VWAP. A pullback to the mean (VWAP) is to be expected in any ascending, or descending move… However, when longer-term CCI is indicating that the instrument is still trading outside of the 1st-standard deviation, or below the mean, we know the trend is still in effect. Then, if mass (as measured through WAVE • PM) still has room to widen ***and*** short-term volatility spikes outside of longer-term volatility, we know to immediately take positions with the trend, to capitalize on another bolt of price action.

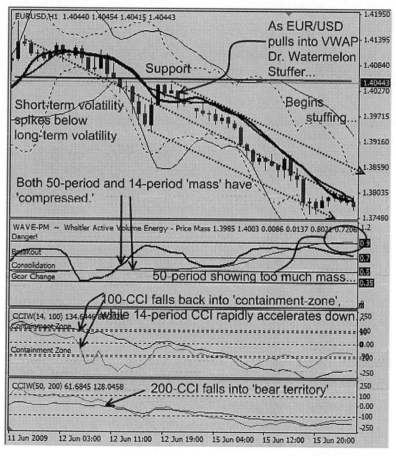

Figure 12. 4

Mark Whistler   •   Volatility Illuminated   •   Page 401 of 466

Again, we can look for true 'vigor' where a move starts and ends, through the expansion of short-term volatility, outside of long-term volatility, and conversely, where lateral trading (back to VWAP or a larger reversal) may take place, through short-term volatility compressing back underneath longer-term volatility.

Moreover, in Figure 12.4, you will notice I have marked longer-term (50-period) WAVE • PM as seemingly dangerous, when it was trading above 0.9.

What the occurrence meant to us was the distribution was too wide, meaning it had too much mass, and the likelihood of consolidation, or a reversal was highly likely.

In the above case of the EUR/USD, exactly such happened, as just after the 50-Period WAVE • PM line started to fall back below 0.9, meaning the distribution was compressing, the EUR/USD experienced a rugged period of lateral/choppy trading.

Personally, during periods of longer-term distributions compressing (after a large upward or downward move), I prefer to just sit out of markets and let the other guys slug out choppy sideways trading…

Then, when both the 50-period and 14-period distributions have again consolidated, I will look for short-term volatility spiking outside of long-term volatility (and a breach of major support, or resistance), to take a position 'with the trend.'

In essence, we should refuse to take positions when 'mass' is too large and the risk of mean reversion choppy trading is substantial...unless of course, we are specifically attempting to take advantage of a mean-reversion type of position.

In the end, when we apply volatility/probability to the larger concept of subset distribution *mass* compression and expansion, we not only are able to navigate markets with incredible perception, but are able to transcend intraday volatility that kills most traders.

CHAPTER THIRTEEN

THE DYNAMIC MOVEMENTS OF SUBSET DISTRIBUTIONS

Within the following pages, the concepts presented are intended to not only challenge the reader's perception of traditional descriptive statistics and distributions even further, but the greater awareness volatility and probability within markets as well. Moreover, the application of volatility/probability to markets was actually derived through countless hours of philosophical-reasoning behind the 'theory' of the concepts at hand.

Beyond math, the principals within the final chapters of Volatility Illuminated are intended to invoke fresh conversation about common perceptions of accepted standards of price movements within markets.

It is the author's intention to show that both empirical and non-empirical events within time, existence and markets are comprised of both normal and non-normal distributions, whereby the identification of an imperfection within the smaller subset of distributions surfacing in the larger skewed distribution of markets (and time) is actually the 'imperfection of perfection' that must remain for time to persist, markets to move, and stretching to the bounds of philosophy, to empirically prove some of the toughest questions regarding *price action*, all at the same time. In essence, identifying imperfection within subset distributions validates volatility and movement within markets, time, and history.

Furthermore, the author will show that volatility within distributions is relative only so far as probability -measured in standard deviations– infers information (and subset distributions) can never maintain a static state. However, much like time will not cease to progress, neither will the movement of information affecting markets and life; thus the traditional perception of risk probability and standard deviations as static...is flawed.

Within distributions –and the outliers of volatility– resides variance, or the probability of tails. However, when understanding that markets will never remain stagnate, one comes to terms with the understanding that 'outlier variables' are actually the pivot points whereby markets shift, prices move, distributions evolve and time progresses.

Historically, participants have approached markets (in terms of descriptive statistics) with the perspective that one may continually rely on mean-regression empiricism to 'contain risk' and perceive outliers of volatility, through probability. Much like time, the validation of a mobile mean propagates that markets, or the actions of participants will follow the mean itself. However, within markets, mean follows price (and the larger shift of distributions), which can only surface when outliers of traditional probably fail.

The author challenges whether it is truly probability that fails at these extreme points within distributions, or rather, whether the greater perception and implementation of probability, which is/was perhaps, flawed from the start?

THE NEVER-ENDING SEARCH BEHIND PROBABILITY DISTRIBUTIONS

Probability theory is generally thought of as the identification and measurement of events within random phenomena, in an effort to unveil statistical patterns and transparency within the seemingly arbitrary occurrences at hand.

It is important to understand that markets transcend rational probability analysis of 'games of chance', as the underlying fundamental events are really not 'random' whatsoever.

As Jaume Masoliver, Miquel Montero and Josep M Porra stated in the December 1999 paper A Dynamical Model Describing Stock Market Price Distributions,

"One of the most important problems in mathematical finance is to know the probability distribution of speculative prices."[53]

The authors explain traditional Gaussian measurements often fail in markets as, *"Gaussian models are thus widely used in finance although as Kendall first noticed, the normal distribution does not fit financial data especially at the wings of the distribution."*

The aforementioned authors hit the nail on the head, in that traditional implementation of a Gaussian distribution within financial markets fails to consider the extensive volatility produced outliers that commonly surface.

Moreover, within the Central Limit Theorem, Wall Street has historically made the mistake of assuming a finite mean *and* variance, which repeatedly falls victim to unanticipated risk, losses and default as the distribution at hand slides away from the preconceived outliers of normal probability.

The issue at hand within traditional analysis of probability and volatility is simply the continued attempt to measure finite variance in an effort to locate mean and outliers of probably.

Even when attempting to apply multi-dimensional alternatives like a multivariate Gaussian distribution, or matrix normal distribution, markets seemingly incorrectly assume price action is linear, or in effect: not.

The same problem is again encountered in the previously mentioned models, in that when one attempts to identify the variance in distributions at all, the conclusion is a failed measurement of deviations from normality.

Within this line of thought, the same problem arises repeatedly...that regardless of man's attempt at identifying probability and volatility within any given distribution, the grave mistake of assuming a finite variance has been, or is to be, made.

Referencing the paper from Masoliver, Montero and Porra again; the authors conclude, "*Summarizing by means of a continuous description of random pulses, we have obtained a dynamical model leading to a probability distribution for the speculative price changes.*"

To rephrase, there is substantial brilliance within Masoliver, Montero and Porra's modeling; when considering a larger failure of understanding is taking place within most statistical thinking -regarding markets- whenever considering markets are static, or that distributions are not constantly in motion...

Continuing our discussion of the historical study of price distributions and probability, it can be said that the larger goal of most eco-physics statisticians has historically attempted to identify potential tails for prices and returns within distributions.

Case in point, quoting the paper *Stock Market Return Distributions*: From Past to Present submitted to the Institute of Nuclear Physics, Polish Academy of Science in 2007 by S. Drożdż, M. Forczek, J. Kwapień, P. Oświe̦cimka and R. Rak, *"Much effort has been devoted on both the empirical and the theoretical level to such phenomena like fat-tailed distributions of financial fluctuations, persistent correlations in volatility, multifractal properties of returns etc. Specifically, the interest in the return distributions can be traced back to an early work of Mandelbrot, in which he proposed a Levy process as the one governing the logarithmic price fluctuations."*

The authors continue with, *"This empirical property of price and index returns led to the formulation of the so-called inverse cubic power law, which was soon followed by an attempt of formulating its theoretical foundation. Subsequent related study revealed that, opposite to the earlier outcomes of, the tail shape of the return distributions might no longer be so stable along time axis."*

The aforementioned study of price action examined American Stock Market companies from 1994-1995 and 1998-99, but then extended to examine 1000 of the largest American companies. The authors concluded, *"The difference of the results for the same market but for different time intervals might suggest that the scaling behavior is not stable and depends on some crucial factors as, for example, the speed of information processing which constantly increases from past to present."*

Despite all of the incredible breakthroughs in financial modeling over the years, it may be possible one aspect of 'modeling' statisticians have missed is one of simplicity, in that prices, given the continual urge of men to profit, will never remain stagnate and thus, with each passing day, present a new 'paradigm' of subset distribution movement.

Thus, perhaps true understanding to movements within markets (past, present and future) simply because, as is the nature of man, overcomplicating matters seemingly creates validity, especially if the true answer is/was in plain sight from the start. In reality, the answer to many of market's failed risk modeling is not in the larger consideration of the macro picture, but in the oversight of the power within smaller subset distribution movement.

To shed a slight bit more light on this understanding, the author would like to politely request the reader to keep an open mind to a potentially larger paradigm shift in the preconceived understanding of probability/ volatility and distributions, as a measurement of tails, risk and returns. Instead, our greater understanding of dynamics behind the movement of subset distributions altogether may just very well be the key unlocking answers to all of the above.

CHINESE RESTAURANT PROCESS, PROBABILITY/ VOLATILITY AND DISTRIBUTIONS

To find a greater understanding of market movement's we must keep Levy processes in mind; however, the true answer within probably, volatility and distributions may actually be found in the evolution of techniques used to derive machine learning.

As a brief definition, machine learning is the intersection of computer science and statistics. Computer science is the measurement of data and statistics apply probability. Ironically, while many academic institutions and Wall Street quant teams have long-since focused on Levy-based models, the actual answers to currency market movements may actually be within machine learning, whereby we are able to identify clusters of market data and then make good decisions with poor and uncertain (noisy) data.

The evolution may have come about as traditional Levy models have assisted in the pricing of risk, the same models perhaps failed in predicting the larger movements of distributions (and markets) overall.

Historically, with the implementation of statistics in markets, quantitative analysts have assumed pricing data within markets as random variables with real vectors. However, within the framework of the theory presented here, price action within markets is actually comprised of complex data structures requiring more evolved methods of measurement and inference.

Nonparametric Bayesian Methods eloquently help us see why this progression in thought is necessary. Within Nonparametric Bayesian Methods, as price data surfaces, we begin to see 'clusters', which statisticians historically have used in an attempt to 'break out' Gaussian models. The unknowns within cluster centers are known as theta, while the size of each cluster, is better known as π.

Cluster centers

$\theta \in R^{\wedge}2d$

Whereby we attempt to locate theta within the script, assuming the data is two-dimensional.

Cluster proportions

$\pi \in R^{\wedge}d$

Thus, we attempt to locate theta within the script, assuming the data is two-dimensional.

$X_{(i} \sim) \; N(\theta_{(j,)} \; \sigma^2 I)$

With probability π_i

$P(\theta, \pi)$prior

By using Nonparametric Bayesian Methods the outcome is similar to Bayesian inference, but with an infinite amount of parameters. The overall goal is to use the clusters to dissolve the larger model, which in terms of price data, can be inferred as the geometric presence of a one-dimensional chart.

Stock market data is similar to stick data and can be measured via Dirichlet Process, thus creating a 'picket fence', or random probability distribution summing to 1. As the data grows, the coherence of the probabilistic model also continues to gain momentum, as much like protein folding and density estimations, we are able to move beyond the historical attempt to measure risk and valuation.

Rather, we may instead be able to locate order flow and volatility transparency through subset distributions (clusters of price data), seeking out angles of movement through density of order flow, potentially surfacing within currency markets.

In essence, when we begin to transcend the thought process that price data is flat, we can begin to measure the total mass of clusters and thus, the density and angles of potential movements at hand.

At the end of the day, when one is able to perceive 'density' within markets ahead of the game, the larger paradigm of risk modeling quickly changes, all at the same time.

Before beginning the larger discussion of Beta Processes, we will first quickly cover the Poisson Process and Levy Process. The Poisson Process allows us to identify random points falling into an interval, thus deriving intensity and density within a distribution.

We must find the "measure" within the Poisson Process, which gives the 'mass' to a set, thus providing density within the data set.

PROBABILITY DENSITY FUNCTION (PDF)

Much like the decay of atoms holds a significantly large number of possible events, each being rare, so does the larger set of outcomes within any given period of price action within markets.

With a greater understanding of the Poisson Process, we are able to derive even more information from the Levy Process, whereby we derive stochastic time series, or random processes.

As information evolves, we will break out Brownian motion, thus invoking the Langevin equation as well.

Before moving too quickly (circling back to Levy Process) one might think of market action much like atomic structure, in a discrete distribution, when we measure mass of price data unfolding in markets, we find independent conclusions, with the data sets as disjoint.

Thus, the Levy measure allows us to locate mass over omega Ω, which in the case of currency markets, would be time. The Levy measure becomes the base measure of the

Poisson Process, whereby mass is the weight of data in time intervals. Because two prints within markets cannot occur at the same moment in time, and must fall into a time sequence, we are able to rationally justify this thought process.

The Levy Measure then helps calculate the mass on omega, deriving intensity, whereby be arrive at the Beta Process, while pulling in the concept of Brownian motion all at the same time, and in essence, creating a type of superprocess.

To back up for a moment, the Levy process (holding the Levy measure within a Poisson Process) allows for inference of a random discrete measure presenting mass to disjoint sets. However, much like atoms are not fixed, neither are markets.

With the aforementioned in mind, we will find some clues within the Beta Process, whereby we discover similarities of market movements, volatility/probability and pricing with that of atomic structure. Similarly, as Brownian motion gave birth to Particle Theory, and continuous-time stochastic processes, Beta Processes hold that the data within a distribution can be continuous, discreet, and mixed. The initial inferences derive that all values can only sum 1, with all points presented as real numbers.

Bernoulli Sampling allows us to break out individual distributions within the larger infinite time scale, thus bringing us to "Indian Buffet Process." Within the Indian Buffet Process (Chinese Restaurant Process), one can think of the market as a large restaurant, where customers step in to try an infinite amount of dishes, whereby each customer can try a dish on the buffet line, at random. When a customer tries a dish (buys a currency) his likelihood of trying that dish is equal to the probability of those who have previously tried the same dish, which is the partial explanation for momentum within markets, when breakouts and breakdowns occur. However, when ranges move, the process invokes the Poisson Process whereby "new dishes" (market ranges) are introduces as clusters of data within the larger time series of trading.

Moreover, because trading is an active process, whereby one can buy, as quickly as he, or she may sell, we also invoke "exchangeability" within the larger concepts of measuring density and intensity within the cluster movements (known as the "hierarchies of Beta Processes.)

As a quick, though loose example, assuming we have two days of market data, measured in clusters, or distributions, we are able to infer the first of the two days as our base measure of data. The second day allows that trades can take place at the same data points; much like the motion of atoms. Because the data sets are disjoint, our goal is to create an inferential algorithm for the clusters that have been created within the market. In other words, by quantifying subset distributions, we are able to create probability modeling for movement within markets, major pivot points within ranges, and potential intensity of breakouts and breakdowns…when the distributions shift.

While market data is not truly a "nested clustering problem" as known in the Dirichlet Process, the conceptual framework behind the data sets remains the same. However, by categorizing hierarchies of clusters, we are able to create 'classes' of probable movements and outcomes potentially about to unfold.

At this point, we find ourselves at the measurement of variance an Integer Attributable Models, or our Inference Algorithms of market movement. Using Levy Measures, the author concludes that we may be able to find rare occurrences of data within the cluster data sets, which derive probability of, and into, movement.

Accordingly, we evolve our Levy Process thinking to Gamma Processes, whereby we are able to begin seeking 'jump probability.'

In 2004, David Applebaum wrote that the gamma process can be written as $\Gamma(t;\gamma,\lambda)$, it is a pure-jump increasing Levy process with intensity measure $v(x) = \gamma x - 1\exp(-\lambda x)$, for positive x.

Because the Gamma Process may be measured in terms of the mean (μ) and variance (v) per unit time, we find market action unfolding as:

$\gamma = \mu2 / v$ and $\lambda = \mu / v$.

Conceptually, while we would like to measure the movement of the mean, the author's recent research is instead focuses on the rarity of data clusters, and or possibility of standard deviations actually surfacing not as larger points of regression, but instead, the precise points where ranges shift, or 'jump.'

Within currency markets, by measuring the clusters in terms of omega (time) in terms of each market as linear, we may derive that density both implies probable intensity of jump and capacity of range 'locking' at the same time.

To date, the author has spent considerable time with a team in China creating code to locate the clusters of data, which is now complete. We are now applying jump-probability via the Beta process, while also seeking to attempt to find volatility and probability of movement, or not, within the cluster subsets of market action.

All of the aforementioned –again- serves as a hopeful *'jump point'* to open further discussion of the movement of subset distributions within financial markets, as one of the larger clues to the seemingly random prices surfacing day-after-day and year-after-year.

In the end, the larger principals behind Volatility Illuminated and the possibilities of…reside more in challenging traditional paradigms, with the hope retail traders will begin thinking of price action more in terms of *physics and quantitative-statistics*, over historical methods of mere 'technicals-based' buying and selling.

One would think that as all things in this universe hold energy and matter, price action, if even seen as a derivative of human emotion, would hold some of the same attributes.

With all that I have mentioned, I would like to politely challenge readers to reshape conventional views on market and trading action from that of *'the old standards'* of technical and fundamental analysis, to *'the new standard'* of the expansion and compression of energy as seen through volatility, probability and the movement of subset distributions.

Finally – thank you so much for your time and support!

Mark Whistler

RULES OF
TRADING DISCIPLINE

1. NEVER OVER-LEVERAGE

2. Know the Economics.

Do not place a trade if you don't understand why the trade is being made.

3. <u>NEVER EVER</u> leave a position unattended without some sort of stop in place.

4. NEVER OVER-LEVERAGE

You will compromise your account by taking on a position that is too large to think clearly.

5. When in Doubt Get Out.

If you can't sleep at night, get out of the trade.
Trust your instincts.

6. Missed Money is Better than Lost Money.

If you have a negative gut feeling about a trade setup, stay out. There will always be opportunity to make money, but not if you don't have any.

7. Send the Trade Away, Live to Trade Another Day. If it doesn't look, or feel right, get out.

8. The First Loss is Always the Smallest Loss.

It's hard to take a loss, I know, I've taken plenty of them. I can tell you firsthand, you will save a ton of money by taking the first loss - at your predetermined stop - rather than letting your emotions keep you in a position.

Stop losses are a critical rule of money management.

9. Little Loss… Little Loss… HUGE WIN.

We must understand that there will be losses in trading.

We will accept small losses, even if there are a string of them, knowing that a big win is on the way.

We will <u>never take a large loss</u> by violating out stops, because doing so, would void the trading plan we are working so hard to execute.

If you think small, you will get small.

Traders who constantly take little winners off the table eventually blow up.

10. Lazy is Crazy.

At every turn, we will work hard to improve our trading knowledge by reading and studying everything we can.

SIX CORE PRINCIPLES
OF TECHNICAL
ANALYSIS

Charting, like all technical analysis, must be understood for what it is. The core principals to understanding what technical analysis is and why it is important are:

1. Charting and technical analysis are lagging indicators, meaning that they display information about an event that has already occurred.

2. Using technical analysis alone, without regard to fundamentals, or news…is lazy, and will often cause losses.

3. Technical analysis should be used as a "beacon in the night", signaling that an event, or shift (fundamental, or news-oriented) within the market, or stock has occurred.

4. Often, technical analysis relies on 'self fulfilling prophecies', meaning that many people must be

watching, believe in, and act on the same data for signals to become accurate.

5. There is no 'secret code' to markets. Some technical signals work better than others do, but none will work *"all of the time."*

6.   Traders who utilize technical analysis (while also paying attention to fundamentals and news too), but fail to remember simple *'common sense'*, will eventually get killed.

A deep understanding of the above principals is vital to trading with technical analysis. One must understand technicals for *what they are*, while keeping a clear head as signals come about on a day-to-day basis.

In the end, common sense is king.

ADDITIONAL DISCLAIMER

Mark Whistler, fxVolatility, WallStreetRockStar.com and 2034thecorporation.com ("Company") is not an investment advisory service, nor a registered investment advisor or broker-dealer and does not purport to tell or suggest which securities or currencies customers should buy or sell for themselves. The analysts and employees or affiliates of Company may hold positions in the stocks, currencies or industries discussed here. You understand and acknowledge that there is a very high degree of risk involved in trading securities and/or currencies. The Company, the authors, the publisher, and all affiliates of Company assume no responsibility or liability for your trading and investment results. Factual statements on the Company's website, or in its publications, are made as of the date stated and are subject to change without notice.

It should not be assumed that the methods, techniques, or indicators presented in these products will be profitable or that they will not result in losses. Past results of any individual trader or trading system published by Company are not indicative of future returns by that trader or system, and are not indicative of future returns which be realized by you. In addition, the indicators, strategies, columns, articles and all other features of Company's products (collectively, the "Information") are provided for informational and educational purposes only and should not be construed as investment advice. Examples presented on Company's website are for educational purposes only. Such set-ups are not solicitations of any order to buy or sell. Accordingly, you should not rely solely on the Information in making any investment. Rather, you should use the Information only as a starting point for doing additional independent research in order to allow you to form your own opinion regarding investments. You should always check with your licensed financial advisor and tax advisor to determine the suitability of any investment.

CUSTOM
INDICATOR
CODE I

WAVE • PM

Copyright © Mark Whistler 2009 / fxVolatility.com.

```
//+---------------------------------------------------+
//|Whistler Active Volatility Energy - Price Mass     |
//| Price Mass WAVE-PM                                 |
//| Copyright 2009, fxVolatility.com                   |
//| Authors: Mark Whistler/EcTrader.net               |
//| Mark@WallStreetRockStar.com                       |
//|www.WallStreetRockStar.com|www.fxVolatility.com.   |
//+---------------------------------------------------+
#property copyright "Copyright 2009, Mark Whistler"
#property link "http://www.wallstreetrockstar.com"

#property indicator_separate_window
#property indicator_buffers 6
#property indicator_maximum 1
#property indicator_minimum 0
#property indicator_color5 Blue
#property indicator_color6 Red

//---- indicator parameters
extern int    ShortBandsPeriod=14;
extern int    ShortBandsShift=0;
extern double ShortBandsDeviations=2.2;
extern int    LongBandsPeriod=55;
extern int    LongBandsShift=0;
extern double LongBandsDeviations=2.2;
extern int PERIODS_CHARACTERISTIC=100;
//---- buffers
```

```
   double ShortMovingBuffer[];
   double LongMovingBuffer[];
   double ShortDev[];
   double LongDev[];
   double Shortoscillator[];
   double Longoscillator[];
//+----------------------------------------------------+
//| Custom indicator initialization function           |
//+----------------------------------------------------+
int init()
   {
//---- indicators
   SetIndexStyle(0,DRAW_NONE);
   SetIndexBuffer(0,ShortMovingBuffer);
   SetIndexStyle(1,DRAW_NONE);
   SetIndexBuffer(1,LongMovingBuffer);
   SetIndexStyle(2,DRAW_NONE);
   SetIndexBuffer(2,ShortDev);
   SetIndexStyle(3,DRAW_NONE);
   SetIndexBuffer(3,LongDev);
   SetIndexStyle(4,DRAW_LINE);
   SetIndexBuffer(4,Shortoscillator);
   SetIndexStyle(5,DRAW_LINE);
   SetIndexBuffer(5,Longoscillator);
//----

SetIndexDrawBegin(0,ShortBandsPeriod+ShortBandsShift);
   SetIndexDrawBegin(1,LongBandsPeriod+LongBandsShift);

SetIndexDrawBegin(2,ShortBandsPeriod+ShortBandsShift);
   SetIndexDrawBegin(3,LongBandsPeriod+LongBandsShift);

SetIndexDrawBegin(4,ShortBandsPeriod+ShortBandsShift);
   SetIndexDrawBegin(5,LongBandsPeriod+LongBandsShift);
//----
   return(0);
   }
//+----------------------------------------------------+
//| Bollinger Bands                                    |
//+----------------------------------------------------+

int start()
   {
   int    i,k,counted_bars=IndicatorCounted();
   double deviation;
   double sum,oldval,newres;
//----
   if(Bars<=LongBandsPeriod) return(0);
```

```
    //---- initial zero
        if(counted_bars<1)
           {
            for(i=1;i<=ShortBandsPeriod;i++)
               {
                ShortMovingBuffer[Bars-i]=EMPTY_VALUE;
               }
            for(i=1;i<=LongBandsPeriod;i++)
               {
                LongMovingBuffer[Bars-i]=EMPTY_VALUE;
               }
           }
    //----
        int limit=Bars-counted_bars;
        if(counted_bars>0) limit++;
        for(i=0; i<limit; i++)
           {

ShortMovingBuffer[i]=iMA(NULL,0,ShortBandsPeriod,ShortBands
Shift,MODE_SMA,PRICE_CLOSE,i);

LongMovingBuffer[i]=iMA(NULL,0,LongBandsPeriod,LongBandsShi
ft,MODE_SMA,PRICE_CLOSE,i);
           }
    //----
        i=Bars-ShortBandsPeriod+1;
        if(counted_bars>ShortBandsPeriod-1) i=Bars-
counted_bars-1;
        while(i>=0)
           {
            sum=0.0;
            k=i+ShortBandsPeriod-1;
            oldval=ShortMovingBuffer[i];
            while(k>=i)
               {
                newres=Close[k]-oldval;
                sum+=newres*newres;
                k--;
               }

ShortDev[i]=ShortBandsDeviations*MathSqrt(sum/ShortBandsPer
iod);
            Shortoscillator[i]=OscillatorLine(ShortDev,i);
            //UpperBuffer[i]=oldval+deviation;
            //LowerBuffer[i]=oldval-deviation;
            i--;
           }
     //----
```

```
        i=Bars-LongBandsPeriod+1;
        if(counted_bars>LongBandsPeriod-1) i=Bars-
counted_bars-1;
        while(i>=0)
          {
           sum=0.0;
           k=i+LongBandsPeriod-1;
           oldval=LongMovingBuffer[i];
           while(k>=i)
             {
              newres=Close[k]-oldval;
              sum+=newres*newres;
              k--;
             }

LongDev[i]=LongBandsDeviations*MathSqrt(sum/LongBandsPeriod
);
           Longoscillator[i]=OscillatorLine(LongDev,i);
           //UpperBuffer[i]=oldval+deviation;
           //LowerBuffer[i]=oldval-deviation;
           i--;
          }
    //----
      return(0);
      }

    double OscillatorLine(double indicator[], int StartBar)
      {
         double S=0;
         int ArrayLong=PERIODS_CHARACTERISTIC;
         double Result;
         for(int j=StartBar;j<ArrayLong+StartBar;j++)
           {S+=MathPow((indicator[j]/Point),2);}

         S/=ArrayLong;
         S=MathSqrt(S)*Point;
         if(S!=0)
           {Result=indicator[StartBar]/S;}
         Result=MathTanh(Result);
         return (Result);
      }
   double MathTanh(double x)
   {
      double exp;
      double returnNum;
      if(x>0)
        {
          exp=MathExp(-2*x);
```

```
            returnNum= (1-exp)/(1+exp);
            return (returnNum);
        }
    else
        {
            exp=MathExp(2*x);
            returnNum=(exp-1)/(1+exp);
            return (returnNum);
        }
}
```

CUSTOM INDICATOR CODE II

DUEL CCI WITH SIGNAL

```
//+-------------------------------------------------+
//| Duel CCI w/Signal                               |
//| Copyright 2009, fxVolatility.com                |
//| Authors: Mark Whistler/EcTrader.net             |
//| Mark@WallStreetRockStar.com                     |
//|www.WallStreetRockStar.com|www.fxVolatility.com. |
//+-------------------------------------------------+
#property copyright "Copyright 2009, Mark Whistler"
#property link "http://www.wallstreetrockstar.com"



#property indicator_separate_window
#property indicator_buffers 4
#property indicator_color1 SteelBlue
#property indicator_color2 Red
#property indicator_color3 OrangeRed
#property indicator_width3 2
#property indicator_color4 MediumSpringGreen
#property indicator_width4 2
//---- input parameters
extern int CCIPeriod1 = 14;
extern int CCIPeriod2 = 100;
extern int Num_CountBarOf220To64=10000;
```

```
extern int Num_Bigger=220;
extern int Num_Smaller=64;
int count;
//---- buffers
double CCIBuffer1[];
double CCIBuffer2[];
double CCIArrow1[];
double CCIArrow2[];


//+------------------------------------------------+
//| Begin Custom Indicator                         |
//+------------------------------------------------+


int deinit()
   {
    //ObjectsDeleteAll();
    return(0);
   }
int init()
   {
    string short_name;
//---- indicator line
    SetIndexStyle(0, DRAW_LINE, STYLE_SOLID, 1,
SteelBlue);
    SetIndexStyle(1, DRAW_LINE);
    SetIndexStyle(2,DRAW_ARROW);
    SetIndexStyle(3,DRAW_ARROW);
    SetIndexBuffer(0, CCIBuffer1);
    SetIndexBuffer(1, CCIBuffer2);
    SetIndexBuffer(2, CCIArrow1);
    SetIndexBuffer(3, CCIArrow2);
    SetIndexArrow(2,234);
    SetIndexArrow(3,233);
//---- name for DataWindow and indicator subwindow label
    short_name = "CCIW(" + CCIPeriod1 + ", " + CCIPeriod2
+ ")";
    IndicatorShortName(short_name);
    SetIndexLabel(0, "CCIW(" + CCIPeriod1 + ")");


   SetIndexLabel(1, "CCIW(" + CCIPeriod2 + ")");
    SetIndexLabel(2, "CCIW(" + "CCIArrow1" + ")");
    SetIndexLabel(3, "CCIW(" + "CCIArrow2" + ")");
//----
```

```
      SetIndexDrawBegin(0, CCIPeriod1);
      SetIndexDrawBegin(1, CCIPeriod2);
      SetIndexDrawBegin(2, CCIArrow1);
      SetIndexDrawBegin(3, CCIArrow2);
   //----
      return(0);
      }




   //+----------------------------------------------------+
   //| CCI                                                |
   //+----------------------------------------------------+



   int start()
      {
      int i, counted_bars = IndicatorCounted();
   //----
      if(Bars <= CCIPeriod1)
          return(0);
   //---- initial zero
      if(counted_bars < 1)
          for(i = 1; i <= CCIPeriod1; 1++)
              CCIBuffer1[Bars-i] = 0.0;
   //----
      i = Bars - CCIPeriod1 - 1;
      if(counted_bars >= CCIPeriod1)
      i = Bars - counted_bars - 1;
      bool success1=false;
      bool success2=false;
      int j=1;
      while(i >= 0)
          {
          CCIBuffer1[i] = iCCI(NULL, 0, CCIPeriod1,
PRICE_TYPICAL, i);
          CCIBuffer2[i] = iCCI(NULL, 0, CCIPeriod2,
PRICE_TYPICAL, i);
          if (CCIBuffer2[i]<=Num_Smaller &&


    CCIBuffer2[i+1]>=Num_Smaller)
              {
              for (j=1; j<=Num_CountBarOf220To64; j++)
                  {
                  if (CCIBuffer2[j+i]<Num_Smaller)
```

```
                    {
                       success1=false;
                       break;
                    }
                  if (CCIBuffer2[j+i]>=Num_Bigger)
                    {
                       success1=true;
                       break;
                    }
              }//}
           if (success1==true)
             {
                CCIArrow1[i]=CCIBuffer2[i];
                count++;
                success1=false;
             }
           else
             {
                CCIArrow1[i]=EMPTY_VALUE;
             }
         }


        //-----------------------------


         if (CCIBuffer2[i]>=(-1*Num_Smaller) &&
   CCIBuffer2[i+1]<=(-1*Num_Smaller))
             {
                for (j=1; j<=Num_CountBarOf220To64; j++)
                  {
                     if (CCIBuffer2[j+i]>(-1*Num_Smaller))
                       {
                          success2=false;
                          break;
                       }
                     if (CCIBuffer2[j+i]<=(-1*Num_Bigger))
                       {
                          success2=true;
                          break;
                       }
                  }//}
               if (success2==true)
                 {
                    CCIArrow2[i]=CCIBuffer2[i];
                    success2=false;
                 }
               else
```

```
               {
                   CCIArrow2[i]=EMPTY_VALUE;
               }
           }
       success1=false;
       success2=false;
       i--;
   }

 return(0);
}
```

CUSTOM INDICATOR CODE III

WVAV

Copyright © Mark Whistler 2009 / fxVolatility.com.

```
//+----------------------------------------------------+
//|Whistler Volume Adjusted Volatility - WVAV          |
//|                                                    |
//| Copyright 2009, fxVolatility.com                   |
//| Authors: Mark Whistler/EcTrader.net                |
//| Mark@WallStreetRockStar.com                        |
//|www.WallStreetRockStar.com|www.fxVolatility.com.    |
//+----------------------------------------------------+
#property copyright "Copyright 2009, Mark Whistler"
#property link "http://www.wallstreetrockstar.com"


//----
#property indicator_chart_window
#property indicator_buffers 5
#property indicator_color1 Red
#property indicator_color2 DarkGoldenrod
#property indicator_color3 Black
```

```
#property indicator_color4 Black
#property indicator_color5 Black

//---- input parameters
extern int MA_Ticks = 10000;
extern int MA_Shift = 0;
extern int MA_Start = 500;
//---- indicator parameters1
extern string aa="*****************************";
//---- indicator parameters
extern bool MidBandVisible=false;
extern int    BandsPeriod=14;
extern int    BandsShift=0;
extern double BandsDeviations=3.2;

//---- indicator buffers
double ExtMapBuffer[];
double ExpVolBuffer[];
//---- buffers
//---- double MovingBuffer[];
double UpperBuffer[];
double LowerBuffer[];
//-------------


//+----------------------------------------------------+
//||Custom Indicator Initialization                    |
//+----------------------------------------------------+


int init()
   {
//----
   SetIndexStyle(0, DRAW_LINE);
   SetIndexShift(0, MA_Shift);
//---- indicator buffers mapping
   SetIndexBuffer(0, ExtMapBuffer);
   SetIndexStyle(1, DRAW_NONE);
   SetIndexBuffer(1, ExpVolBuffer);
   SetIndexDrawBegin(0, 0);
//---- initialization done
//---- indicators
   SetIndexStyle(2,DRAW_LINE);
   SetIndexBuffer(2,ExtMapBuffer);
   SetIndexStyle(3,DRAW_LINE);
   SetIndexBuffer(3,UpperBuffer);
   SetIndexStyle(4,DRAW_LINE);
```

```
      SetIndexBuffer(4,LowerBuffer);


//----
      SetIndexDrawBegin(2,BandsPeriod+BandsShift);
      SetIndexDrawBegin(3,BandsPeriod+BandsShift);
      SetIndexDrawBegin(4,BandsPeriod+BandsShift);
      return(0);
   }


//+----------------------------------------------------+
//|Custom Indicator Initialization                     |
//+----------------------------------------------------+


int start()
   {
   int counted_bars = IndicatorCounted();
   int rest  = Bars - counted_bars;
   int restt = Bars - counted_bars;
   double sumVol;
   int ts;
   int evol;
   int volsum;
   int j;
   int i;

   //--------------Begin Add MA----------------------
   double deviation;
   double sum, oldval,newres;
//----
   if(Bars<=BandsPeriod) return(0);
//---- initial zero
   if(counted_bars<1)
      for(i=1;i<=BandsPeriod;i++)
        {
         ExtMapBuffer[Bars-i]=EMPTY_VALUE;
         UpperBuffer[Bars-i]=EMPTY_VALUE;
         LowerBuffer[Bars-i]=EMPTY_VALUE;
        }
```

```
    int limit=Bars-counted_bars;
       if(counted_bars>0) limit++;
       for(i=0; i<limit; i++)
           {

ExtMapBuffer[i]=iMA(NULL,0,BandsPeriod,BandsShift,MODE_SMA,
PRICE_CLOSE,i);
           }

       //---------------End Add MA-----------------------
    //---------Begin Volume MA-------------------------

       while(restt >= 0)
          {
            volsum = 0;
            for(int k = 0; k < 30; k++)
                volsum += iVolume(NULL, 0, restt + k*24);
            ExpVolBuffer[restt] = volsum / 30;
            restt--;
          }
    //----
       while(ExpVolBuffer[rest] == 0 && rest >= 0)
           rest--;
       rest -= MA_Ticks / 200;
       if(rest > MA_Start)
           rest = MA_Start;
    //----
       while(rest >= 0)
          {
            sumVol = 0;
            ts = 0;
            j = rest;
            while(ts < MA_Ticks)
               {
                 evol = ExpVolBuffer[j];
    //----           Print("Evol = ", evol);
                 if(ts + evol < MA_Ticks)
                    {
                      sumVol += evol * Open[j];
                      ts += evol;
                    }
                 else
                    {
                      sumVol += (MA_Ticks - ts) * Open[j];
                      ts = MA_Ticks;
                    }
                 j++;
```

```
          }
        ExtMapBuffer[rest] = sumVol / MA_Ticks;
        rest--;
      }

   //---------------------End Volume MA-----------------
   //--------------------Begin Bollinger Band-----------

   //----

    i=Bars-BandsPeriod+1;
    if(counted_bars>BandsPeriod-1) i=Bars-counted_bars-1;
    while(i>=0)
      {
       sum=0.0;
       k=i+BandsPeriod-1;
       oldval=ExtMapBuffer[i];
       while(k>=i)
         {
          newres=Close[k]-oldval;
          sum+=newres*newres;
          k--;
         }
deviation=BandsDeviations*MathSqrt(sum/BandsPeriod);
       UpperBuffer[i]=oldval+deviation;
       LowerBuffer[i]=oldval-deviation;
       i--;
      }
  //----
   //---------------------End Band--------------------
  //----
    return(0);
   }
```

BIBLIOGRAPHY /
RECOMMENDED
READING

Recommended Reading: Statistics

- Best, Joel (2001). Damned Lies and Statistics: Untangling Numbers from the Media, Politicians, and Activists. University of California Press. ISBN 0-520-21978-3.
- Desrosières, Alain (2004). The Politics of Large Numbers: A History of Statistical Reasoning. Trans. Camille Naish. Harvard University Press. ISBN 0-674-68932-1.
- Hacking, Ian (1990). The Taming of Chance. Cambridge University Press. ISBN 0-521-38884-8.
- Lindley, D.V. (1985). Making Decisions (2nd ed. ed.). John Wiley & Sons. ISBN 0-471-90808-8.
- Tijms, Henk (2004). Understanding Probability: Chance Rules in Everyday life. Cambridge University Press. ISBN 0-521-83329-9.

Recommended Reading: DotCom Bubble

- Cassidy, John. Dot.con: How America Lost its Mind and Its Money in the Internet Era (2002)
- Daisey, Mike. 21 Dog Years Free Press. ISBN 0-7432-2580-5.
- Goldfarb, Brent D., Kirsch, David and Miller, David A., "Was There Too Little Entry During the Dot Com Era?" (April 24, 2006). Robert H. Smith School Research Paper No. RHS 06-029 Available at SSRN: http://ssrn.com/abstract=899100

- Kindleberger, Charles P., Manias, Panics, and Crashes: A History of Financial Crises (Wiley, 2005, 5th edition)
- Kuo, David dot.bomb: My Days and Nights at an Internet Goliath ISBN 0-316-60005-9 (2001)
- Lowenstein, Roger. Origins of the Crash: The Great Bubble and Its Undoing. (Penguin Books, 2004) ISBN 0-14-303467-7

Recommended Reading: Algorithmic Trading
- MTS to mull bond access, The Wall Street Journal Europe, April 18, 2007, p. 21
- Sornette (2003): Critical Market Crashes, Sornette (2003): Critical Market Crashes
- Trading with the help of 'guerrillas' and 'snipers,' Financial Times, March 19, 2007
- Rob Curren, Watch Out for Sharks in Dark Pools, The Wall Street Journal, August 19, 2008, p. c5. Available at WSJ Blogs
- Artificial intelligence applied heavily to picking stocks by Charles Duhigg, November 23, 2006
- Carney, John (June 26, 2009). "UBS Accuses Three Quant Traders Of Stealing Its Secret Code". The Business Insider. http://www.businessinsider.com/ubs-accuses-three-quant-traders-of-stealing-its-secret-code-2009-6. Retrieved on July 14, 2009.

END NOTES

[1] Richard S. Newman, *Transformation of American abolitionism: fighting slavery in the early Republic* chapter 1

[2] Results from the 1860 Census: The Civil War Home Page. CivilWar.net. Accessed: June 2009. http://www.civil-war.net/about_us.asp

[3] Remembering 1975 – The Majority was Wrong – The Good News Economist. December 11, 2008. Accessed June, 2009.
http://mast-economy.blogspot.com/2008/12/remembering-1975-majority-was-wrong.html

[4] Buffet, Warren. Buy American. I am. October 16, 2008. The New York Times. http://www.nytimes.com/2008/10/17/opinion/17buffett.html

[5] Loftus, Elizabeth F. Make-believe memories," *American Psychologist* (November 2003).

[6] Cozens, Claire. Ads Can Alter Memory Claim Scientists. UK Guardian. September 4, 2001.
http://www.guardian.co.uk/media/2001/sep/04/advertising

[7] "Make my Memory" in Psychology & Marketing (2002)

[8] Stewart's Beverages - Then & Again!
http://www.drinkstewarts.com/history.aspx

[9] Dot-com bubble. (2009, June 6). In *Wikipedia, The Free Encyclopedia*. Retrieved 23:16, June 6, 2009, from http://en.wikipedia.org/w/index.php?title=Dot-com_bubble&oldid=294871219

[10] Wolff, Michael Dot-Com Bomb. New York Magazine.
Published Apr 24, 2000.
http://nymag.com/nymetro/news/media/columns/medialife/2
978/

[11] Connors, E., Lundregan, T., Miller, N. & McEwan, T. Convicted
by Juries, Exonerated by Science: Case Studies in the Use of DNA
Evidence to Establish

Innocence After Trial (National Institute of Justice, Alexandria,
Virginia, 1996).

[12] Loftus, Elizabeth F. "Our changeable memories: legal and
practical implications," in *Nature Reviews: Neuroscience* (2003).

[13] Loftus, Elizabeth F. "Memory Faults and Fixes" in *Issues in
Science & Technology* (2002; publication of the National Academies
of Science)
http://faculty.washington.edu/eloftus/Articles/IssuesInScience
Technology02%20vol%2018.pdf

[14] Loftus, Elizabeth F. "Memory Faults and Fixes" in *Issues in
Science & Technology* (2002; publication of the National Academies
of Science)
http://faculty.washington.edu/eloftus/Articles/IssuesInScience
Technology02%20vol%2018.pdf

[15] Understanding Your Fears – Author uncited. John Wiley &
Sons, 2003.
http://media.wiley.com/product_data/excerpt/28/04712727/04
71272728.pdf Accessed: May 2009.

[16] Injuries in Athletics: Causes and Consequences **Slobounov,
Semyon** 2008, XV, 544 p. 39 illus., 4 in color., Hardcover ISBN:
978-0-387-72576-5

[17] **Title 18, U.S.C., Section 241**
Conspiracy Against Rights .S. Federal Government, <u>U.S. Department of Justice</u>.

http://www.fbi.gov/hq/cid/civilrights/statutes.htm#section241

[18] Loftus, Elizabeth F. <u>Make-believe memories</u>," *American Psychologist* (November 2003). Accessed: May 2009.

[19] Greg Sandoval Start-up with pricey Super Bowl ad goes bust Staff Writer, CNET News June 14, 2000 2:00 PM PDT
http://news.cnet.com/2100-1017-241907.html

[20] Loftus, Elizabeth F. <u>Make-believe memories</u>," *American Psychologist* (November 2003). Accessed: May 2009.

[21] University of Michigan: Consumer Confidence: Philadelphia Fed

http://www.philadelphiafed.org/payment-cards-center/tools-for-researchers/data-dictionary/Umich-CCon_4-11-04.pdf
Accessed: May 2009.

[22] ST311 Introduction to Statistics Steve Stanislav Lecture Notes Accessed: May 2009.

http://www4.ncsu.edu/~sjstanis/notes.pdf Accessed: May 2009.

[23] Creative Research Systems: Sample Size Calculator. Accessed: May 2009. http://www.surveysystem.com/sscalc.htm Accessed: May 2009.

[24] An Overview of The Study of Economics Principles, Concepts & Applications - The Study of Economics is a new concept in learning Economics. Accessed: May 2009.

The McGraw-Hill Companies.
http://www.dushkin.com/connectext/econ/help.mhtml
Accessed: May 2009.

[25] Assets and Liabilities of Commercial Banks in the United Seasonally adjusted
http://www.federalreserve.gov/releases/h8/Current/

[26] Ecnonomy.com. U.S. Crisis Response. June, 2009.
http://www.economy.com/dismal/pro/data/us-financial-crisis-response.asp?edition=1

[27] Max Planck The Nobel Prize in Physics 1918. The Official Web Site of the Nobel Foundation

http://nobelprize.org/nobel_prizes/physics/laureates/1918/planck-bio.html

Accessed: May 2009.

[28] Gorard, Stephen. Revisiting a 90-year-old debate: the advantages of the mean deviation. Department of Educational Studies, University of York. Paper presented at the British Educational Research Association Annual Conference, University of Manchester, 16-18 September 2004. Accessed: May 2009.
http://www.leeds.ac.uk/educol/documents/00003759.htm

[29] Elementary Statistics – by Mario F. Triola, **Eighth Edition** DEFININITIONS, RULES AND THEOREMS

[30] How Stock Indices Work - WIKINVEST.com - Accessed: March 2009.
http://www.wikinvest.com/wiki/How_Stock_Indices_Work
Accessed: May 2009.

[31] New Dow Divisor for Dow Jones Industrial Average. June 9, 2009. http://www.cmegroup.com/trading/equity-index/files/Dow_divisor.pdf

[32] Einstein, Albert (1905-06-30). "Zur Elektrodynamik bewegter Körper". Annalen der Physik 17: 891–921. http://www.pro-physik.de/Phy/pdfs/ger_890_921.pdf. Retrieved on 2009-02-02. Accessed: May 2009.

[33] Einstein, Albert, 1926, "Space-Time," Encyclopedia Britannica, 13th ed. Accessed: March 2009. http://www.britannica.com/EBchecked/topic/557482/space-time Accessed: May 2009.

[34] "Theory of relativity." Wikipedia, The Free Encyclopedia. 7 Apr 2009, 22:47 UTC. 11 Apr 2009 <http://en.wikipedia.org/w/index.php?title=Theory_of_relativity&oldid=282439495>. Accessed: May 2009.

[35] http://www.telephonetribute.com/timeline.html Accessed: May 2009.

[36] Schwartz, David A. Schwartz. How Fast Does News Travel? The Public Opinion Quarterly, Vol. 37, No. 4 (Winter, 1973-1974), pp. 625-627 (article consists of 3 pages) Published by: Oxford University Press on behalf of the American Association for Public Opinion Research Stable URL: http://www.jstor.org/stable/2747864 Accessed: May 2009.

[37] connected-earth.com

http://www.connected-earth.com/Galleries/Ourworldoftelecommunications/Atadistance/Communicatingathighspeed/index.htm Accessed: May 2009.

[38] Newton's Three Laws of Motion. NASA, Glenn research Center. Accessed: March 2009. http://www.grc.nasa.gov/WWW/K-12/airplane/newton1g.html Accessed: May 2009.

[39] Britton, Erin. Newton's Laws of Motion

The Relationship between Forces and Motion Explained. December 14, 2008. Accessed: March 2009. http://physics-history.suite101.com/article.cfm/newtons_laws_of_motion Accessed: May 2009.

[40] Walsh, Mary Williams. A.I.G. Uses $61 Billion of Fed Loan. The New York Times. October 3, 2009. Accessed: March 2009. http://www.nytimes.com/2008/10/04/business/04insure.html

"Moody's downgraded A.I.G.'s senior unsecured debt on Friday and said it might downgrade other types of the company's debt, which could make it more expensive for A.I.G. to borrow money and do business."

[41] American Cultural History 1960 – 1969. Kingwood College Library. Accessed: May 2009. http://kclibrary.lonestar.edu/decade60.html

[42] Brain, Marshall, 12 New Technologies in the 1980s. How Stuff Works, Inc. Accessed: May 2009. http://electronics.howstuffworks.com/gadgets/other-gadgets/80s-tech.htm

[43] Descriptive statistics. (2009, May 12). In *Wikipedia, The Free Encyclopedia*. Retrieved 21:58, May 12, 2009, from http://en.wikipedia.org/w/index.php?title=Descriptive_statistics&oldid=289555419

[44] Bollinger, John. Bollinger on Bollinger Bands. 2001, McGraw Hill, New York, New York. Page 70.

[45] Bollinger, John. Bollinger on Bollinger Bands. Kurtosis, Page 72: "What is a non-normal distribution again? And what has a fat tail? The graph in Figure 9.2 illustrates the concept nicely. The taller hump is a normal distribution, the way things ought to be. The shorter hump is a distribution like the stock market's, less small changes than one would expect and more large changes. The amount of difference between the two humps is known as kurtosis and it is a significant quantity for stocks."

[46] American Educational Research Association, American Psychological Association, & National Council on Measurement in Education. (1999). *Standards for educational and psychological testing*. Washington, DC: American Educational Research Association.

[47] Concurrent Validity. Online Medical Dictionary. Mondofacto Ltd. Accessed May 2009. http://www.mondofacto.com/about/about.html

[48] Bollinger Bands. Definition: InvestorWords.com. Accessed: May 2009. http://www.investorwords.com/518/bollinger_bands.html

[49] Physics of High Altitude Automobile Operation *Why that Mountain Monster hits so hard.* Mile High Saab. December 14, 2005. http://web.archive.org/web/20051214181804/http://www.saab club.com/242/altitude.htm#physics Accessed: May 2009.

[50] Bank for International Settlements' Triennial Central Bank Survey (Foreign exchange and derivatives market activity in 2007), Bank for International Settlements' Triennial Central Bank Survey Accessed: May 2009.

[51] Retail Forex Volumes Keep Rising Due To Market Volatility Wall Street Journal. APRIL 21, 2009. http://online.wsj.com/article/BT-CO-20090421-715659.html Accessed: May 2009.

[52] Harris, Larry. Trading and Exchanges. Market Microstructure for Practitioners Larry Harris ISBN13: 9780195144703 ISBN10: 0195144708

[53] A dynamical model describing stock market price distributions, Jaume Masoliver, Miquel Monteroa and Josep M. Porràa, b. Departament de Física Fonamental, Universitat de Barcelona, Diagonal, 647, Barcelona 08028, Spain. Gaesco Bolsa, SVB, S.A., Diagonal, 429, Barcelona 08036, Spain

karma

3479117

Made in the USA